Keep the Days

CIVIL WAR AMERICA

Peter S. Carmichael, Caroline E. Janney,
and Aaron Sheehan-Dean, editors

This landmark series interprets broadly the history and culture
of the Civil War era through the long nineteenth century and
beyond. Drawing on diverse approaches and methods, the
series publishes historical works that explore all aspects of
the war, biographies of leading commanders, and tactical and
campaign studies, along with select editions of primary sources.
Together, these books shed new light on an era that remains
central to our understanding of American and world history.

Keep the Days

Reading the Civil War Diaries of Southern Women

STEVEN M. STOWE

THE UNIVERSITY OF NORTH CAROLINA PRESS

Chapel Hill

This book was published with the assistance of the
Fred W. Morrison Fund of the University of North Carolina Press.

Designed by Jamison Cockerham
Set in Arno, Dear Sarah, Jenson
by codeMantra

The University of North Carolina Press has been a member
of the Green Press Initiative since 2003.

Cover photograph: Rachel Young King Anderson, ca. 1860,
holding the diary she kept during the Civil War.

LIBRARY OF CONGRESS CATALOGING-IN-PUBLICATION DATA
Names: Stowe, Steven M., 1946– author.
Title: Keep the days : reading the Civil War diaries of
Southern women / Steven M. Stowe.
Other titles: Civil War America (Series)
Description: Chapel Hill : University of North Carolina Press, [2018] |
Series: Civil War America | Includes bibliographical references and index.
Identifiers: LCCN 2017048916| ISBN 9781469640952 (cloth : alk. paper) |
ISBN 9781469640969 (pbk : alk. paper) | ISBN 9781469640976 (ebook)
Subjects: LCSH: United States—History—Civil War, 1861–1865—Women. |
United States—History—Civil War, 1861–1865—Historiography. | Women,
White—Southern States—Diaries. | Slaveholders—Southern States—Diaries.
Classification: LCC E628 .S76 2018 | DDC 973.7082—dc23
LC record available at https://lccn.loc.gov/2017048916

For Naoko, with love

CONTENTS

Words of War

The American Civil War ran wildly across the landscape and through people's lives. It also swept into their words. We know a lot about the transformation of lives and places. My aim in this book is to show how a certain kind of writing matters, too, for knowing about the war—for reading words of war and bringing ghosts from it into our lives. This is a book about the personal diaries written by well-to-do white women in the American South as the Civil War blew through everything they trusted in life. The Civil War: the Union survives, enslaved people become free, and, wrapped around this, a universe of death and loss, and inside *this*, Southern diarists writing as the air is sucked out of the known world. They wrote the day, and the next day, too.

It was a quiet thing to do in the midst of war, but amazing when you think of it: making time to write when the whole world gaped and time scattered. I wonder about this diary writing as an everyday act that somehow stood apart from the ordinary, and the wonder and pleasure of reading diaries is a big part of the story here. Every diary seems familiar but is always surprising. Each one brings ghosts of the past into the *now* with an easy touch and an open face. One reason to love diaries is that they don't pretend to do more, though the varieties of their plain style were strangely freshened by war and the consciousness that war brought. So this is a book about a way of writing the Civil War and of reading it, too. I aim to tell a story made up of diaries' small stories and to think about how wartime diaries—and through their pages, the war itself—are made by the happy compulsions of writers and readers.

The women who wrote the diaries were from the Southern planter class and lived on wealth brought to them by the work of enslaved African Americans. They are the "belles" of Southern sentimental mythmaking, but now we see them in the light of how they helped manage and preserve, through intricate daily practice, a system of violent human bondage. When the war came, these women worked to keep the Confederacy strong and their men focused, and although there is disagreement about how much women doubted the wisdom of the war even as they helped keep it going, no one thinks they were merely ornaments of the Confederate state. They were central to its course and character, and they took hard its eventual wreckage. They are not sympathetic figures, and their lives are compelling because they are not. Life as a mistress of slaves was not a woman's simple lot in life, nor her misfortune. It was her pride and her blindness; it was her work. It was a life founded on injustice, but that is not what makes me curious. The injustice of slavery is beyond any doubt, and it is good to never lose sight of this—slavery's evils extend into the present day. But this book is not about affirming the injustice again. Rather, I want to know what we can learn from reading these women who lived the wrong life as *my life*, beheld and cherished, and who became the authors of their lives just as their lives fell apart.

It matters that the diarists are women, not men. People in the nineteenth century thought that women had a talent for sympathy and an affinity for all things moral, and planter-class women worked hard to make enslaving others morally right. Or if not that, then something natural, like the weather, where personal responsibility was not the point. These are terrible, murderous contradictions, I say. Our lives, say the women. This difference between us is part of what I want to understand. Another gap interests me, too: the one between slaveholding women and their men. Planter-class women were astute and powerful, but not powerful like the men, who knew how the wide world worked and on whom women were compelled to depend or wished to depend, or both. Women's experience of men's power, and of using it for their own convenience or advantage or enlightenment, gave women a hybrid life—in the ruling class, but ruled—that deepens what there is to know about their time and place. And women are interesting because they were writers of a certain kind. They wrote easily and expressively (especially fiction and everyday writing like letters and diaries) in ways that still speak powerfully about the play of language and past life's subjective touch. Women rose to meet the Civil War with words. I am moved by this, being a writer, too. And I am moved by what they found out: they were certain that they were living the right life, and then that life blew up. We must be lucky and watchful that we do not discover the same.

With this in mind, I read women's war diaries with an eye for empathy. Empathy—a grasp on what another person's experience feels like—is difficult and imperfect. Historians make an empathetic move gingerly because it might suppose too much or yield too little. It seems a particularly risky or suspect thing to do when it comes to mistresses of slaves. Empathy means that anyone's point of view is a treasure, even a slave owner's. Empathy means that everyone's feelings are in play—the historian's, too. Empathy invites me to go a long way before I simplify, or discard, or pass final judgment on someone else's slant on things, even one I despise.

But empathy is not sympathy, which thrives on closeness and caring. Empathy is about the difference between me and the other person. Empathy *requires* difference, the whole effort being to find a way into a foreign sensibility. The evil done by mistresses was not only brutal, it was sweet-faced and dissembling. It was clear skies and cloudy. It was everyday. Empathy's gift is to show some small part of how this life made sense to them. At the same time, looking for empathy shows us that difference does not mean distance. Seeking empathy for a mistress of slaves does not push her away or quarantine her as a unique figure of evildoing. She stays around, we get to know her.

This is empathy's mode, an uncomfortable one that might seem open to the old lies about needy slaves and wise masters. But I don't see it that way. I seek empathy to understand slaveholders' lives soaked with their power but also to see how slaveholding women could believe their lives were *good* lives. I look to empathy to sharpen war's cutting edge, letting me see war and emancipation taking down these lives piece by piece. And I look to empathy to reveal ways I can think about myself as living and writing in my own time, likely blind, too, to how the *good* of my life is not such a sure thing after all.

Diaries are good guides in all of this. They invite us to imagine and do not press us to be satisfied with passing judgment and moving on. They invite us to picture *scenes* and to hear people's conversation, broken and true, and the private thoughts that follow conversation. There is in-your-face immediacy but also room to think when reading a diary; there are few, if any, author-laid traps. Diaries' start-and-stop prose lets us say "let us say . . ." and speculate. Let us say that it happened this way, or it did not, or it happened another way. . . . Let us say that she felt this, or that, or maybe both. . . . Diaries give us the words people used—the vernacular rhythm of the times—without much screening or self-protectiveness. Riffing on this language is an empathetic move. I have chosen a small way to do this, which tests the distance and the difference between the diarists and me, between slavery's times and our own. Consider: a planter-class white woman was never called a "woman." She was a "lady," a term taut with meaning in 1860, but which seems dead or comical now—or damning. Enslaved African Americans were called "servants" in polite, white talk, a term we now shun as a slaveholder's euphemism.

And enslaved people were called many other things in white diaries—slaves, Negroes, Cuffee, blacks, Africans, Ethiopians—that today sound insulting or quaint or puzzling. I've chosen to range through the mix of terms for both women and enslaved people. Using the mix is a way to keep alive the difference and distance between our world and theirs and to not let the difference and distance automatically serve as my judgment on the past.

So when I reach for empathy in reading diaries, I have to be patient with the full and prickly life a diary points to—a life as real as my own. I have to expect that slave mistresses can show me something more than why they deserved to lose, something about understanding the past—about reading and writing the Civil War, writing in the present moment about other present moments, snaring ghosts, and other aims of doing history. And when the diarists come up against the limits of their own moves toward empathy—with men, and especially with slaves—I test the limits of my effort to know them. My thought in all this is that empathy does not follow understanding but comes before it. We do not understand in order to empathize; we empathize in order to understand.

My focus is on the later war years, 1863 and after, when the bloom was already off the Confederacy. The diarists here are few in number, but nearly everyone who reads about the war will, sooner or later, read passages from these journals. All of them have been published, most for a generation or more, and are part of a canon of personal sources relied on by historians and enjoyed by readers of all sorts of Civil War history. These diarists lived throughout the South, mostly in the Carolinas, Georgia, Virginia, and Mississippi. Most of them were young and unmarried, though a few were middle-aged and had husbands. Some of the women had kept prewar journals and some continued writing after the war ended. But most began writing because the war happened to them, and when the war stopped, they stopped.

These ladies did not write for us. We know this, but it is easy to forget, and if we do, we forget how our irrelevance matters. The Civil War raged on, and so do our histories of it. Arguments are marshaled and sources are massed in formations following sound historical practice. Diaries are lumped together as a kind of historical source—behold the "Civil War diary"—and read with an eye to making an argument larger than any diary. Quotations are removed from them and dropped into academic histories. Days are trolled for examples of this or that. And so, as readers and writers, we streamline diaries to fit our interests and our uses, one more kind of fuel for the great engine of big-picture Civil War history, the kind we call monumental, sprawling, the tale of generals and soldiers, landscapes and campaigns, heroic and poignant struggle. And diaries satisfy. As historical sources, women's diaries give us sharp moments and personal words about topics we have learned to want to know about: the home-front scene and women's war work; tales of battle as seen from the dooryard; nationalist ambition shockingly transformed into devastated homes. The local imprint of General Sherman's vengeance? Emma LeConte's diary is a source, and Grace Elmore's and Mary Mallard's, too. White women as refugees? It is there in Mary Chesnut, Kate Stone, Sarah Morgan. Our sources, ours to use.

But before they were our sources, diaries were texts, peculiar, uncertain texts, with no thought of us. They lived alone, you might say, sure of themselves and unsure of the world. The page of a diary steps forward as the woman writes it, and then it is revised or reversed by the next day's entry. The diary is made for permanent impermanence, *for the time being.* The act of writing, this pace of things—the stumbling, the honesty—lies underneath all of the diarist's opinions and descriptions. Her authorized voice, seized upon by historians, was first of all a cry in the wilderness, and still is. Write what you know, say the teachers of creative writing. Diarists did not see any choice and wrote little else. *We* have a choice, though, and mine is to not lose the distinction between what diarists wrote and what we modern readers want to know, between text and source. Take a historical issue argued about in our present day—the gendered politics of the war and whether Southern ladies' support for it weakened because they lost confidence in their men. Diarists may be found on both sides of the "Have our men failed us?" question, and we bring them forward as sources with weight-bearing quotes for the histories we need to write and love to read. As a text, though, a diary usually shows the diarist *taking* both sides of the question. Diarists contradict themselves, like anyone, because days pass, things change, and what was bad or good one day shifts some days later. Or it just disappears. A woman writes her text, holds her pages close, and what she writes has no consequences in the world. She experiments over the days, makes secrets, writes mysteries. Maybe she forgets what she said last week, or maybe she recalls it but still cannot make up her mind. All of this can look cluttered and in need of a historian to see the text as a "source," to make it into something useful. But the jumbled look of the diary, wild eyed and sleepy at the same time, is the diary itself. Do not turn away! See the text, true to uneven life, and sail on by our poor desire for neatness and clarity.

Not that diarists were untroubled when their texts appeared before them wobbly and disheveled. Diarists themselves put limits on the diary's messiness. They start to care about their writing and notice gaps and illogic. They frown when their opinions go askew or their judgment wavers, and they think about having readers, or about themselves as readers, and they reach out to grasp the war and want to tell it true. But, in the end, a diary is a piece of writing more deeply felt than deeply considered. There cannot be a grand plan. As we read a diary, we are reading this: a woman sits down to write, and in her head is *what happened today* and also *this is my diary*. The diary's plain, absorbing, and contrary ways begin with the perfect, unselfconscious snapping together of these two thoughts. Here the diarist begins working to find out what the war means in her life, and here, too, through her text, arises the chance for empathy that opens up this work, this war, this life. Reading the diary—our work—is the act that joins us to her. There are not many other ties to be had with a long-dead slave owner. But the scarcity of ties between us has an advantage. The *pastness* of a life—a ghost that lives in all texts—speaks strongly from her pages because she is so foreign. An opening for empathy: we do not mistake her life for our own.

Reading this way, seeing diaries as texts, does not privilege certainty. It does not privilege the purposes of our time and place, our Civil War interests, our moral rightness. But if I am in this book saying that the lack of certainty that diaries inspire is a good thing, a challenge and more than that, a pleasure (and I *am* saying this), it is not in order to be indecisive about what the past can mean. There are arguments to be made, weaker or stronger, based on evidence deep or shallow. And yet the greater certainty is that historical meaning is not a steady beacon but a kind of constant flickering in the darkness. Diaries are good with this kind of light. The writer Margaret Atwood likens writing to descending into a half-lit underworld of experience and imagination both. Writing is taking a trip "from *now* to *once upon a time*" and not being "captured and held captive" by either. It is a trip where a writer's invention appears clothed as discovery. The diarists lived and wrote the war this way—their diaries mime it—and we, too, discover and invent the war when we read it and write it, too. In the big-picture view, the Civil War was a huge thing that ate up the lives of Americans, consuming or transforming them. A diarist's journey through her pages shows us this craziness of war and then, in a flash, fits the whole massive thing within the circle of one life. It was *her* war, and it is the war I am looking for.[1]

By now it is plain, I hope, that I am holding to a personal voice in this book. I am a reader and lover of historical diaries, and in a book about these plain and complicated texts, the women and the war that made them, and about historical empathy, it seems a bad idea to stand behind a curtain. I am a white man from California, who came to study the South nearly fifty years ago because it was a troubled and vibrant place that held the past close, as California did not. I thought the South might be a place to find keys to understanding my country's troubled, vibrant history. My way of stepping into the South's past has been to get to know something about historical people I do not admire or even like, and to let the intellectual tensions that follow have their free rein; then I explore these tensions and people as far as I am able. I *do* like and admire other historians, but my aim in this book is to stand a little outside the tribe. Though I have always loved conversation and how historians choose in various ways to put everything into words, my choice here is to travel light along the landscape of diaries to see what conversation I can have with the diarists about writing and war, without the usual respite of having colleagues in my pages. This means that footnotes and the tribal talk they invite are scarce here, but how much I am part of and beholden to other historians and readers of the Civil War, women, and diaries, I try to make clear in the closing note on reading. And when I talk about "us" in these pages, when I say "we," I mean anyone who knows about or wants to know about diaries, the Civil War, Southern women. I mean you, dear reader.

What follows is a cast of characters introducing the twenty diarists (more about their diaries and their lives is in an appendix, "Guide to the Diaries and Diarists"). Chapter 1 is about the diaries as they are today, about picking them up as they are and reading them. It is not a tutorial, but a tour of how a diary entices and persuades, the textual moves it makes, and the ambitions it kindles in readers. It is also about how these texts have been taken out of their time and turned into published historical sources, disciplined to be well behaved—easy to read, clear, and focused on *our* interests. So this chapter is about some of the strange things that have happened—and still happen—to diaries as they pass through the not-always-gentle hands of editors and readers who struggle to fit a diary's unruly pages into big-picture Civil War history. In Chapter 2 the focus shifts from reading diaries to the women writing them. *I am keeping a diary!* they all wrote in one way or another. Said with surprise, or responsibility, or amusement. Or with dismay and embarrassment: was diary keeping the act of a witness to a world turned upside down by war, or was it a compulsion, unproductive and much too self-revealing? Of course it was both. On the women wrote: what they said about writing and the war was never enough for them, and at the same time it was too much. This was the quiet drama that made the Civil War into the diarist's war.

Chapters 3, 4, and 5 take up themes women found inexhaustible in fashioning the war into their war: violence, men, and slavery. Or that is how I choose to read their pages. There could have been chapters, instead, on family, religion, nationalism, and the public realm. Or on travel, or on money and land. Or on clothes and food. On the sense of humor. My choice follows from what I read as a diarist's best moments of doubt and play on the page, and as the diary's wonderful mix of the known world and the world seen for the first time. These are themes that trace the line between loss and anticipation, a line so thin that maybe it isn't there. Domestic life is featured, and so is the shock of war as an unprecedented turn toward chaos and darkness. I hear the intensity in the women's words most surely here, though I know the intensity is partly my own. One of the reasons to love reading diaries is to find this synergy. Chapter 6 is about the diarist as she saw herself. Sometimes this happens up front, mostly it is roundabout. A diary begins as a first draft and pretty much ends that way, and it is a rare diarist who steps outside this raw writing to sum up her diary keeping or herself. Instead she becomes a kind of willing ghost in her own pages filled with ghosts, which is a diarist's way of giving us her war by giving us who she thought she was, over and over again.

As an editor, I have made myself scarce. When I have excerpted quotations from the diaries, I indicate these in the usual way, by ellipses. I have let stand misspellings and odd usages, and I have not used "*sic*" unless it seemed necessary to avoid confusion. My few interventions are noted by curly brackets { }. Editorial interventions by each of the volumes' editors are noted by square brackets [ ].

ACKNOWLEDGMENTS

I have been helped in many ways, over many years in this and other projects, by archivists, librarians, and editors who studied and worked with the diaries and diarists in this book. In one way or another, they steered me right. At the University of North Carolina Press, Chuck Grench gave me good advice and all-around support for how to think about this book. Mary Caviness skillfully moved the manuscript through to publication.

I tried out a few early ideas with colleagues in the Indiana University Department of History in a 2010 "retirement talk" and received engaged responses and helpful questions. I'm grateful, too, to Kristine McCusker for her invitation to be a Strickland lecturer at Middle Tennessee State University in 2012, and to her and her colleagues who took the measure of the project as it then stood and helped it to develop.

More than ever before, I imposed on friends and colleagues, within Southern history and without, to read the entire manuscript in one take or another. I am so glad that I did. Some had praise, some had doubts, many had both, all gave encouragement. I always went back to my pages with energy and much to think about. I am indebted for generous and critical readings to Stephen Berry, Emily Conroy-Krutz, Laura Edwards, Martha Hodes, Charles Keith, Edward Murphy, Suman Seth, Lewis Siegelbaum, Michael Stamm, David Thelen, and Jamie Warren. Among these readers, but really in a class by himself, was the late Michael O'Brien. Michael's friendship, unsparing critical eye, and love for Southern texts helped me in ways that cannot be replaced and so can only be deeply missed.

Historians Margaret Abruzzo and Anya Jabour, once-anonymous readers for the Press, weighed in with their knowledge of nineteenth-century writing, women, and the crisis over slavery. They handed me encouragement and some pointed questions. The book became stronger through their focused, subtle readings.

Keeping the days with me was Naoko Wake, my partner in all things historical and otherwise. She read the manuscript many times with an eye for what I saw and didn't see, and she helped me make some hard critical turns. Amid the brainstorms, dead ends, and the tide of everyone's words, her light shone. I look up, and she is there.

The Diarists

Eliza Frances Andrews

She begins her diary late in the war, at the end of 1864, moving to and from her home in Wilkes County, Georgia, staying with kin to keep away from the enemy. She is twenty-four. She thinks her marriageable years are slipping away. But she says this is of no consequence, and she never marries. The vast and formative war needs explaining, and she looks to do it through her diary. She keeps the days by keeping her eyes on solid events and away from vanity and trivia. She argues with her Unionist father, and she grows closer to her sister. She gives each day its own clear entry.

Lucy Breckinridge

At the start of her diary she imagines a listening friend, a woman older than the nineteen years she has seen at her family's place, Grove Hill, near Fincastle, Virginia. She imagines someone sympathetic who is eager to hear emotions put into words—this is what diaries do—and to follow the sudden, sharp-angled turns she makes as she writes. She writes of war's destruction, which she never sees close up though two brothers are killed. She is courted by a soldier, quarrels with him, marries him. She stops writing her pages on Christmas Day 1864. Five months on, the war winding down, she suddenly falls ill and dies.

Lucy Buck

There are soldiers in the yard more than once, looking for food and safety. She gives them breakfast, keeps them outside. Her father's place near Front Royal, Virginia, is in the channel made by the armies flowing up and down the Shenandoah Valley all through the war. She starts her diary when she is nineteen. She hears the cannonading and her heart beats fast, and she begins to think about her country, the enemy, and the cold greatness of the world. One afternoon General Lee and his aides ride up and take refreshment on her father's porch, and when the Confederacy sinks she despairs and cannot write for a while.

Mary Boykin Chesnut

She turns forty midwar, a childless woman married to a U.S. senator who resigns as their South Carolina secedes from the Union. She is a woman used to upper-echelon society and its privileges: slaves to stir the humid air with fans, the gatherings of the few and the clever, the sense of being well placed to write stories of wartime. Well placed, but dancing on the tightrope, as she likes to say, now that war is the choice. Her pen skips across the page with dashes instead of full stops. Her words, cutting or ironic (never tender), mingle with others' words, and her scenes vanish to become other scenes and—always—conversations. Sometimes she keeps her diary out in the room for people to notice.

Floride Clemson

A tall young woman, she feels she is awkward and in some ways the family's black sheep. Maybe writing the war will help focus things, so she starts keeping a diary in 1863 at age twenty. She is the granddaughter of South Carolina's most famous public man, John C. Calhoun, a decade in his grave when the war begins. With this family tie, the Clemsons might become targets of Yankee revenge, so the war means traveling from home in Pendleton, South Carolina, to various havens in Maryland. It means gardens abandoned before the flowers bloom, and it means smiling through afternoons at the young men who come calling in Bladensburg and Beltsville. The war pops into her pages, but often it is not there for days at a time.

Pauline DeCaradeuc

She writes as if diary keeping is there to be enjoyed, war or no war, though two brothers die in the fighting. When she turns twenty in 1863 and begins her diary, she hopes that the war will resolve itself without leaving many more wounds in Aiken, South Carolina. She writes with ease, skipping days at a time without apology, free to speak in the diary's vernacular and to write about men if she wishes to, or about her spiteful feelings, Christmas, travel, and her full-of-questions mind. The war must fit itself in.

Catherine Devereux Edmondston

She loves her Looking Glass plantation in Halifax County, North Carolina, not far from the sea, and she loves her husband, who leaves her surprise gifts in the summerhouse where she writes her diary. She is thirty-seven years old when the war comes, married fifteen years. They have no children. When her husband travels, she is the lone white person among her slaves. She thinks that she is protected because they need her. She eagerly reads newspaper reports of armies, generalship, fierce battles. She writes about the daily things that the war is changing, and she reads diaries she kept as a younger woman and finds that she has changed. She worries that if the Yankees come, her diary will fall into their hands.

Grace Brown Elmore

At home in Columbia, South Carolina, she is twenty-one when Fort Sumter in Charleston Harbor is fired upon, and she feels Carolinian pride and foreboding for having started the war. With her mother and sisters she lives an urban life, facing wartime shortages, taking in boarders, wondering if the slaves will take themselves off. The war does not initiate her diary but enters into one she's been keeping for some years. She finds that she is likely to write when she is sad or when she doubts the strength of her religious faith. She thinks that her sisters find her officious, cold. There is a man who shows that he loves her, but she feels unlovable.

Anna Maria Green

Her father manages a lunatic asylum in Milledgeville, Georgia, and there she will meet the man she marries, though he is no lunatic. She begins her war diary at the beginning of the war, at age sixteen, thinking the war will hand her plenty to write about and writing will give her a more mature character. She wants to improve herself and grow to be a good person, and she wants to know men and why war. Her pages mingle her wonder at life with days or weeks where she writes nothing at all. She is not a writer who reaches back to recover unrecorded times, but she can hand over the writing moment as fresh as she found it.

Emily Harris

Her husband has kept a farm journal for years, and now that he is away from time to time on war's errands, he asks her to log the work routine of their place in Spartanburg District, South Carolina. She is in her midthirties and writes easily, as if diary keeping were her idea and not her husband's. She observes the weather and how the crops fare and how market talk is shaken up by the war and the slaves stirred up by it. Purchases made, harvests sized up, what the neighbors are saying, children hard at work. The war is out beyond the fields and she does not travel to find it. She writes the war almost before she knows it, as it takes on the face of the everyday.

Emma Holmes

She lives with her widowed mother in Charleston, South Carolina, and she turns twenty-three in 1861, no longer one of the young women. The war takes her only a few miles away, to Camden, when Charleston is threatened by the enemy. But she feels that wartime change is vast and intricate, really beyond imagination. She hires herself out as a teacher. She becomes a seamstress, making clothing to make money. She falls in love (though she doesn't call it that) with a captain in the Confederate army. She holds her diary close, taking it everywhere, hiding it from the Yankees when they ransack her employer's house. When she is unable to write, she goes back and fills in the missed days with all that she can remember.

Elizabeth Ingraham

She resides in Claiborne County, Mississippi, a day's travel south of Vicksburg, a woman in her midfifties with an older husband. When the Union army lays siege to the city in 1863, she begins writing a daily account, meant for her daughters, of the wildly changing world and perhaps her doom. It is a kind of diary, and she thinks aloud in it. She thinks about the slaves who steal her clothes and about the slaves who tell her they are on her side. She wonders how long Vicksburg will hold out and whether she has drinking water to last. Her husband seems feeble or distracted. Union soldiers ride up to the door, push her aside, run through the rooms taking things she never thought any thief would take.

Mary Jones and Mary Mallard

They are mother and daughter. In 1864 Mary Jones is fifty-six years old and the sole mistress of Montevideo plantation in Liberty County, Georgia, now a year since the death of her husband, a planter and Presbyterian minister. They had been married thirty-two years. Mary Mallard, twenty-nine and pregnant, also is married to a minister, though he is away. When they hear that Yankee troops are nearby, they both resolve to keep diaries. To keep a history of what happens, to not forget, to give witness to God's mercy and to conquer fear. They write long afternoons of rumor and waiting. When the soldiers show up at the house, they take what they want but leave the women unharmed. In the midst of these days, Mary Mallard gives birth to a daughter.

Emma LeConte

She begins her diary in December 1864, just after her seventeenth birthday, at her home in Columbia, South Carolina. She adores her father, a scholar and physician who has bolstered her courage now that the Yankee army, after marching across Georgia, is descending on the city. Friends have left town, slaves are disappearing, Charleston is lost. She reads the newspapers and re-members the details, and she talks rumors with friends. From her porch she hears Sherman's artillery fire, and at night her anger deepens as she sees the city burn. She thinks that the war has robbed her of girlhood's carefree years.

Cornelia Peake McDonald

The children will be safer at home, she thinks, so she stays for as long as she can in the house in Winchester, Virginia, as the town changes hands more than once in the course of war. She turns forty years old in 1862, the year she begins her diary, which she loses and then begins again. First she writes at her husband's request that she keep a record of their days apart, but soon the diary becomes her project and a keepsake of the momentous times. She makes deals with Yankee soldiers for food, and she puts on her bonnet and takes herself to the Union general's quarters to request his protection, hoping he will prove to be a gentleman. Rude enemy soldiers are everywhere, in the town streets, outside her windows.

Emilie Riley McKinley

She comes to Mount Alban, Mississippi, from Pennsylvania to tutor the children of several planter-class families. She in her late twenties and writes little about her past or her future plans. She takes up diary keeping when nearby Vicksburg comes under siege, the sound of cannon a backdrop to the armed men of indeterminate loyalties who are on the roads. Her teaching stops, and she thinks about how war monopolizes everyone's time and what it does to manhood. She trades news with neighbor women and her employers, putting it down in dialogue on her pages. She thinks she can never go north again, so full is her heart for the Confederate cause.

Sarah Morgan

The war is dreadful and absurd and a curious thing, too, and she is curious about whether she can stand it as the war enters its second full year and she enters her twentieth. She writes to be able to stand the war, wrapping it in words. There are the travels with her mother and sister between New Orleans and Baton Rouge, Louisiana, and back. There are her brothers in mortal danger, then dying, and her family home sacked by Union troops. There are the slaves, unreadable, perhaps more interesting now. She writes reasons to accept and to resist what the world calls fate. She writes about eligible men, and married ones, and ones she never thought she would speak to. The world opens up, then encloses her, then opens again as she writes the amazing scenes and her transparent self.

Emmala Reed

She feels wartime Anderson sinking along with the rest of South Carolina. War empties the churches of men, brings abrasive Yankees, makes profound uncertainty out of everything familiar. She turns twenty-six in the last year of the war and she feels old. She writes dense pages of underlined sentences, with many questions, solid days and frantic ones bundled together. There are gardens to write about, and her music, and the failing Confederate will. There are friends, conversation, and the lover who returns from battle but does not call on her.

Kate Stone

She begins her diary at Brokenburn plantation, a day's ride northwest of Vicksburg, Mississippi. With her family, she aims to sidestep the armies by moving first to Texas and afterward to Louisiana. She is twenty-one years old in 1861. Her pages are made of large events and small, the death of a brother, the way gossip runs through the neighborhood, camping on the road west. There are treacherous slaves and slaves she is sorry to see go. There are times she calls exciting: enemy soldiers try to steal her horse, and as she moves to stop them, one pulls a pistol and points it at her head.

Ella Gertrude Thomas

She has kept a diary since 1848 when she was fourteen years old, and her diary keeping will outlast the war years. In wartime, she is sometimes with her husband, sometimes without, as the war demands, in the environs of Augusta, Georgia. Children and enslaved servants crowd into her pages, along with her worries about them and her impatience and her doubt. Her wish is to be a better person. She makes decisions alone, counts her cash, and will not, at first, take seriously the word that Lee has surrendered. God moves in mysterious ways which no one should question, though she does have questions that she cannot answer except by writing on.

Keep the Days

CHAPTER ONE

Reading the Diary

A diary is a balky thing to read, only half-awake to our concerns. The clearest thing it says is about each moment of its own creation. *It is today, and I am here.* This seems simple but it is not. The diary is a self-absorbed piece of writing and gets wound up in its ways, but it is not transparent or innocent. It holds its own ground among other texts from the past, and this is the ground I want to travel. I travel as a reader, so I begin this book on Civil War diaries thinking about reading. Maybe this seems like an odd move, putting the war a little to the side and taking up a text. But this is what a diarist did each time she wrote, and the diary is all we have between us. Begin with it.

All the diaries here, brimming with the war's history, seem to await the reader eagerly. They are familiar and trusted as historical sources, so it is easy to step around the body of each diary—the handwritten volume, and the published volume, too—without giving it any thought and move into the content—the stories, the history. The impulse is to read the past through the diary as if the volume in our hands is a simple pipeline to the diarist and the war. As if the saga of her bound-together body of words, making its way to us through years of miraculous survivals and calculated maneuvers, does not matter. But it does matter. The particular substance and shape of any diary and how it got here should be more than an afterthought or an afterword in a book about Civil War diaries. It should be the first thought, and one taken along for the ride.

The diaries in this book are read as "war diaries," even though the war shows up in their pages in ways that do not flow easily into great-event, big-picture Civil War history. A diary is insistently personal and satisfied with being so. This can make readers (and editors) want to skip around in it to find pieces of the big picture, the familiar wartime action. Resist doing this and you will see the diary's peculiar artfulness, which is to make the diarist the center of everything while also keeping her apart, busily at work with words within the bubble of her subjectivity. She witnessed the war. Something of what that meant to her clings to how she wrote it. She wrote her way ahead into the day, the week, the people and the slip-sliding events, and she did it solo because a diary does not, like a personal letter, seek out and take strength from correspondence. A diary is more like a broadcast than a dialogue. The diarist speaks into the air, so to say. We read her, hear her, but she keeps her own company, fills all space, and the war fades in and out as she sees fit.[1]

Some of the diarists here, Emma Holmes and Catherine Edmondston, for example, feasted on specifics by following the war in the newspapers and reporting on troop movements, battles, and generals up or down. Stretches of their writing read like a primer on the course of the war, or the outline of a war memoir. Other women had little to say about wide-angle "war news," and for some, like Sarah Morgan and Floride Clemson, the war dropped completely out of sight for days at a time. So the war in these diaries is a presence, not a plot. In a way it seems all the more powerful for this, and more mysterious. As we read, the war shifts its shape. It is sublime and then it is familiar. It is terrifyingly beyond words, and then, in a blink, it is perfectly suited to the diary page. The war reads as pathos and bathos, the twins of improvised writing, and many other points in between that the diarist touches, or passes by, feeling her way ahead in the day, on the page—as I do when reading her—and sometimes she understands. If I have nothing else in common with these slave-owning, worldly-wealthy, nineteenth-century Southern ladies, I have this desire to write the war, and to read it. I have this text in front of me.

VOICE AND STORY AND THE SCALE OF THINGS

A diarist's war has her tone of voice, and I read to get to know it and find the war—her war—through it. Anyone who writes about the war has a voice, so this is a patch of shared ground. A diarist's voice is partly her conscious choice, but it also comes from the sheer momentum of writing—from the page right to the ear. Consider passages from three diarists. Young Grace Elmore, doubting her faith in God, thought about Christ at Easter time in 1864 and wondered, "Will I ever, be proud, indifferent, cold, untouched by his holy life, his awful death, his glorious resurrection{?} . . . Shall I never find time to think of Christ, the mysteries of his gospel? Shall I ever be in too much hurry to rest?" She wrote on in this vein. There was bad war news from the West; there was new trouble at home with the servants. But Elmore did not mention these things here, and in fact her religious doubts carried over from her prewar diary. So how do we read her self-reproach in this passage—as something stirred up by new, war-sown tensions, or as Elmore stepping outside the war to revisit old, long-standing sorrows? Or maybe this distinction was something the war—and diary writing—was subtly erasing in the lives of introspective women.

In another part of the forest is Emily Harris; reading her is not like reading Grace Elmore. "PLANTED IRISH POTATOES" begins an entry in Harris's diary in the early spring of 1865, as Sherman's army was heading toward her farm in Spartanburg, South Carolina. Harris was well aware of Sherman, but she was keeping the diary for her absent husband's later edification, and, for him, the potatoes were first things first. Yet the diary was *hers*, too; more and more the entries show it. "Had a fight with our girl, Ann," Harris goes on, factual and determined, "which ended in my tieing and whipping her with the assistance of Mr. Bagwell. Some remarks of the children about the affair have hurt Mr. Bagwell's feelings. He Knows nothing about the management of negroes." A brutal time, an intense day. The big war of Sherman's advancing army is only on the edges of the truly dangerous war, Harris's war: making do as mistress, wife, and mother in the wartime absence of a husband who should have been there. This day, Harris is unable to beat the enslaved woman Ann without calling on a man, and she calls on the wrong man. He is hapless, and the children rude about it. Ann fights back, then slips from view. All of this is the war, though Harris does not say how the events sorted out in her mind. The power of her blunt voice is in the factual weight of the chosen moments she hands over without dressing them up. *What happened today* joins the line of what has already happened, day after day. This is the war; read on.

Then there is Floride Clemson, a South Carolinian, like Elmore and Harris, who was out of harm's way in Maryland when she turned to her diary one October day in 1863 to write, "I have just planted out many roses, bulbs, & shrubs, & have trimmed the hedges &c. I also attend much to the horses. I am very busy. . . . Hurrah for Charleston yet! I have had two more teeth filled." Here the big-picture war—Charleston holding out against the Yankees—pops up briefly in the stream of Clemson's daily tasks—or, literally, her slaves' tasks. Charleston's long resistance to the Union siege was another thing that happened today, put in place exactly where it belonged, next to gardening and dental work. Clemson's voice? I hear the satisfaction that comes from habitual diary writing, half-automatic but taking pleasure in channeling the day's notable happenings into a single stream within the page's comforting confines, and giving Charleston the exclamation point.[2]

So we read to find diarists giving voice to the war as they take it into their lives, alongside God, whippings, and teeth. Sometimes we read from the centers of their days to the edges, and sometimes it goes the other way. A diary is shot through with the woman's shifting attention that moves like light over a landscape. We read the war through the quirkiness of this one voice, and I take pleasure in how odd and open her choices are, *telling* many things as they occur, and *showing* many other things in the telling. I like critic Sharon Marcus's idea of the "just reading" of a text, with "just" taken in two ways. It suggests making an effort to be just, or true, to the text's integrity and the author's grasp on her writing. And it also means just (simply) reading: engaging with the surface and shape of a diary, rather than searching for "hidden master codes" beneath the surface or valuing clarity over the diary's clutter. This doesn't mean that a diary is simpleminded or can be read by suspending interpretation. Quite the opposite: just reading means recognizing that diaries, like all texts, are in themselves "complex and ample." They will take any kind of reading, from skimming to burrowing in. And no matter how we read, "interpretation is inevitable" so that "even when we are attending to the givens of a text, we are always only—or just—constructing a reading."[3]

In this light, I read a diarist's voice as a guide to how one day followed another for her, and how voice shapes a just reading by its tone. Diaries are busy with life's moments seized or slipping by, and each diarist makes her own way in the surprising variety of expression open to solitary authorship. And I read knowing this: the diarist's eyes are never on me—never. I am completely unknown, not there for her to please, and she is not there to please me. That is the power of the diary.

Not that we should read a diarist with the idea that she thought of her writing as a dark secret. As we will see, some women shared their diaries with friends or husbands and got some praise or some laughs in return. Some women enjoyed having a literary alter ego. Ladies knew the diary as a genre of writing with a particular kind of intellectual-intimate charge. They had read famous diaries and knew novels where women kept diaries with passion and purpose. They knew that journal keeping probably should be an act of self-improvement. And they knew of other women keeping war journals. We read a diarist's voice on this ground, and we also read it for the way her writing scoops up her personality and shakes it out, her prides and her prejudices. Sarah Morgan pinching herself and others for emphasis; Emmala Reed singing her heart out; Pauline DeCaradeuc checking out the men; Lucy Breckinridge checking out the men and the women; any number of women saying "silly me!" and "woe to the race of Yankees." We read to see what she will write next, and how her voice lifts and carries her world.

And so we read for stories. Without the urge to tell stories, no diary thrives. A woman might lose her narrative thread for some pages and write about what the newspapers are saying, or about her Christian passion, or her desire for a lover, and go adrift. But she will come back to stories. Stories told and, wrapped inside them, stories more shown than told. A diary is a permissive text, off guard and impulsive. Read diaries expecting to plunge into more than one layer of storytelling at a time. Purposeful stories ride in tandem with unintentional ones; we ride both shallow and deep. Mary Jones and Mary Mallard, mother and daughter, went, as we will see, through days of Union troops arriving at the front door wanting things, or wanting to do things. The women faced them, endured the trashing of their house, and wrote stories about conversations with the trashers, tricks played, insults suffered and given, jokes made, strategies for next time. Inside the action, or maybe rising above it, is another story, one about religious faith: for these two women, God was present through each harrowing moment, and this was the story that covered all.

So, too, as we will also see, did Emma Holmes, Gertrude Thomas, and other women managing households when emancipation came write narratives of the changed domestic scene, the old smooth-seeming days now corrugated by kitchen conspiracies and the sudden personalities of the black people who had always done the work. As Holmes and Thomas wrote their stories of negotiating with "the servants," who had morphed into wageworkers sharp for their own advantage, they were also writing another story of *everyone* struggling to come to terms with the people they knew who had turned out to be only partly known—slaves and mistresses made strangely vibrant or opaque by war. And by writing this, Thomas and Holmes also sketched their prewar world as a kind of by-product of their wartime diaries—bits here and there of a life that now seemed to be ending and would be replaced by who knew what. Replaced, maybe, by naked will and the open struggle for advantage that marked the changed politics of servitude. We read everyone struggling over race and wondering what it was all about; whether race was about something they knew, or about something that substituted for knowing.

Stories of all sorts, fierce and gentle. Suddenly, as we are reading along, the moment becomes weirdly elastic. The scale of events, of life generally, recalibrates before our eyes, and the war's enormity folds into a single image of personal terror, sadness, or relief. The entire war is compressed into one hour, one encounter, even one image. For Kate Stone: a black Union soldier looks her over, coming so close to her that he stands on the hem of her dress. For Emma Holmes: when—*when*—will the captain come again? For Elizabeth Ingraham: the soldiers leave the house upended and the yard ravaged, but what she writes about are the missing cups, the small red cups. Diarists inscribe such things freely, even haphazardly, but I read them and stop in my tracks. Their words carry small events past all thought of proportion, and this unintentional exaggeration of a moment makes the war seem preternaturally present and *strange*. Or it may be that the shift in scale reveals the real but forgotten proportions of life in war and now we actually see them. Either way, the scale of things shifts drastically so that instead of the war engulfing the woman's life, her life stands for all of the war, unashamed.

It is a slight thing to hold onto, but along with voice and story, finding the scale of what I want to see and say about the war is something I have in common with the diarist. These things shaped her pages, and they play with the writing and reading of history, too. We, she and I, fit "what happened" to how we want to read and write—to witness, to give comfort or pleasure, to stir up, revise, or reform. To just *get it down*. I read her—feel her caught up in her words—as another writer carried along by the flow of the page but making choices, too, and even if her choices would not be mine, I can make an opening move for empathy. It is a frontal move, a choice to keep reading her and not put her aside. A move to face the wrong she did as a slaveholder and stay in its presence, and so be open to the buzz of implications in her days that showed her the seriousness of her wartime self.[4]

Subjectivity is the currency here. The diarist's subjectivity flows through her discoveries and satisfactions as a writer, and the play of it, mostly careless and unremarked, gives us the pleasure of feeling *this close* to the past because we feel closer to a person. Subjectivity is strangely perishable in the face of harsh scrutiny by readers, or in the face of the diarist's own embarrassment. It is easy to mock. But it can rise up unexpectedly with surprising force. Because these are diaries of nineteenth-century women, subjectivity opens onto a gendered world where women inhabited a "natural" feminine realm of their own. The public imprint of gender is not as much in the foreground of this book as individual women's subjectivity, which, admittedly, can be ambiguously rich and privately weird. Even so, it is inner life that I read for in the heart of a diary; subjectivity as the essence of gender, rather than the other way around. I use the diary—just reading the diary—as a kind of rope line into the subjective darkness. It has strength and a no-nonsense feel. I follow it along as far as I can, as the diarist herself did, her words revealing her world and, in the same moment, making the world anew on the page.

Strangely, diarists are not much help here, at least not directly. The diary plays with both surfaces and depths, and there are many pages where the surfaces of things are enough for the diarist. Subjectivity? "My subjective days are over," wrote Mary Chesnut, the most famous of Civil War diarists, in a famous passage. She hoped that writing would get her outside of her own head and end her habitual "*silent* eating into my own heart." She thought that writing in her diary would be akin to speaking out, though there is not an obvious likeness between them at all. Still, "entirely *objective*" was what she aimed to be. Yet her accounts of war and war talk, of men and women sparring and gossiping, of things political and things social, are bound together by nothing so much as her own subjectivity. Instead of freeing her from subjectivity, her diary gave a shape to it. Her subjective days, released from wordlessness by her writing, were just beginning. A reader has to look for a diarist here, planted in her subjectivity, where she writes not at all to help readers along. In fact, she makes demands on readers. Subjectivity is the currency, and it might be unwelcome for a reader to find that it calls for a payback: her subjectivity is warm and elicits ours. This, from a slave mistress, might be unnerving. And a reader might become impatient with reading a text where the big-picture historical payoff is often pretty thin and the diary's limits as a historical source are many. But such demands, if that is what to call them, are part of the good work of reading diaries and looking hard for the diarist.[5]

INTO PRINT: PLAY AND POSSESSION, ORIGINALS AND READABILITY

There is a woman writing. Her head bends to her work. The diary is on a small desk, and she sits a little to one side. It is moving to be able to hold in my hands the volume that was once on that desk. It's called the "original." There is no happiness like having a manuscript's weight and fragrance, its marginal ephemera (as the archivists say) right where they belong, in actual margins. No happiness like the manuscript's folds, nicks, ink blots, erasures, doodles, and sometimes, close to the binding inside, the stubs of razored-out pages. The woman's cursive hand, its slant and height, the form of its vowels, the sense of the pressure of her pen, the crossing of t's and the dotting of i's are the diary's birthmarks and the manuscript's beauty. All of these things carry a slight charge from her time to ours. Diary-reading paradise is this: we have the manuscript diary straight from her hands, from the moment she last put down the pen—the original. We lose this, and we accept that we do, or we think that we accept it, when the diary is transcribed and put into print.

Into print: accessible, shareable, requiring no special handling. The diaries here have these features, and one happy result is the large number of readers who have come to them and how easily others will discover a diarist's voice, her stories, and the scale of things from her eye level. Good things all, but the way publishing a diary hands them over to readers is not all good news for the text. Think of the diary as a text peculiarly open to a reader playing with it and possessing it; one invites the other, easily but disquietingly. The diary's frank openness makes it not too sober a text to take up in a friendly, familiar way. The diarist herself did so day after day, each written moment fresh and available as she filled in the order of things, tried out scenes, remembered conversations, scratched out, amended—played with the diary. She kept possession of it, too, making time to write, rereading, hiding it from her sisters. At these times her old-hat diary might turn into something intensely dear. *Dearest Diary*. These qualities of a diary's creation cling to it when she rereads it after the war and when it is read by others, including us. Readers take up the diary—or think they can—as the diarist did during the war, fond of its ordinariness, valuing it as a comfortable text not at all profound or brilliant. And so, open to possession and play.

It might begin right after the war, but usually it is many years later. The woman sees that the pages of her diary are brittle and fading, and she recopies it to pass along to her family. Or she has ideas about the meaning of the war and thinks that publishing her diary would be a good way to express them. Or a son or a granddaughter believes, after her death, that publishing the diary would be a way to honor her and keep a memory of the war. More years pass and scholars and editors are intellectually impressed or emotionally moved by a first edition of the diary, or they discover such a diary in an archive, and they set about having it published. All of these people, and the diarist, too, are readers who do what readers do: form likes and dislikes about the text, see places where it might be *improved*. Everyone—especially that fiercer kind of reader, the editor—plays a bit with the text, possesses it, imagining how the diary might say things about the war more clearly, be more dramatic or more succinct. Good, practical reasons for doing this sort of thing are plenty: such texts attract other readers and sell more copies. Seldom does anyone making these maneuvers have ill intentions, and not all of the outcomes are bad. The diary, gentle text, tolerates the playing and possessing, and it abides—sort of.

It is poignant, funny, sometimes frustrating, even harrowing, this journey of the diary from the woman's text to a published volume and then to us. Family members and editors tell us only what they please about how they have tinkered with the pages. Many say nothing at all about how they altered the text, and their silence impoverishes our reading. The saga of a diary's transformation should be part of what we know about it. Edited diaries shift their shape and take some strange turns, as we will see, and part of the pleasure of reading a text so vulnerable yet so solidly within itself is to know that the act of reading, like editing, is an act of play and possession. And to keep in mind that inside this published volume, this "historical source," the changed and still-changing text is always there.

Pause in this transformation tale for a question: as the diary travels away from its author, her desk and pen, and the time of its creation, does the original manuscript still matter? I am going to say it does. When published, a diary loses all of its manuscript texture, but if published complete and unaltered, it remains "original" and privileged. It still has some of the heat of its creation, the perfect sense of an imperfect woman laboring away to the best of her limited but relentless ability, day after day, entry after entry, even lapse after lapse. There is another view of this, though. This view sees the "original" text not as the obvious place to start reading, a critical baseline, but as a way of bestowing authority—too much authority—on the *earliest known* text. It is a mistake, in this view, to give iconic standing to such a text. Diarists are famous for writing on scraps of paper, losing them, beginning again. They are erratic and forget things. They start or stop writing without giving notice. Emma Holmes sometimes entered a week's worth of dated entries at the end of the week, but silently; only a later slip of her pen revealed the smoke-and-mirrors postdating. Catherine Edmondston copied into her volume passages she had written elsewhere in haste but does not say when or where. Grace Elmore kept two diaries simultaneously in 1864 without saying why. Who can know if what seems to be the earliest text actually is "first"? And think of how diarists are always revising their thoughts as they go through the days rereading what they have just written. At what point is a diary "finished" so as to become the "original" text? Isn't it misleading to treat the diarist as if she were a historian or archivist by holding her to documentary standards that don't apply to her freelance scribbling? Suppose she revises her text a few years later and changes some entries. Isn't it overreaching to criticize her for falsifying or tampering with her own "original" words?[6]

Seeing things this way is of interest because it highlights the diary as always under construction, maybe uniquely so among texts. But this view veers close to seeing the diary as so unremarkable a piece of writing that it does not matter how it came to us—and how it began. So I want to hold on to the idea of an original diary text, not as something empirically uniform from diary to diary, but as a *choice* we make to notice the earliest-written manuscript, and to say: this is it, as far as we know, this is how she said it. Diaries are about uncertainty and time, and about reading one's way through both of these. The original is important not as an icon but as a vantage point on all the subsequent textual playing and possessing. I make the choice to see whatever the diarist herself wrote—her insights, mistakes, monotony—as unlike anything that might come after. And better. No words cut, no words altered. Bare and complex. It's the "original," the text when questions come up to "go back" to.

A diary is about time in another way; its first suit is immediacy. And because we know what it is like to live in a "present," we read a woman's diary in a special, approaching-empathetic way. The text now in front of us was written from *her* here and now. The essayist Annie Dillard describes wanting to write in such a way, a diary-like way, so as to "depict precise moments precisely, in the hope that a collection of such moments might give an impression of many sharp points going in different directions—might give a vivid sense of complexity." We read diaries for their sparkling play with the immediate moment, which can be sketchy and confusing, too. There are errors of fact, strange juxtapositions, lost skeins of thought, events without outcomes. Some diarists see this and, dismayed, point to the "trash" they are putting on the page. *This is not the best me.* But if we have patience and stay with it, this roughness lets us grasp something of the diarist's emotion and judgment and imagery on the fly: her world *now* with its "many sharp points going in different directions."[7]

A person takes shape gradually but forcefully as she writes from her immediate moment, especially in an original, complete diary. It is one of the diary's best gifts. Emmala Reed, conversational with her diary as with her friends, is a hearty, agitated writer. She is barely able to wait out the war in the South Carolina Upcountry, so she searches each day for signs and underscores word after word—*what, what will happen next?* She pummels her pages with words as she sees fall the two pillars of her life: the South and her sweetheart's love. Catherine Edmondston, middle-aged and without children in North Carolina's so-far-it's-quiet Halifax County, goes to the summerhouse to make entries in her diary, presides over it, calling herself "Mrs. E" when she reprimands or condescends to herself or otherwise observes the observer. Mary Chesnut, also in middle age, loving wartime excitement and fearing its cost, speaks in fragments and takes a little opium on the side. War brought a new kind of life, which surprised her by turning into a *new life*; she writes on, disheveled, but engaging for that, a little gnomic, breathless. Anna Green stirs a dialogue with her lover, Samuel Cook, into her entries, allowing him to write lines in her book, the two of them talking to each other on the page.

So the original diary's completeness and immediacy pull us to the page and to the woman writing away, afloat on her abilities and imperfections. She is pulled to her diary by these same qualities years later when she decides to preserve it, and these qualities attract her children or scholars, who then decide to put the diary into print. So the play and possession begins, and it is here that something strange happens. The immediate unspooling of days and thoughts and personality starts to seem cluttered and exhausting to read. Or so someone thinks when they think about publishing an original diary whole. The subjectivity that makes a diary compelling seems from another angle to be the very thing in need of fixing—the strong personal voice rambles too much; the sense of time passing seems to set us adrift; immediacy trails off into trivia. Diarists repeat themselves! They make mistakes! So the qualities of the original text harden into flaws, and editors, or sometimes the diarists themselves, think about cutting passages or pages, neatening it up, making it more *readable*.

Some see the danger in letting impatience or a desire for "readability" override the peculiar mix of inscribed moments in each diary. But the editorial urge to streamline a woman's voice by cutting and polishing her words is powerful, especially when it would make for easy coherence, a shorter published volume, and a larger readership. Not talked about, or not talked about enough, is how altering a diary in the name of readability quietly soaks into everything we think about diaries and the women who wrote them. Both become neater, thinner in profile, more recognizable. And although it may take time for this to trickle through the pages of dozens of diaries, the Civil War gets changed, too, in the same way. It becomes more like the war we have already imagined.

What is this thing, "readability"? Publishing a diary alters its private heart and yet in a way oddly seems to fulfill it, so strong was the diarist's drive to *tell*. But while writing, she did not have so strong an urge to be *readable*. Readability is our creation, the nemesis of "just reading" the diary. Readability is our knowing better than she what she has to say. It is taking a diary text out of itself to make it more finished or entertaining or logical—more like other kinds of texts. It is making the "good read" of our time the good read for all time, including the diarist's. The editorial work that has shaped the diaries here ranges from the gentle and careful to the gross and misleading, but in the end the commitment to readability means cutting the past to fit the pattern of the present. The vast field of Civil War history has room for many different characters and texts, but readability favors those that speak in familiar voices on the known stage of big-picture, battle-and-emancipation history. There is an already-primed excitement in reading a diary that hooks right into history as we know it. A diarist writing from the hot wartime action in middle Virginia in 1862 is pretty much going to be more "readable" as a war diarist than a woman in the quietude of northeast Texas. The thoughtful, clear, but witty diarist is hard to beat, too, and one who writes every day is a plus. We want the familiar weight of a well-worked historical source, and we want to be entertained.

It is a comforting thing, sometimes exciting, to have a text satisfy these desires, and it is a good thing if just reading the diary hands them over easily. But if editors of a published diary have had little faith or time for just reading, then we should know something about how they have tinkered with the text to make it more "readable." The text's journey to us along the editorial road is a saga we should know about. Examples of the editorial knife at work, performing readability, will follow, and there are many more eye-widening sagas of transformation where diaries emerge from editorial makeovers not as themselves but as something diary-*like*, trim and eerily vivid, the textual equivalents of androids. But, for now, it is enough to say that if editors (some diarists, too, and not a few readers) apply any single standard for readability, it is to root out, dress up, or lacquer over "trivia," which usually means playing with passages where the diarist repeats herself, multiplies details, copies out a favorite poem, tells a long story without a clear point, mentions people she does not identify, or mentions going to church or a neighbor's and includes the names of everyone who was there. Editing out trivia leads to modifying obscure sentences and long ones, or sentences where the diarist's logic turns without signaling, and other things the editor thinks are distracting and add up, in the editorial mind, to days—pages!—where *nothing happens*.

But wait. How can we justify so transforming a text that is supposed to be a true primary source of the past? There is a lot of trivia in official military accounts of the Civil War, and yet no good editor would think of preemptively cutting these accounts in the name of "readability". It is not just that a diary has trivia, it is *personal* trivia, the diarist's unmade beds and unmet needs. Gender plays a role here, as a woman's "trivia" is, or used to be, devalued in the same way as women's "gossip" as peripheral, or as so ordinary as to be not pertinent, or with a different dismissive spin, as the timeless stuff of womanhood. In any case, whatever is called trivia seems expendable because it is not what we want or expect to read about the Civil War, the big-picture war we have in our heads and that we have come to love.

There are other, less open reasons for cutting out "trivia." Passages of routine personal busyness or the diarist noodling over her half-formed wishes and fears are marked for editorial oblivion because a diarist, or her kin, or a later historian-editor does not want her to seem an unfocused, boring person who now, in a published book, will inflict boredom on readers. And even boredom is not the worst fate to be avoided by playing with diaries and possessing them as texts that can be made *better*; it is embarrassment that everyone flies from. Personal life is keenly awkward and has too many primary colors when it rolls uncut from the diary page. So it is not only repetition and routine that are excised, but some of the deeper reaches of a woman's subjectivity, especially religious faith and romantic love. It is fascinating that the religious and romantic words that embarrass (and yet bore) many diarists when they reread their pages are the very words that bore (and yet embarrass) scholarly editors a century later. The urge to cut words about overflowing hearts and dark nights of the soul goes beyond their supposed tenuous link to big-picture Civil War history into some critical place where religion and love are too nakedly revealing to be looked upon for very long. They are too close to the diarist's present moment; too much *in need*. But such passages are among the best diaries have to offer. Ducking boredom and embarrassment keeps the diary "readable" when, instead, we should be facing the reality and having the pleasure of staying with the diary's *now* and moving at all costs into another person's amazing life.

INTO THE HANDS OF OTHERS

Now consider particular sagas of transformation where the present puts its playful, possessive hands on Civil War diaries. A diarist rereading her journal years later and making marginal notes is the beginning of one saga; editors begin another by thinking about larger contexts, explanatory notes, and readability. Readers set up transformations, too, as they lower themselves into the pages expecting to find their idea of enjoyment, information, the *past*. There is reason to be hopeful that keeping a diary alive by publishing it, to borrow Michael Holroyd's observation about biography, "gives an opportunity to the dead to contribute to the living world." I believe this, or want to, but it is too simply said when it comes to diarists. Did a diarist want her diary to fall into the hands of others? Did she want to make a contribution to our world? Most never say, and the silence lets the "living world" of readers and editors throw its weight around and take the diary for a text-altering ride.[8]

An editor (a kind of supercharged reader) is a master of ceremonies who is eager for readers to learn something about the diarist and *from* the diarist about the Civil War. About heroic Southern womanhood, let's say, as it was thought of in the white, postbellum South, or by the 1970s, about women's gendered experience of the war. Doing good editorial work is tough, and the point here is not to find fault. But an editor, even a careful one, edges toward becoming a kind of ghostwriter, an amanuensis with an agenda. Think of editors as themselves historical actors, carrying the diary from one time to another, one literary atmosphere to another, leaving signs of their possession. Readers do this too, in a way. At every point in the saga, layers of text are stirred up, absorbing new hopes and intentions sparked by new times. It can be frustrating to read a diary while looking out for these things; it can make the diary seem to be a moving target, a historical source that will not sit still. But all historical sources are unquiet and only seem to be at rest. A just reading of a diary text that extends into its published form welcomes the restlessness. The sagas of editorial transformations become, over time, part of what a reader learns to be curious about. And this helps readers take pleasure in the ways a text is *not* fully knowable, just as the woman's full subjectivity never will be, and filled with wonderful things rooted in its own time and the time (or times) of its editing. With patience for the tales of transformation, it is possible to see that diaries "contribute to the living world" not once but many times.[9]

To reach for all this is to reach back through the text for contact with the diarist. I seek to feel the directness of her pages as if it were a stare. To hold her eyes, face her as someone who lived the wrong life by our lights but who lived it as fully as we do our own. If you highlight her wrongness, you see a *type* of woman. If you lean toward her life, you see a person. A diary opens up the angle between these two views as an angle on knowing the past. There is the empathetic intensity of staying engaged but staying apart while reading. There is also the determination to understand how hard it is to map the editorial adventures of a text but to see why it is worth doing, and more than that, why it is a pleasure to do it—the odd sort of pleasure that comes from mixing surfaces and depths.

A sample from the diaries here will give an idea of what there is to know. For color and drama, begin with two worst-case editorial sagas, wrought by the editors of early published versions of the diaries of Sarah Morgan and Mary Chesnut, both of which later landed happily as well-edited, uncut texts. Ben Ames Williams, a writer of popular fiction, brought out an edition of Chesnut's diary in 1949, now known as one of the most extravagant escapades of editorial overreaching. Morgan's manuscript came into the hands of her son Warrington Dawson when she died in 1909, and he published his version of it in 1913. Dawson's manipulative editing is less well known but no less extreme than Williams's possession and play with Chesnut. Were these men in some way authorized by the diarists to publish? Not Williams, who reshaped Chesnut's diary long after her death. He worked from an earlier, also drastically altered volume, published in 1905 by an editor-friend of Chesnut's. Dawson does not say whether he discussed publication with his mother, though he does say he talked her out of having her diary burned after her death.[10]

As diarists, Morgan and Chesnut, despite twenty years of difference in age between them, share a liking for language and the description of scenes. They lean toward the reckless, or like to seem to. Both love irony and hyperbole, and both sometimes fear writing merely froth and trash. Both love to find fault. Morgan's voice often rises at the absurdity of things; Chesnut's is lower but no less keen. Each loves the bon mot, Morgan's coming amid long, unspooling paragraphs that gain power from their density and speed, while Chesnut is epigrammatic, her words achieving force by being hard and few. Both women are impatient with, and given pleasure by, the wartime parlor gatherings of their upper-class kind. They inscribe evenings and personalities marked more by heat than light, but want light, especially from men, who always fall short.

As editors of these emotional but word-anchored ladies, Warrington Dawson and Ben Ames Williams might seem an odd couple—the dutiful son and the next-century novelist—but they are not so strangely paired. Both men step forward as admiring protectors, gentlemanly handlers, bringing the women forward to a modern readership. Passion for the Civil War as a romantic, tragic time translates into an almost eerie gallantry. Both men speak of their personal attachment to the women, and about the diaries as neglected gems of literary creativity. Williams is fascinated by Mary Chesnut's intelligence and wit and moved by a vision of a lost "Southern society where remote and untouchable ladies in crinoline relish a scandalous piece of gossip or a *risque* jest, and where gentlemen may share these well-spiced conversations." This is the world he found in the manuscript diary, which he used, he says, to restore many passages elided in the 1905 edition. Williams mixes his enthusiasm with piety. As a writer of historical fiction, he tells readers, he needs sources such as Chesnut's diary to keep him on the straight and narrow as he "seeks out and respects the truth" of history. Williams is reassuring but vague about his editorial practices. He *did* make changes of his own, but only to excise trivia, "incidents lacking either human or historical interest." *Are* there such incidents? He sails on: "The attempt has been to make the Diary easily readable, without doing violence to Mrs. Chesnut's own words; so occasionally a noun or verb has been supplied, or a phrase inserted or transposed." So Williams, the cultivator of readability, slips smoothly into the driver's seat of this editorial saga. Warrington Dawson also writes of treasuring his diarist, his mother, Sarah Morgan, as a lovely, proud creature of a lost South. She was a fine prose stylist, Dawson says, and so "I have taken no liberties, have made no alterations, but have strictly adhered to my task of transcription" of the diary. He sends up a warning but quickly takes it down: yes, he did some editing of trivia, "merely omitting here and there passages which deal with matters too personal to merit interest of the public." He almost rises to his feet: "I pledge myself here to the assertion that I have taken no liberties, have made no alterations" in the "pure" quality of Sarah Morgan's prose.[11]

In fact, Dawson and Williams engaged in multiple, heart-stopping interventions in the Morgan and Chesnut diaries. We know this because the original manuscripts are still around for checking. Both men speak reverently of the originals, but each cut the diarist's text by about half without mentioning it. The cutting is insistent, on nearly every page. They silently trimmed paragraphs piecemeal and moved whole passages from one place to another. They inserted their own words as if they were the diarist's; their occasional use of ellipses for deleted text only makes more deceptive the times they intervened silently.

It was free play, but not without a purpose. Both men's interventions brought the big-picture Civil War to the foreground by toning down the diary's daily voice—"trivia"—which might interfere with the narrative of robust and tragic warfare. Both men buffed up what they took to be the diarist's attractive femininity. Williams highlighted (and sometimes invented) Chesnut's eye for the sexual games played among her crowd. He liked, as he said, "well-spiced" encounters. Dawson worked in the opposite direction by removing his mother's sexual moves and musings. In all of this, Williams and Dawson were not innocents in the editorial shop; both knew the value of an original text. But once inside the unsuspecting pages of the diary, instead of collaborating with the diarist, each man became the lead actor in the saga of its transformation: Williams half-avuncular, half-infatuated with his spicy Chesnut; Dawson floridly—and creepily—false in his declarations of faithfulness to his mother's writing. At the same time, though, I don't doubt that both men were truly moved by the women's strong voices, their stories and sheer style. But in loving these so much, the editors took possession of the diaries, each with the thought that the text could be made truer to his ideal of the woman, and to his idea of large-scale, *readable* Civil War history.

We can see them at work close up in the way they altered the first words of each diary. We might pick up any diary expecting a woman to self-consciously *commence* her wartime diary keeping, and some do. But more often women just begin with the day or a thought. Sarah Morgan draws a bit on both modes when she opens her diary by telling of her brother's death, then her father's, the previous year. She begins on January 10, 1862: "A new year has opened to me while my thoughts are still wrapped up in the last; Heaven send it may be a happier one than 1861." The phrasing about heaven is a little strange, but this is a classic opening for a diary: a new year, new hopes, and (as she goes on to say) a new book to write in. Morgan's pace is slow, a little formal, then sentimental, as she moves into the deaths of her menfolk. A loving memorial of father and brother gives weight to her venture into writing. Without a hint, her editor son lops off this beginning along with the first several pages of the diary, substituting for them the entry of March 9, 1862: "Here I am, at your service, Madame Idleness, waiting for any suggestion it may please you to put in my weary brain, as a means to pass this dull, cloudy Sunday afternoon." One of Morgan's voices is this snappy, mock-arch one. It is easy to see why Dawson liked it as an opening. But the somber opening he deleted is Morgan's voice, too. Erasing it dismantles the memento mori with which she eased her way into diary keeping by *not* writing about herself. Dawson's intervention picks up the pace so that Morgan's self-dramatizing seems present from day one, instead of being a voice she discovers as she becomes comfortable writing.[12]

Ben Ames Williams's version of Mary Chesnut's diary opens with a completely fabricated entry: "I came to Charleston on November 7th and then went to Florida to see my mother." The next sentence, also not to be found in Chesnut's manuscript, sweeps readers efficiently into a familiar Civil War narrative, as aboard a train "a woman called out: 'That settles the hash! . . . Lincoln's elected.'" Compare, as Williams doubtless would have done with a frown, the actual opening sentence of Chesnut's diary, on February 18, 1861: "Conecuh, Em's." These mysterious words come from a place far inside Chesnut's world. Be patient with the mystery. Then, learn that Chesnut called her mother "Em," and that she was living in Conecuh County, Alabama. In his zeal to get the Civil War train moving, Williams put forward a readable Chesnut for modern times. And so he erased a diary's inside references and insider's voice, the best it has to give. In my reading, the intrusions of both editors stem from their impatience with the actual opening lines and how embarrassing it would be to present such a clunker to readers. Morgan's hopes for a better year: too slow, too generic. Chesnut's "Conecuh, Em's": what does *this* say? The men push their way past these beginnings, which say: come to know me.[13]

The poet Anne Carson thought that using other people's words is like taking "a cut, a section, a slice of someone else's orange. You suck the slice, toss the rind, skate away." It's a "sense of banditry," a joyride, to play with the words of others. This is what Dawson and Williams gave in to, loving the diarist, loving history, but laying waste. If they were looking for empathy, the impulse got out of hand. Their play and possession of the text shows us something important about diaries. The diary's peculiar mental world, on the surface and yet subjective, is in a way defenseless. It is insular. It does not seek the light of other diaries as novels play on other novels, or histories build on other histories. A diary seems a happy innocent, a fool: I am forever and complete. Not so, it turns out. If you revise a history, it stays a history; rewrite a novel, and you still have a novel. But redraft a diary and it will turn into something else.[14]

Williams and Dawson were bandits, but even careful editors take a slice of the orange. If a diary is not to be published complete, some words must go. Whole days, maybe weeks, are tossed, time stutters, rhythms of voice vanish, the oxygen of daily routine becomes thin. Knowing this—that even good editing is bad news—we can be smart and curious about reading edited diaries that have sagas of transformation that put a further spin on the idea of "just reading." We can see the historical source (the edited volume) as being braided together with the text (the original), which had a life somewhere before and beyond the source and is maybe still out there in the world. Careful editors give a glimpse of how these two fit together, as far as they know, and tell us what part they have played. They have good reasons for their editorial manipulations, but they know it is bad news anyway. In the end, inevitably, the diarist appears in our world altered, or exaggerated, or partly erased.

So the published diary we pick up is alive with ghosts and gives off an aura of sadness for what has been lost over time, yet it is freshly eager to be read, right now. There are as many sagas of transformation as diaries themselves, and the reader will always be somewhat in the dark, as I am here in this book on diaries. Reading is reaching out, an act of communion (I'll risk the grand word) and, in light of what we can't know, an act of will, too. We know it is a ghost we are seeing; we decide to go with her, and so begins her story and ours.

We do not know what, if anything, Gertrude Thomas, Emma Holmes, and Anna Green planned to do with their diaries after the war. But we can know something about their diaries' sagas because we have original manuscripts as a baseline, and each diary had only one brush with editing. None of their editors took liberties anywhere close to those of Williams and Dawson. All of them, though, became attached to "their" diarist through their grasp of the diary's text and the moves to be made in transforming it. All of them struggled to make the diaries more "readable" Civil War sources, and so all took advantage of the welcoming nature of diaries, their openness to other hands and times, and their openness to being possessed and played with.

Gertrude Thomas kept her diary for forty-one years, so the Civil War just passes through it on the way from 1848 to 1889. About 70 percent of the diary's 450,000 words were cut when it was published in 1990, and it still makes a large book. The editor is clear about her interventions and straightforwardly tells of the "agonizing" cuts she had to make, removing "entirely or in part" passages "dealing with clothes, parties, shopping, college, and the constant visiting among friends and relatives." Also deleted were passages dealing with "weather, time, and place," including "totally irrelevant sentences" about visits with people or church bells tolling. When Thomas was "worried or depressed," her editor observes, she "wrote at length of everyday occurrences until she had calmed her emotions." These entries, too, "have been deleted or shortened." The editor avoids the word "trivia," but that word describes what guided her cutting. Thomas's visits, shopping, emotions, and the church bells, all worth the diarist's notice, do not, the editor explains, "contribute measurably to Thomas's story." Which story is this—or whose? Thomas's, yes, but also the editor's story of *her* Thomas, a story where editorial choices seek to pull from Thomas's pages "the essential plot and themes of historical significance," meaning the big-picture Civil War, for one. It is a reasonable way to go about editing such a huge text, just as it would be reasonable for a reader of the uncut diary to skip over the same things while looking for "themes of historical significance." It is a consensus choice, really, almost invisible because it seems so sensible. But still a choice—and a trade-off. The stuff of days—weather, people, states of mind—become puny things—trivia—when set alongside the war, *our* Civil War and our pride in its significance.[15]

Emma Holmes's editor takes her diary in a similar direction and shortens the long text by one-quarter, eliminating, for one thing, many passages "that merely catalogued names." This sounds harmless, and the editor leaves careful signs of his interventions, but wait—why would Holmes, or anyone, merely catalogue names? They turn out to be the names of people Holmes saw, wrote to, or thought about every day—friends, family, visitors, slaves, people newly met. It was her social world, the everyday: who was there or not there, who wore what, who deserved a letter. The editor takes all of this apart. And quiet and unlooked for, such close work with another person's words brings about something like intimacy with a diarist. Sometimes there is a personal edge to what Holmes's editor says about her. He criticizes her, for instance, for being often inaccurate—"very inaccurate"—in her reports on battles and other large events of the war. And so she is; she had a knack for it. She read the papers, talked with people about battles and politics, but many times got outcomes and actors wrong. Her editor cuts many such mistaken accounts, as if readers would of course be more interested in an accurate Civil War source than in Holmes the person and would not want to be embarrassingly misled by her. Making worse her errors was her misguided support for the Confederacy. "Miss Holmes did not consciously distort information," but readers should be on the alert for her partisan opinions. "I have not attempted to debate the Civil War with Emma Holmes," her editor says, though it seems he would have liked to.[16]

Anna Green's editor is even more confrontational, in an oddly patronizing way. He tells readers not to expect too much from Green's writing because it is shallow and often repetitive. He seems almost embarrassed to be editing her and eager to be understood as not implicated in the personality he found in her pages. He sums it up: Green "remained throughout her life the pathetically irresponsible, though generous and gracious soul which her writing reveals." He is particularly affronted by the romantic yearning possible in the life of an eighteen-year-old living in the Georgia Piedmont. He deletes many of her thoughts on (trivial) love—she thought a lot about love—including dialogues written with her lover, whom she later married. It is a good guess that the cuts were made with the thought that love talk tells readers nothing about the Civil War. But the cutting slides past that reason into possession of the diary and the diarist, too. Once, someone, presumably the editor, made an editorial move that makes Green sound less thoughtful about love than she was. She wrote one day, when love and marriage were on her mind, that it was important to think about what was happening among the young women she knew. She gave herself counsel: "Two of of {sic} my schoolmates have been married in the past month, and though I do not want to get married indeed would prefer remaining single until twenty one or two years old yet still I long for one manly heart to love and care for me." Does Green sound pathetically irresponsible? Well, playing with her words can make her more so! Her advice to herself to remain single for a while longer was deleted, so the published sentence reads: "Two . . . schoolmates have been married in the past month, and . . . I long for one manly heart to love and care for me." *Now* she's the lovesick girl we can fully possess and rest easy in our condescension.[17]

So editorial choices make a diarist in the mind—the editor's mind. Editors tighten their hold on the diarists, and this is how we lose them. We lose how the long day passed, and how long it was, and how the diarist circles a thought, almost how she breathes. Emotional and social worlds are rubbed out, and a diarist's "story" clusters into an "essential plot" conforming to what is already known and expected of a Civil War diary. Gertrude Thomas's callers, her parties and clothes, her troubled and inconclusive thoughts, church bells tolling all become distractions, when for her, they were life—her life standing up to war. Anna Green *was* passionate about love and men. The Civil War made love and marriage even more of a puzzle for a young woman, and this is something to learn from her as she writes about this war, her war. Emma Holmes knew she was making factual errors and says so, and with a diarist's good practice, she wrote from one day into the next, correcting herself when she could. In any case, her mistakes were more than simple errors of fact. Her mistaken accounts of Confederate victories were her imagination of ultimate victory, her deep wish for it, and they still carry her passion for the Confederacy and the South. Remove the mistakes and you remove this passion. Remove the underbrush of the woman's world, all the growing things a diary makes a place for, and you remove her struggle to *write*, one of the few handholds on her life that provide a chance for empathy. Ignore her "trivia" and she seems to live only for the war—the big war, our inherited story of it—and my darkest thought is that we do all this removing and ignoring so that we can have the last word about her and the past. We want to make her ours, so we make her like nobody is, simple and trivia-free.

Holmes, Green, and Thomas are ghosts, but ghosts with original manuscripts. Other diaries here have editorial sagas with much fainter trails from the woman to publication to us. They are in the darkest part of the editorial forest. No original manuscripts are known to exist, and some diaries were edited more than once, by taciturn editors with nothing to say about what they or others did to possess the text. This page in front of the reader: what, and whose, fears of boredom and embarrassment—or dreams of Civil War significance—changed it after it left the diarist's hands? There is only silence. Still, there are pieces of such sagas to gather up and keep, each one adding to the minimalist pleasure that comes from accepting how unstable these diaries are under their solid-seeming, published surfaces.

For Elizabeth Ingraham's diary, ghostliness is almost the whole saga. With the Union army making its move on Vicksburg in the spring of 1863, Ingraham wrote a series of daily letters to her daughters. The entries *read* like a diary, though it is easy to see that Ingraham was talking to someone besides herself. What is not known is whether the daughters ever received the letters, so the text is a kind of diary by default. We also don't know whether the text we have is complete. It makes its first, unexpected appearance in print as an appendix to an 1866 biography of the last wartime governor of Louisiana written by a friend of Ingraham's. The diary is an odd little light at the end of the biography, quiet and unexplained, and completely irrelevant to the last wartime governor of Louisiana. Here it lives a secluded life until it is pulled into view by an academic historian who publishes it in a scholarly journal in 1982. He, too, says nothing about the decision to bring the diary forward and nothing about what happened to the original text—or to Ingraham, for that matter. The diary just appears, as it did in 1866, riding on the coattails of the big-picture Civil War. The text is self-evidently interesting because the war is always interesting. No editorial need to say more.[18]

Pauline DeCaradeuc's daughter carried her mother's diary part of the way to us, typing it and giving copies to a small readership in 1928. We don't know anything about how she went about her work or what happened to the original manuscript. The published diary's editor, a historian, ran across the typescript in a historical society a half century later. She is optimistic, as editors usually decide to be, that "presumably" the daughter did not change much, or anything, in her mother's pages. We have to trust her, the now-deceased daughter, to have been—what? We trust her to have been patient with her mother's words and her world; to have handed over a complete text with only a few judicious interventions, and to have trusted readers (and herself) to rise above boredom and embarrassment. But the truth is we have no idea what DeCaradeuc's daughter might have changed. *Presumably* is a kind of prayer, trust over doubt, but it would be a near miracle of self-restraint for a daughter to change nothing as she typed her mother's words. We readers and editors just decide to take the text as DeCaradeuc's diary—decide to because it reads like other diaries we know, keen on the war, gossipy, and gap riven. It *seems OK*.[19]

Knowing more about a diary's saga may not make everything about it clearer. But it can reveal the eye-opening ways a diary can shoot the rapids of time and survive. Mary Jones and her daughter Mary Mallard wrote their now-lost pages during days of high anxiety in Georgia as the next bunch of Union troops rode up to the door. Like Ingraham and DeCaradeuc, Jones and Mallard said nothing (nothing that we know of—always this gravitational drag toward mystery) about plans for readers or publication. The handwritten text we have is a copy, made by Jones, which suggests a plan or a promise for a future, maybe a drift from diary toward memoir. How far did she drift? There is still more to wonder about if we enjoy the surprising turns a text makes as it stays alive. Jones's copied text combines the writing of both women, each working from an unknown number of earlier texts. There exist what might be original pages by Mary Mallard, which cover barely a week of the women's terrifying eight-week adventure. Mary Jones began the surviving text—the composite diary—by copying Mallard's diary and allowing these pages to flow into her own (copied) diary. Mostly. Sometimes Jones copies from yet another text by her daughter, now lost. On top of all this, there is a typescript of Jones's composite text, of unknown origin by a mystery typist, which differs in small, unexplained ways from Jones's handwritten text.[20]

The editor of the diary's first published version, working in the 1950s, skips over the complexity. From oversight or confusion, impatience or embarrassment, or from the sheer relief of just asserting editorial possessiveness and getting on with it, he mentions the two diarists, but slides past the copying and the missing originals. Jones's text, the one he chooses to publish, is clearly a copy of *something*, as the pages have two voices but only one handwriting. And yet he calls this text an "original," holding it up for readers to see, a text "written in a clear hand on the yellowed pages of an old ledger book," the very image of an authentic, single text we don't have to worry our heads about. But it's a ghostlike text after all. There are shadows of lost texts, if we look for them, falling on ye olde (copied) ledger book to show us that if we love Civil War diaries we must love the ghost.[21]

Ghostly hands—her own and later historians'—are present in Emma LeConte's diary, too, which is a copy she made late in life. One way we know it is a copy is that LeConte tells us it is. Early on in the diary, in the entry for January 2, 1865, an older LeConte suddenly pops into her wartime text in a parenthetical note from some point in the future, saying that she is, at that very moment, copying the diary. She was copying with an eye toward making her diary more readable and the war more understandable; you can almost hear her clearing out the "trivia." For one thing, she writes, she removed a January 2 passage "filled with speculations on and arguments for and against the immortality of the soul, etc." She is amused by her youthful self, and gentle, too, and she seems to reach out to us. She is, maybe, a bit troubled by her cutting. Why else mention it? (Years later, she again acknowledges, a little ominously, copying the diary—"at least most of it.") Her first historian-editor, in 1957, calls the copied text an "original" and says that in his hands it "has been reproduced exactly as Emma wrote it." Not quite. Someone, probably he himself, silently deleted LeConte's parenthetical acknowledgement of her self-editing. Possession: editing bent on erasing signs of previous editing!

I read him as giving in to the allure of an original, untouched text, something so desirable that he passed over the chance to collaborate with LeConte, who wanted it known that she had been fussing with her pages. A second modern historian, re-presenting but not reediting the diary in 1987, does mention LeConte copying her diary, but does not mention the January 2 note excised by the first editor. Only LeConte reaches out, her note a small flare of authorship by way of self-censorship, an invitation to know her, and a nod to her youthful self, the girl who wrote about the soul's immortality as war came to town.[22]

Eliza Andrews introduces her younger self, too, gives her a pat on the head, and sends her packing. Andrews is the only diarist here who brought her own diary to publication, in 1908 at age sixty-eight, and she notes that she edited her youthful text in proper and well-considered ways, thank you. She deleted "personal" matters, though she did let stand some of her youthful impulsiveness (like calling the U.S. flag "a hateful old striped rag") to keep the flavor of the time. More extended girlish trivia—"tiresome reflections, silly flirtations, and the like"—went under the knife. Like later historian-editors, Andrews wanted her diary to fit into a big-picture vision of the Civil War. Her youthful self would only "interfere . . . with the fidelity of the narrative" she now wished to tell, a narrative of a South driven to inevitable conflict by the economic tensions of slavery. The rise and fall of the Confederacy was the valuable story Andrews found inside her diary, and for richer or for poorer, it is the one that drives the text we have today. The 1908 volume was reissued in 1960 with introductory words by a Civil War historian, and again in 1997, this time reframed by a historian of women and gender. The second historian only obliquely mentions the first (his remarks, and thus his place in the saga, are entirely removed from the new edition), and neither historian raises questions about how far Andrews's self-editing may have carried the text over the murky boundary between diary and memoir. We will never know this, but Andrews's neat daily entries, all of similar length, never a day missed, make it hard not to wonder. Things diarists usually scooped up as they wrote the day—observing the weather, feeling ill, eating dinner—are nearly absent. Were these things trivial, like "silly flirtations," and therefore properly removed? Or did Andrews simply never write about such things? It is Andrews's secret. But her self-assured diary with its buffed-up feel is, in its way, as ghostly a presence as the sudden, mysterious appearance of Elizabeth Ingraham's fragment at the end of her friend's book.[23]

For Cornelia McDonald, the story is different. She makes her diary's survival of the war part of the story, a diary-keeping saga of loss and recovery worth telling. It was worth it, too, for her modern editor, and the two joined forces to out the ghosts, so to say, and make the unstable text more enjoyable in its instability. McDonald's diary keeping was born of the war and knocked around by it, a story better told than neatened up. When the war moved close to her in 1862, McDonald grew worried about her diary's safety and surer of its value, writing in praise of her small daughter Nell for taking the initiative to hide it from the Yankees when they came. Keeping a diary was not McDonald's idea, not at first; she wrote because her husband asked her to. After writing for some months, she says, she lost a portion of the text and began again. Before the war ended, she made time to reconstruct the lost part from memory and added it to the existing daily record. After the war, she added a third bit of writing, a memoir to fill the gaps, and then she put everything into a composite volume, inscribed duplicate copies, and gave them to her children. She titled the volume "A Woman's Civil War," calling it "a diary with reminiscences," which seems just right, and she is frank (if not always clear) about how the three texts fit together and which of them the reader is reading.[24]

At some point after she made the composite text, all of the prior texts were lost. Again, layers vanish. Then, after her death, new layers were added. A son put the composite diary together with other family memorabilia (and maps and illustrations) into a lavish doorstop of a book he published in 1934. He told readers that his mother's text "has been adhered to in words, spelling, and punctuation." This sounds suspiciously oblique, and it turns out to be far from true, as McDonald's second editor discovered some fifty years later. Beginning with his mother's title, the son silently rearranged many things, removing entire passages and altering the grammar and punctuation of much that remained. (Can't sons be trusted as editors?) But because McDonald's second editor had one of the untouched composite volumes as a baseline text, and because she was under no pressure to make editorial cuts of her own, she was able to undo the son's interventions and recapture McDonald's own text. The editor takes seriously—and takes pleasure in—the text's permutations as a mark of the war itself, of diary keeping, and as a means of reaching out to McDonald and the ways she had circled through her pages. If the diary lost some of the heat of its first inscription, it gained back some warmth from the empathy surrounding McDonald and her editor as both tell the diary's saga of coming through times past. This is what is left to us, and it is a lot.[25]

The short-story writer Alice Munro, exploring her family's past, was impressed with how doing history, "rifling around in the past," was a strange experience of "being joined to dead people and therefore to life." Working with diaries, especially published ones, means being joined to the diarist and to other people, too, mixing motives and iterations of the text, the dead and the living together. With this odd and moving collaboration in mind, understanding what diaries say about the past is not the only aim; what we *feel* when we understand is worth finding out, too. For this, diaries have a special comprehensiveness. The diarist needed to create what she did, and reading her through layers of text, we discover a corresponding emotional need and satisfy it. We read and are pulled closer to the diarist's time and place even as the diary's indecisive story lines and unexplained turns—and the known and unknown morphing of its text through the years—show us how far away the past is and always will be. In the peculiar mix of right here and far away is the pleasure of reading a diary: neither one privileged, neither denied.[26]

And so it is with doing Civil War history, too. As we now move into the wartime experiences these Southern women inscribed, look to be patient with ghosts, to wade into daily routines, to anticipate trivia, brush against subjectivity, and be on the watch for the "too personal" things running all the way through the big-picture war that raised the Confederacy and brought it down. Wonder about possessing the diary and playing with it, and stay with the lively ghosts. Do this with a will to see diaries' native messiness not as something to tidy up, but as the very imprint of war burned into the text. Take pleasure in a diary's awkwardness and brilliance and boredom in the midst of war, and make an opening for empathy there. The diarist: a person, but not one to be imagined as simply "like us." She is a kind of artifact of the empathetic urge, a subjective figure to whom we can move this close but no closer. She is there in her pages, there to be read, but apart, like her war—the real, tumbling thing she tried to write.

CHAPTER TWO

Keeping the Diary

"Keeping a diary" is a curious turn of phrase. You do not "keep" a letter as it's being written or keep a sermon or a speech; but you do keep a shopping list or a promise. Something personal, something *now* and with a future. As they wrote, the women came unexpectedly face-to-face with keeping a diary, with the novelty of being moved to stop everything and write, and with the prehensile world of paper, pens, and reason and time to write. Their curiosity about the act of writing, sometimes the wonder of it, threads through the subjects and scenes that fill their pages and will concern us later on: the war's violence, men, slavery, and self. The women discovered what we need to remember as we turn their pages: the diary-inscribed war and the act of writing cannot be separated—were not separated in these women's minds— and this helps us think about why they kept coming back to their journals and how we should read them. They wrote about the conditions for writing, the emotional atmosphere of it, the pages achieved. They imagined readers and critics; they reread themselves and judged what they read. They thought about the distant war and the war up close and about how the "habit" of writing had made them care about the *now* of writing. They played and possessed the ways in which the diary played with events and revealed the mind's play. They sewed the war into their daily lives with their own hands.

The ladies can write in a stagey way about writing—look at me!—and soberly about the intellectual effort. I am more taken with the times they are caught off guard by how much the act of writing the war matters to them. Their diary keeping surprises them and latches on. For Emma Holmes, one day it is a wonder "how attached I have become to this record of the passing hours." So, too, for Pauline DeCaradeuc: "It's a comfort for me to write. . . . My desk is *so* private, so entirely my own." They can seem "obvious," whatever that means, or "trivial," but these times of noticing the pleasure of diary keeping are not simple. The diarist is not exactly being self-reflective, and she certainly is not performing. She is not just passing the time, either. She is savoring the act of writing, stepping back a half step to appreciate it. It is a frank, personable gesture, vain but unselfconscious, like catching a look at herself in the mirror as she leaves the room. It lets me have a look beneath the face of the page and the busy stories, and a way for empathy opens. Why? Because such brief appreciations of writing are awkward in their openness and make her vulnerable in the pleasure she takes in them. They are moments instantly recognizable to writers and not to be denied. They are mine, too.[1]

As diarists wrote the passing hours, they found that they were also just writing the moment, always writing it, and here is further ground for empathy. In one way or another, diarists discovered that the act of writing did not lead to a goal—a brilliant perspective on the war, let's say—that steadily came into view. Writing was *it*—means and end—the daily scratching out of words at odd moments. I know something about this. I write my stories, my histories, *tend* to them by taming the writing moment to my subject. The subject must prevail on the page, not the days I spent writing about it. Still, those days never go away. They stay inside whatever I have written, a ghostly crew. The diary's implacable *now* is greedier, and I reach for a writer's empathy in order to grasp how a diarist lived with this avid *now* filling her pages, *making* the page. Diary keeping might have given her something to lean on, but she also struggled with how the pages called out to her to act, to *write*.

Consider, for example, the diary's sturdy daily pace and readiness to be accurate in the midst of cascading events. Diarists varied, but most of them took pleasure in carefully dating entries and correcting errors when they found them. They referred back to their pages to find out exactly when something happened and promised themselves to verify or revise questionable reports. They summarized events when they missed several days of making entries. Diarists made these retrospective moves in different ways, but all showed how insistent was the daily pace as the diarist's metronome, and how easily it might be lost, or how it actually might conceal the hours spent writing. Some diarists, overwhelmed by events or out on the road, fell back on weekly entries instead of daily ones. They made the new, slower pace obvious and even apologized for it. Others, like Emma Holmes in March 1865, tried to keep on writing while caught up in the rush of things. She struggled amid the slippage of missed entries and resorted to retrospective summarizing under a single date; her long March 4 entry includes a subterranean flow of two weeks' time. Others kept up an orderly façade of daily dates, like

Gertrude Thomas in September 1864, but as you read, it becomes clear other days are hidden inside a single date. Her back-to-back entries dated Friday the 23rd and Friday the 30th include references to other days she has absorbed into these two dates without saying anything about them. So diarists rode their devices, and wrangled their days, in the face of the diary's *now*, an obvious part of diary keeping and yet—strange paradox—something was always being overwhelmed: now but gone; now but not now. It is the struggle of anyone who makes stories about time passing, and so while diarists are "sources," they are also our companions in the land of history writing.[2]

Why write? This is the warp-and-woof question of diary keeping and of this chapter. Because it's war, diarists say; because these are exciting times, without precedent. The unimaginable and terrible war, and the fact that they were witnesses to *noble sacrifice* and, they hoped, the Confederacy's survival, made wanting to write it seem self-evident. But the women also wrote because they became *diarists*; because, once begun, the daily journal became a story and a habit, a confidant and a mirror, and a touchstone for each day. They began to love the act of writing and, from here, to love the book they had made. And writing for whom? Women wrote for posterity, "for the benefit of the children" as Gertrude Thomas thought in 1864, and maybe for history's benefit, too—it was not too much to think that her writing "may prove interesting" when "we of this generation shall have passed away." A woman wrote for herself: Sarah Morgan wanted to make "a souvenir of my dark days" for later in life, and Floride Clemson wrote for her "old age, my future self." In all of this, writing scooped up something less easily grasped than war's events: a subjectivity without predictable shape or limits. What is the heart of diary keeping? Mary Chesnut thought it was about "spinning my own entrails." A gut-level image, vaguely unsettling but just right. The stuff of writing came from deep within and it might not be pretty, not to the diarist and not to us who read her. The war and the diary-kept war cannot be separated, and we readers find what the Civil War showed the diarist: this is who she wrote herself to be. Now, what do we let ourselves think of her?[3]

IN EXCITING TIMES, A RECORD AND A RELEASE

Diarists discovered an appetite for recording war's riveting events, and by writing, soon enough discovered the subjectivity that presents itself to all writers whether or not they do anything with it. A diarist found her record of the war surrounded by a haze of personal feelings, and becoming a writer meant holding the two in awkward balance. Writing, wrapped up in the *now*—wartime's dangerous, exhilarating now—pulled on her emotions even as it distanced her from the very moment she was inscribing. The critic George Steiner thought that "all commentary is itself an act of exile" marked by "distance and banishment." Gertrude Thomas felt this distance when, writing about some exciting events, she suddenly found herself instead "thinking of my journal and wondering how I was engaged this time last year or how I will be engaged next year." Her thoughts turned from war's urgent moment and fastened onto the act of writing and the subjectivity it invited. She wrote the *now* and then she banished it.[4]

Ladies took up their pens, and their satisfaction varied. Edmondston had "many times" begun a journal as a younger woman only to drop it, "perhaps from weariness, perhaps from an absolute dearth of events," she did not know. Perhaps she had not worked hard enough at it to benefit from what diaries were supposed to do: refine the diarist's observational powers and give her an easy, confident style of self-expression. When she decided to keep her war diary, Anna Green expected it to be a "vast means of improvement" on both fronts, and Eliza Andrews remembered having the same idea when she began her journal. So, too, Lucy Breckinridge believed that keeping a diary would be "good employment in these war times" when so much that was new collided with all that was known. The decision to keep a diary was a personal declaration made in war's presence, with personal hopes for some instructive, lively pages ahead. "For a journal to be readable {it} ought to have plenty of Plums in it!" Edmondston thought, reflecting on her earlier, dreary diaries. The war would take care of that.[5]

When a battle came near to home and enemy troops were in the neighborhood, or when a brother, a father, or a lover headed into far-off battle or came safely out, writing was irresistible, and making time and finding words for the desire to *tell it* seemed a natural thing to do. But there was something else, too, a pleasure in writing synthesis and thinking about national fortune. Diarists lived in a culture of reading where novels and histories told of glorious nations and peoples emerging from storied war, and where newspapers excitedly tracked this war's course. The women read the papers and took in local talk about leaders and strategies, politics and predictions. "News! News! News!" Edmondston wrote in July 1863. "There has been a battle, a terrible battle at Gettysburg in Penn. . . . Meade is falling back to Baltimore & Lee pursuing him. . . . The slaughter terrific both sides admit. The bridge over the Susquehanna at Wrightsville has been destroyed, whether by us or them I cannot understand." Us or them, and terrific slaughter all around. During the same stretch of days, Emma Holmes looked west as she read the newspapers.

"There seems no doubt that Vicksburg has fallen after all our sanguine hopes and expectations. . . . The garrison were exhausted with starvation, & [with] mines being sprung. . . . The garrison, 17,500 men, are all paroled & allowed to come over into our lines, the officers retaining side arms & baggage." Keeping a diary gave a woman the voice of someone who knew things. There was a journalist's urge to report the factual weight of triggered mines and demolished bridges, while keeping only a little apart from the partisan and other passions just underneath the narrative stream. For some diarists, the excitement of telling these big-picture things leaned toward writing a history, or at least collecting the makings of a history. Modesty would say otherwise, but many diarists had begun writing in hopes of finding a clear, personal vantage point on raging war that would pull a powerful narrative out of the storm.[6]

It was not an easy thing to do well, it turned out. Catherine Edmondston loved to recount battle stories offered up by newspapers, but she worried about accuracy in the short run and the futility of journalism overall. So she reined in her reportage on the war in Louisiana one day: "{Gen. John} Magruder . . . is said to be within five miles of N O, but rumours are as plenty as Blackberries, so I will not fill you O! my Journal today with what I may have to contradict tomorrow." Even this kind of braking did not always let a diarist avoid the thought that maybe she lacked skill as a writer. The war blindingly filled the days, and a good writer would give stirring voice to a stirred-up world. But rereading her pages in 1863, Gertrude Thomas was appalled to find that so many of her entries in "the most eventful period of my life" were so poorly written that "the absorbing theme of war" barely came through. Edmondston was dismayed that "my journal is becoming a mere chronicle of battles, bloodshed, & death" and concluded that she was writing too much about such things. A couple of weeks later, she criticized herself for not writing *enough*, or well enough. The war breathed tragedy and pathos, but everything she wrote seemed "bald, meagre, & flat." So the women struggled to be writers who faced war and made their own record of it, and when they fell short they wondered about themselves *and* writing. Maybe the act of writing itself was inadequate. Thomas thought that the war was perhaps too overwhelming, too enveloping, to be written well by anyone. A diary could scarcely keep up, stolid and labored amid flashing events. Maybe war's "absorbing theme" was "one to be talked of better than written about."[7]

So a diarist came to a certain emotional edge in her diary keeping where the fierceness of war and the small, plain act of keeping a diary blended strangely and uneasily together. It seemed that diary keeping put events at a remove only to reveal how inadequate this was to the war's terrible proportions.

Keeping a diary stretched time into ungainly shapes, the *now* of writing (here I sit) weirdly tied to the *now* of war (everywhere suspense or chaos), each banishing the other by turns on the page, playing tricks with the scale of things. Look at a page: narratives of battle and national fortune washed to and fro in the tub of daily routine. One got out of bed, sewed at midmorning, and later met with friends in town; in the midst, Stonewall Jackson was killed by his own troops. The proportion of things wildly shifted without warning in one's own journal! Would a diarist have the stamina, the patience, to continue to sit, pull her volume out of the drawer, and take up her pen?

Nothing good came from overflowing emotion. To keep at diary keeping, a woman had to believe that the act of writing, which summoned the exceptionally tender or sharp emotions vouchsafed to women, would also safely guide them. Emotions rose up, were released, and again gathered force as much from the stark strangeness of writing about sewing on one page and death on the next as from the general atmosphere of wartime excitement. Would the diary's attachment to everyday moments check the flow of feelings? Eliza Andrews thought so; writing was a "safety-valve" without which "I believe I would burst sometimes." "I thought I would sew after tea," Gertrude Thomas wrote one evening, "but sewing is poor employment when the mind is disturbed." Sewing made her thoughts wander and emotions arise. So "I turned to my journal, 'ever present help in time of trouble.'" Emmala Reed knew about the safety valve, too. She had "filled up every book with my *silly journalizing* that I could find. . . . I feel that I can scarcely live without giving some such expression to my feelings."[8]

Writing made anticipation from loss, worked this day into the next, better day. On the page, loss and anticipation were pretty much the same thing. Keeping a diary meant writing one's way into this mystery and somehow joining national peril to personal feelings with no plan except the diary's day-to-day pace. Reed's pages joined the Confederacy's slow downfall, entry after entry, to the slowly dawning reality that her lover no longer cared. She mourned each in turn, and each was a stepping stone to writing about the other. Andrews's safety valve blew off the steam from her arguments with her Unionist father that rumble beneath her pages and occasionally come forward in her view of the South's inevitable but, she was sure, not humiliating defeat. Thomas's "disturbed" mind on a given day yielded worries about her family and about estranged, transfigured black people, the veins of her emotion tunneling through the Confederacy's fate.

In all, wartime events and the array of feelings released by pen and page came together to power the flow of a diarist's words, and even for the most levelheaded diarist, this made the subjectivity of diary keeping sometimes hard to face. Emotions were unnerving to write and also embarrassing to see flat footed on the page, and there was but a short step from being a woman of sensibility to being one who was sloppy with emotion. The foundering Confederacy brought this writerly edginess to its sharpest point at a time when the pain of losing the war's gamble was not separable from the pain of wanting to write the whole risky venture *well*. Some of the women were overwhelmed and put their diaries aside; others wrote their way further into the pain. When in the fall of 1864 the war's nearby violence gathered new force in the Shenandoah Valley, Lucy Buck stopped writing. It was not a writer's block; it was a choice she made in the midst of emotions that writing could no longer handle. "My diary was laid by," Buck explained when she took it up again five months later. "Those sad autumn days my heart was too sad." Pauline DeCaradeuc, though, kept writing through crises and seemed more limber and defiant because of it. There was something about the act of diary keeping that gave her emotions shape and reality: "My inner life is entirely & essentially different from my outer. My heart most usually bleeds inwardly, and this Journal is the only thing in this world that ever gets a peep into it." A configuration of war, emotion, and writing kept Grace Elmore at her desk, too, though she lamented the results. "I used to love to write sometimes," she said of the antebellum years, "and put in words either the thoughts of my mind or relieve the heart in that way of superfluous emotion. Then I had time to not only feel but to express the feeling. But now, everything is so changed, everything seems so worthless."[9]

So it was that emotions came unstuck and rattled around when a woman journaled the events of war. Emotions were as much at the heart of diary keeping as were the satisfaction of making a record and being a person who knew things. The solace found in the habit of writing, as women made it a habit, was not easily done without. Still, the same beloved diary might upend emotional life as surely as the war did. The possibilities open to a writer were far scarier than the women had imagined—writing too superficially, going too deep, being overwhelmed by doing either or both. And this: keeping a diary might make war's destruction harsher by giving it a relentless, solo voice—her own—that went far beyond the record of "what happened" into unknown subjective places of the heart. All of this was daunting, and alluring, too, a challenge and a goad. *I will write this day.* Beneath every inscribed page in our hands are the diarist's false starts, her unwritten fears, her forced renewals of will.

Commonplace and exceptional—that was how diary keeping seemed. Impossible, but there it was. Caught by this, women took hold of small rituals of writing that worked below the level of anything we might call inspiration but gave freedom to put pen to paper. These diary-keeping touchstones, ordinary but essential, even lightly magical, nodded to the extravagance of writing the war and thereby domesticated the act. Imagining a listener was one of these small charms, along with cherishing the physical text. Another was putting the actual moment of inscription into words—the moment's "pleasure of writing with good ink." Scattered throughout a diary's pages, these touchstones helped a woman write and helped make the act of writing inseparable from her narrative of war. They are easy to delete as "trivia," but they are the heart of just reading a diary because, in a way, they bring the writing woman closer to us than anything else she put on the page. They hold a plain, everyday sense of her persistence and spirit, and they point to what the act of writing meant to her, and what the war "means," too, as something unprecedented and yet at home (like anything else) on the diary page.[10]

Many diarists wrote while imagining a special friend whose intimacy lovingly absorbed whatever feelings and observations spilled onto the page. From here, the inert pages themselves became a "friend." This was a common practice of diary keeping, well aired by characters in novels and among young women looking to share secrets. It was commonplace because it did important work, carrying the subjective charge of writing into the familiar ground of friendship. Having a diary friend was a buffer against solitude—against the stark, solo act of writing and maybe against a larger surrounding loneliness in life. Having this friend played with the romantic delight women found in correspondence with beloved female friends, the sex that truly listened. It played with the pleasure not of possessing the object of one's desire, but of *reaching* for it. Writing approached and postponed. Diarists created ideal friends in love and pursued them through their pages, anticipation and loss in delicious balance. Lucy Breckinridge imagined her diary as "a female, rather older than myself and a great deal smarter, but whose sweet and gentle disposition shall call forth all my confidence." She named her friend "Harriet" (after a friend of her mother's) and during many months of writing, just as it seems Breckinridge has gone on alone, "Harriet" reemerges, intimate and ready. For some diarists, it was interestingly complicated, as friendships are. Gertrude Thomas had spoken to her diary friend in her antebellum volumes, and yet she sometimes seems tentative or shy in the war years: "I will be confidential to you my journal, I had almost said my friend." Was she at an age when imaginary friends seemed too girlish (though talking to a book was all right)? Catherine Edmondston talked to herself ("Mrs. E") *and* to her journal, whose standing as an intimate changed as Edmondston's moods shifted. She stopped herself from writing too much one day by pushing her friend away: "So, Journal, dont you set yourself up by thinking you are my confidant. I do not tell you one half I feel."[11]

Such friends blurred the lines between diary, letter, and conversation. The confidence and candor of one poured into the others, and solitary diary keeping was placed in the ordinary run of shared expression and feeling. If writing the page suddenly seemed an act of tossing words into a vast emptiness, having a friend brought the words back safely into dialogue. And, for us, there is pleasure in just reading the page's play between diarist and friend as a trace of the lost language of intimacy a woman shared with people she loved. Breckinridge took her love to "Harriet" to find confession and comfort. Elizabeth Ingraham was separated from her daughters by the siege of Vicksburg, but her multiday letter to them brought them closer because it spooled out like a diary. Emily Harris began writing because her husband had asked her to keep his farm journal up to date when he went away from time to time on war's business. He left notes in the pages to prompt her. Sometimes as she set down her daily accounts she replied to him in his book. Or was it her book, or theirs? She wrote (to the page, to him) that he had always demanded a lot as a husband and he was not slackening off in wartime. But they were a pair, all said; he was "a choice, superfine husband." He was away, but he was in the pages they wrote, and she pursued him there. Superfine.[12]

All of this made the act of writing less strange. Conversation pushed the pen along and made subjectivity less stark. Writing became natural, its energy warm. Some diarists responded to it when they came to the end of a volume and felt the sadness of saying goodbye to a friend that stood for the substance of what they had created, and its realness. Gertrude Thomas's parting with a filled book was always a painful changing of partners. "Dear old journal," she wrote as she finished a volume in 1864, "I realy dislike to give you up—to lay you aside and form a friendship with a new one." Anna Green stepped up to the elegiac: "And now my old journal farewell a tried friend hast thou been and it is sad to lay thee with the past and take up a new." Floride Clemson, not one to comment on the act of writing, suddenly spoke to her diary as she prepared to take a trip north: "Good bye dear little volume, I shall not take you with me!!"[13]

There is something funny about this, grown women talking love talk to their books. And modern times receive the syrup of these emotions uncomfortably. *Goodbye! Goodbye!* The impulse is to dilute the words given to intimacy and avoid their embarrassing sugar. Or to read the emotions as simply a conventional gesture, a pose. But don't do any of this. The women's endurance and their tenderness are there, fed by diary keeping and made real. Real and sustained. The women learned to write the war by making their diaries a place for loving loss. The old journal is gone, a new volume awaits. Write it. Loss and anticipation both were sweet, and when she treasured her own words as a "friend," a woman beheld and refreshed herself.

This does not mean that wariness of emotion—of subjectivity—disappears. It always drifts through women's pages. A diarist remained inside her own head with her own "word-pictures," as the saying had it. Feverish imagination. Imagination filled space on the page and made space for new pages. This space was never filled, not for the avid writer, and so the desire to imagine continued unquenched. A diarist came forward with her daily words and wishes, and before she knew it she was attached to her pages in a way not explained by the mere sum of their entries. In wartime the stakes of emotional play grew beyond anything she could have imagined, and sometimes the diary's plain voice strangely exalted war.

For most of the women, the physical volume—*my book, my journal, my pages*—was a kind of anchor for imagination and an object prized as a charm against war. A volume was hidden away each day like a treasure, or put out in view as a reminder to write. Under the gun in wartime, women fled carrying their diaries, buried them, or gave them to others for safekeeping. The physical object was her accessory and her open secret. It lay there on the table and sometimes it seemed to her that her social world circulated around it. Her daily routines rose to the surface of her mind. Not finding the time to sit down with her diary as usual, Grace Elmore realized that "I never knew how much occupied I am until I thought of keeping a journal." The physical book became a signature of sorts, a marker of a woman's peculiar creativity even in war, and while some ladies wrote only when alone, others wrote on trains, in sewing circles, in front of the servants. Looking upon a diary as a friend came full circle when actual friends asked how the diary writing was going. Emmala Reed's friends Theodore and Gibbes admired her discipline in keeping a diary and "both ask why I don't write more." War needed chronicles like hers. Emma Holmes had friends who made suggestions. Dora told her that "I ought to note in my journal" the exorbitant railway fares "as a token of the extortion of the times."[14]

Husbands of married diarists came into the orbit of these objects. Mary Chesnut's husband remarked on her writing, which she notes from time to time, though not to say what he said or to comment on it. It seems husbands found diary keeping a mostly feminine conceit, but they grew curious as the pages filled up. So diary keeping got written into their marriages and, for brief stretches, wrote the marriage. One evening at home, Gertrude Thomas's husband looked over at her and "wished to know why I did not write in my journal" as they both were sitting and reading. "As this is the first time he has expressed such a wish I must take it as a compliment," Thomas wrote a few minutes later, having fetched her diary. Catherine Edmondston wrote, "Last night Patrick made me a present of a nice new blank book in which to write my Journal. I am the more pleased at this, as he takes you, O my Journal, for an object of especial merriment—merriment at once good humoured and pungent." But she figured that he must actually approve, "or he would not aid and abet me thus in keeping you."[15]

Thomas had been keeping a journal for two decades, but only now did Jefferson Thomas ask, Why aren't you writing tonight? Patrick Edmondston laughed at Catherine's writing—borderline mocked it if the word "pungent" means anything—and yet here he was, urging her on with a fresh book. A compliment, said Thomas; aiding and abetting, said Edmondston. Neither searched their men's motives. They were pleased, and maybe there was a dis-believing cast to their pleasure, something that might ripen into irony. But maybe not. Neither woman seemed at all ironic in mentioning that the vol-ume she was writing in was inscribed with her *husband's* name, a personalized ledger that had been intended for his purposes. The men's motives? Probably as straightforward as the women hoped they were. Chronicling the war was a work their wives had taken on, the war was momentous, and there were already pages and pages. Why not give her a book so she could write more?[16]

A book, an ordinary object. Diary keeping seen this way—like seeing it as a "friend"—softened the power of the interiority it opened up. Even in war-time, a woman could tell herself, writing one's thoughts in this familiar book was not extraordinary or boundless behavior. But as the war went on, journals grew in size and energy, filled with first-run emotions and packed with inti-mate, local details. Yankees in the neighborhood gave faces to possible thieves of such an object, and this made it even more dear. Cornelia McDonald's town, Winchester, Virginia, was in the hands of the Union army when, one day, her young daughter Nell saw two Union officers approaching the house. McDonald had left her diary out on a table, and only after the men were gone did she realize that Nell had "first concealed the book and then went to see what they wanted. Great prudence on the part of a maiden of seven years," who told her mother that "she thought there might be something in it the Yankees ought not to see." Nell was prudent, and precocious, too: "I had not thought of her knowing the character of the book."[17]

The diary might be an extraordinary thing, after all. Like a child, her diary might be "carried off" by the Yankees, Emma Holmes feared, with all of its named friends and pro-Confederate thoughts. So Holmes buried her diary when U.S. forces came near and kept an auxiliary journal on a few loose pages she could easily destroy. Catherine Edmondston also hid her diary from Union troops, bidding her "old friend, you my Journal, for a time good bye!" The book was as vulnerable as anything physical to "prying Yankee eyes and theivish Yankee fingers." It amazed her that her thoughts should have become this stark object.[18]

I read these protective, passionate writers and wonder whether I fall among the thieves. Probably I do. *Prying eyes.* I tell myself that the diarist is long dead and gone, though this isn't a very good reason to continue prying. Still, I read on because I have this object in my hands, which against entropy and all the odds, she created in the midst of war's fatal distractions. And I imagine that because of this she would have liked to have readers like me—unimagined readers in other centuries. I'm making this up, but many of the connections we have to people's feelings in the past are made up. We imagine we know certain things about historical people because we choose to believe that certain essential things about people don't change. So I can also imagine having her permission to read her diary, which I realize I would like to have, and from here I think of whether she and I might agree to accept the fact of our unlikely meeting, our otherness, not to mention our disagreement about the war and its outcome, and so find grounds for empathy through the existence of this physical object.

The object: I realize I am thinking of the original volume, which, because she once held it in her hands, conducts a unique jolt of enticement, or reproach, whichever it might be. There is nothing quite like the vulnerable, persistent physical diary to suggest empathy's hard way, whether it ends with a missed meeting of the minds or a connection. The plain fact of a physical volume (even a published volume will do) gives substance to both possibilities even as it represents the gulf of time between us and makes it keenly felt, as it should be. It is a huge gulf, and I picture the fragile diary suspended over it, with all of the meanings we find in it, the respect we think we give it, and the smartness we think we possess because we are right on the issues of the Civil War. It is a gulf so wide that a gesture toward the diarist might go haywire, or it might just fade away.

When Catherine Edmondston imagined thievish Yankees opening her volume, she imagined them reading and laughing at her. "Think how {Gen. Phillip} Sheridan's bumming officers would seize upon the 'Journal of a Secesh Lady—a complete record of daily life spent in the Southern Confederacy from July 1860 to April 65' & how I would feel thus dragged from the recesses of private life & aught I know published for the amusement of a censorious, curious, and critical public?" Imagining such Yankees (and I think I can, too), she hid her diary away. But what is she imagining here? Yankee mockery, yes, and awkward public exposure. But she also comes up with a title (and subtitle) for her diary. And while I am imagining things, I can imagine her surprise that this title, *"Journal of a Secesh Lady,"* in fact became the title of the published diary 114 years later. It does not serve to mock her, of course—but then what effect does it have coming from across the great gulf between us and her? Respect for her words, but a respect having the irony of modern hindsight mixed with a slightly patronizing urge to lighten things up, to have a snappy title that will catch a reader's eye. Would Edmondston feel humiliated by this? Angry? Fulfilled? The grounds for empathy grow less certain amid such questions but still compel, and this, too, represents the power bound up in the physical object, the ordinary and extraordinary diary, which we have taken from her. We can imagine and we can ask ourselves, holding her book, how far we should go.[19]

"It is still raining," Gertrude Thomas wrote one night. "What shall I say as my pen falls idly in my hand." What shall I say. Another diary-keeping touchstone: evoking the act of inscription as it happens. She is place holding, marking time but not being wordless, making a moment for the ordinary but always fresh intimacy of the page. Anna Green wrote about handsome Bryan Thomas, "a man I could admire." Then she checked herself, and wrote on unchecked in a single sentence: "It is unmaidenly to write this and my face burns as I write it." Green's twentieth-century editor cut "as I write it." Maybe he thought the words were superfluous. But read the sentence without those words, then with them. Feel her catch hold—*now*. Such moments only flicker through the pages of diaries, but if we don't skip over them they pull us in. The diarist presents herself. *Here I am. See me writing.* Effortlessly, the written page doubles as the moment of its making. And though we seem to be catching her unawares, we are not. She is holding the moment, stilling it; she is unguarded but unembarrassed.[20]

These are not artless moments, but ones called up by the diary's peculiar mode of artful plain talk. The double vision—the words on the page and the act of putting them there—leads to a kind of circular movement through time that has a ready warmth, a feeling of connection: from her pen to the page, from her page to us, and back to her. Diarists write that they have been *thinking* about writing, or write about missing opportunities for it. "Three days and so many interruptions that I have written nothing," Cornelia McDonald wrote in September 1862. Lapse acknowledged, she was free to write again. Lucy Buck often wrote that she had written, which is strange to read on the very page that would seem to make it unnecessary to say. "Up and had breakfast very early. Confusion and trouble. Sat upstairs reading in my Bible, then came down and wrote in my diary." Buck is right here and at a distance, both. Diarists recorded the *now* for later, and later, brought back the *now* with ease.[21]

Noticing pens and paper—this paper is too thin; my pen has just blotted the page—also yields the just-passed moment as an intimacy. There is a chorus of pen commentary. Depressed, Gertrude Thomas wrote, "I am very weak—twice tonight while I have been writing my pen has fallen from my hands." "In spite of miserable, soft-nibbed pens & consequent bad writing, I think I shall continue," Emma Holmes wrote on a January day in 1865. Sarah Morgan, having written gossip, spoke to her pen late one night to ask it, "Shall we leave off, my scratcher? . . . I dont know which is worse; for me to have such thoughts, or for you to transcribe them." From pens to flashes of the diarist herself, illuminated by the pen moving across the page. In one entry, Thomas was "smiling as I write." Emma LeConte once inscribed herself writing when "the hot tears rush into my eyes and I cannot write." Tired at the end of a day, struggling with the fading light and a bad pen, the women are caught in the act as they sign off. "I knit & read & must *rest* now (so sleepy I could scarcely scribble the above!)." "It is late and I am frightened and sleepy." "Finish this another day."[22]

They write that they write; they write that they cannot write or that they will write. A strange maneuver, this spinning of the wheels and getting somewhere at the same time. The diary's moving parts are plainly seen, and the diarist comes closer as her diary keeping aligns with my reading. It feels something like being trusted by her, or at any rate, that she trusts her page to show that writing is an act that happens in all sorts of *nows* but that it is always just writing. In her openness is the confidence to just read.

WHAT IS THIS THING, THIS DIARY?

We will never know how many women destroyed their diaries, or put them aside to die, especially as the Confederacy was sinking. Some of the surviving diaries we are looking at became feeble, too, at the end. Pauline DeCaradeuc wrote on only seventeen days between January and July 1865. Anna Green made just six entries from mid-January to May 1 of that same year. Even wordier women—Mary Chesnut, Sarah Morgan—slowed down toward the war's end. (There are exceptions: Emmala Reed continued pouring out page after page.) And if an actual diary was treasured, possible diaries were fungible, unstable, tradable. Emma Holmes got the money to buy "the long wished for purple calico" by selling a pair of Confederate shoes and a blank book she had purchased for her diary. Some diarists had written mainly to face down a crisis and probably never intended to take on more. This was so for Mary Jones and her daughter and for Elizabeth Ingraham, too, who all recorded with fierce detail the assault on their homes and families by Union troops. That done, they fell silent.[23]

Still, in the uncertainty of the times, and in the uncertainty of timing, most women here kept on writing, and some began to ask themselves what sort of thing it was they had created, beyond a "friend" and valued object. Is this diary keeping, women wondered, something "good"? Though most of them did not say so flat out, it was partly a literary question. When they looked hard at their pages not only as writers but as readers, too, they saw them as a poor, skeletal thing set against the fullness of their lives. Words that gleamed with the pleasure of writing them were, the next day, sparse and blinking. The powerful *now* looked piecemeal, and the dreaded "trivia" began to show through. The women were disturbed by this, but enticed by it, too. It is the same for us. No matter how rich, a diary skims a life with nothing like balance, maybe especially so in a war the diarists knew they were losing. Whatever was on the day's page, the women knew that the day itself was more brilliant and more dull than could be written, and we can be sure of this, too. Did this make the diary bad writing or good?

It made for frustrating times for sure. Catherine Edmondston made an entry in May 1865 to say that she ought to stop making entries. "What use is there in my writing this record?" she wondered. "What profit, what pleasure, do I find in it? None! none!" "I have lost all interest in keeping this fragmentary record," Emma LeConte wrote that same month. Pauline DeCaradeuc also wrote about not writing, explaining that she had no obligation to explain herself: "I do not often feel like writing here now, there are events enough to record if I choose, people come & go, but I don't care for them, I feel, well it's of no use to say how I do feel." And yet Edmondston and LeConte kept coming back to their desks and pens, and DeCaradeuc surprised herself by falling in love at the end of the war, and as the Confederacy went out her diary stayed lit, though she wrote less often. "I'm either too busy, or too happy or something."[24]

So the women struggled with how to love the always-in-motion, always-uncertain diary, to love it as the ghost of something more—some Excellence or Achievement—that it never became. That's the trick for us, too. A diary is as thin as paper; it never has the substance we want. When Mary Chesnut began writing, it was with the thought that "the present never satisfies." That described diary keeping, too, as it turned out. If a writer is a person who polishes and revises her pages, who runs up against writer's block, and who seeks and suffers critics, then a diarist is not a writer. A diary is about going on, leaving the door open, making your bed but not lying in it. It does not sum up or conclude; it *acts*. The point is that diaries are not first drafts of something better, but perpetual first drafts. This was behind the frustration, the curiosity, and the pleasure a diarist felt, and relied on, too.[25]

Consider diaries' final sentences. These bring the diaries to a close, but they are only final by chance; a line written one day becomes the last line. No concluding and assessing, no cosmetics. They are fragments, perfectly so. Kate Stone came close to ending things deliberately, but she signed off with a question that unsettled her goodbye: "So this is the end—shall I ever care to write again?" Floride Clemson left her diary behind when she traveled, but she gave it a future: "Till we meet again." But most diaries just stop. Last lines come from the middle of a day, or the middle of something, interrupted and half-seen. Read their bluntness as a suspension that speaks of a moment, but also of the provisional flow of moments and days: "Heaven grant me rather the horrors of war!" "Tommy was there!" "Have one of my nervous attacks." "Oh, Journal, just think of it, in three day's time we are to move & to live with Guerard's enormous family, the thought is alarming and [illegible]." "I tried to make the day pass pleasantly and I am afraid we escaped the sabbath." "I don't know the author." "I had a good cup drawn for them and they left before sunset." "No news."[26]

Perpetual first drafts—diarists knew them from the act of writing, if not by design. It is not that their chancy nature closed off other ways of thinking about their texts. Writing for their (future) children's sake or for an imagined posterity had been a first measure of their diaries' value, and many diarists held on to it and later acted on it, as we have seen, by playing with the idea of making their journals into memoirs. Or diaries might somehow stoke one's ability to write essays or fiction. Maybe they were in training to become refined authors; maybe not. Mary Chesnut worked on a couple of novels after the war but did not publish them. Grace Elmore experimented with the elevated comic style of popular writing in a few retrospective pages in her diary about her postwar teaching adventures. But she gave it up. Anna Green had hopes for brilliance, but then had to say, "I do not think my journal bears one idea on its pages." There were no "thoughts of any depth or value." Emma Holmes believed she might have the stuff of a novelist—friends told her she did—but looking over her diary pages she had to say that it did not add up. "I can tell a plain story but cannot draw characters," she decided. "Fiction can never equal reality." She seems to echo Chesnut's famous observation that, in war, "life is so real" that fiction pales by comparison. But I think Holmes is saying something different, that fiction and "reality" cannot even be compared, so different in "talent" were diarist and novelist. In wartime, Holmes thought, "fine materials lay ready at my hand" for wonderful stories, but a diarist was not a creator of a world. She merely lived a life.[27]

Holmes was selling herself and diaries short, but if a diary and fiction were played in different keys, and if a diary was not simply a failed novel or an embryonic one, what was it? Diaries were like histories, some women thought, though even more seriously flawed by the author's limited point of view and without a history's grand ambition. Even diaries kept in earnest ended up wrong about facts, as diarists well knew. And it was more than that. The self-revising *now* of diary writing pointed to the drudgery, maybe the futility, of writing history at all. Reading over what had seemed a satisfying daily record, Holmes discovered "how many N.B.'s I ought to add to correct first reports." Chesnut found that "nearly all my sage prophecies have been verified the wrong way—& every insight into character or opinion . . . turned out utter folly."[28]

Chesnut and Holmes complained about their diaries, but they grasped something, too, about the kind of text they are. It was not simply about a diary being more or less like a novel or a history. I read the women as realistic about what they had made and curious about how hard it was to write a first draft that never ends. Writing page after page meant having the peculiar faith that this would pull something stable from the unstable run of days. Floride Clemson, thinking in 1865 about what she had written, admitted that her diary was little more than bundled rumors. But she came to the realization, exasperating though it was, that the truth of any "fact" in a diary "is not to be ascertained until the fact has lost almost all interest, & novelty." A diarist does not wish to lie, she is saying, but in the course a diary takes, the "facts" stand apart from what the diary does best—play with the moment's interest and novelty. Was it a gloomy thought, or a liberating one?[29]

If a diary stops moving, it dies, and in the end it is the movement that matters. Writing this way, one unrevised *now* flowing into the next, was the only possibility a diarist had for making her war real. And this is what diary keeping tells us about the Civil War, that it is always grasped from inside a life, from someone's passing days. The women saw that their writing shifted in meaning from day to day, embraced rumor, shimmered with indecision. Every day the war was still new. Every day there was the unkempt pleasure and frustration of writing from the gap between *what happened* and the urge to *tell*. Sarah Morgan was surprised, rereading her account of a week's stay in Madisonville, Louisiana, while on her way to safety in New Orleans, to find that her account failed to convey that the week "was one of the pleasantest weeks I have ever spent." I read her passage and have to agree; she sounds more irritable than anything else. Morgan was puzzled by the disparity, and intrigued. Why should her pages fall so short of the experience? Maybe she had been tired when she wrote, or maybe she was an inadequate writer. Or maybe what diary keeping revealed was that writing tracked the reality of evaporating time and was also fooled by it. Anna Green felt the same misfit between the desire to write and the act: "We cannot write down our thoughts whenever the spirit moves us" because, perversely, "the circumstances that awaken imagination to her wildest flights are just those in which we can not take up a pen and write." So the entry will always be a ghost. Catherine Edmondston had the thought that her diary, which both delighted her as she wrote it and frustrated her when she read it later, was best at showing something underneath events and thoughts, something about temperament or personal style: "Journals are not correct exponents of peoples thoughts, wishes or feelings. Why it is I cannot say." But, writing, she had been made aware of "the habit of reticence which from long use I have acquired," which diary keeping challenged. No matter if a writer sought to be open, openness was never the page's simple story; the writer's subjectivity lay waiting between the lines. Morgan understood this, too; whatever she inscribed, in one way or another, arose from the "compromise between laziness and inclination" that marked her as a writer. The diary on her desk, the book in which she wrote, was in fact not her real diary at all. The real diary was the "very amusing one in my brain."[30]

Diaries did not simply capture the war's events or the war's emotions after all, and they were far edgier as texts than any of the women imagined when they first started to write to their "friends." Making daily entries was driven and purposeful, a boring and embarrassing act of coming to terms with loss and turning it toward anticipation, and what resulted could never be simply true. You, the writer, have a vision, says the essayist Annie Dillard. "But you are wrong if you think that in the actual writing . . . you are filling in the vision. You cannot fill in the vision. You cannot even bring the vision to light. You are wrong if you think that you can in any way take the vision and tame it to the page. The page is jealous and tyrannical; the page always wins." Diarists knew this tyranny, and found that their words on the page were not the wonderful offspring of their inspiration, but (as Dillard says) a changeling, a kind of ghost.[31]

Sarah Morgan, though one to find a solemn mood unnerving, quite solemnly decided (for one day, anyway) *not* to worry about why she had put so much effort into her vain, incomplete, untrue, and altogether unsatisfactory diary, "so trite, so stale, so tedious and matter of fact." She was tempted to burn it, afraid that its pages might mislead others in the future and certain that it "would be rather unpleasant to be misunderstood." But she checked herself. In a quieter time, her turgid diary might clarify, and she along with it. More than friend or object, it was a text, and when the war had passed it would, she hoped, "enable me to find a moral for the story of my life, not yet told."[32]

Gertrude Thomas leaned on her diary as a friend, a "soother" and "silent witness," but she, too, saw it grow into a text, something less romantic than a loving friend but better for that. Reading her pages, she read herself, and it was satisfying to do so. She had become newly, particularly real. In her pages were inscribed her many "vows to fulfill my promise to live nearer to God." So now, in war, "when faith falters & grace does not uphold me I sometimes read where I have recorded that God was with me . . . and I grow stronger and better." Day by day, she had doubted her faith; but now she could read that it was there.[33]

The time came, one night, for Lucy Breckinridge to understand that the stories in her diary—and she was an enthusiastic storyteller, speedy and sulky by turns—were not just beads on a string. They were not stories so much as *her story*. Her diary was a text, her text told her life, and "my life is like a plain, little novel, written by a silly, but practical schoolgirl." Not the stirring text she had pictured reading after the war on "a windy night" and not pointing to a bright future: "For me there will be written only the bitter disappointments, the stern realities, the sore trials of life—for my lot must be the common lot of all." Her diary was not her friend or a report or a witness offering some extraordinary hope. It was her story, and the diary was itself, day after day, achieved and open ended. It was staring her in the face: "My lot must be the common lot of all." She was like everyone else.[34]

The page always wins. Amazed, frustrated, but unfazed, the women wrote the war as a way of witnessing and a way of wishing, both. Their diary keeping endured, an act of faith that one day's words will be made better, or hold more, or mean something only by writing the next day's. Faith in ghosts. It is an unlooked-for faith in women so full of themselves, and I feel it pulling me to them despite their vanity and wrongdoing and despite the fact that they wanted to hold on to a world I reject. A diary-kept war goes somewhere but never quite arrives. It feels like life to me, this nonarrival, like embracing loss as something to keep. So there is a whiff of empathy, improbable empathy, for these unsympathetic women.

CHAPTER THREE

Wartime

The women knew it was a war between Yankee and Southerner about history, country, and home. A civil war. They read the newspapers, passed along rumors, talked with people who had been at the front, and as we have seen, liked reporting events and outcomes in their diaries. We know very well how planter-class women stepped up during the war to serve their interests and their values, and we try for a broad and balanced view. It is broad and balanced to say that these women made do amid destruction and dislocation, were surprised by servants gone and glad, and learned to understand war as politics by other means and so learned politics. Women became critical (somewhat) of the men who proved so wrong about secession, war, and the whole tragic mess. A few women ventured to critique slavery, though they did not go very far. A few learned to be (somewhat) critical of themselves and discovered that a lady's realm was not as imposing and complete as they had thought. When we read for these broad and balanced things in women's diaries, of course they are there.

But what shook diarists and excited them to write was the craziness of war, destruction's breath in the very air. So here I read diaries in another way— nothing broad and balanced—to find the sheer strangeness of war as the women found it on their doorsteps, head-on and cockeyed. A war-estranged time called for capture by words. Women wrote war coming inside their lives and tearing things up, soldiers in the house. And more—scenes less gross and frontal but written in the same fierce present tense with an appetite for novelty. They wrote of sharp turns in small routines they would have thought beneath war's notice. Warfare's twins, loss and possibility, came onto the page, and decorous time fell into chaos. Time became wartime.

This wild, personal war is still there in a diary's pages, a ghost inside the big-picture war, the strategic and political war we are accustomed to. War (and her diary) put a lady in the midst of things she never imagined having to find words for: rampant destruction, sad yet funny transformations. Absurdity and naked truth. Diarists did find words for a lot of it; everything they wrote in wartime was about the war in some way—not only pain, suffering, and resolve, but also awkward things, eye-popping things, bouncing over the categories and topics that we moderns have concocted for the war. There were small scenes that meant more than words could give back and so were written with fewer words and plain ones. Catherine Edmondston's friend had her wartime wedding dress made from bedsheets. "Think of that!" Edmondston wrote. Her tone of voice is war's tone, amused and amazed. Here she was, *now*, in a time fabricated by war when brides dressed in bedsheets.[1]

So a diarist made war's collage piece by daily piece at the pace it appeared, or at the pace it could be written. Proportion and meaning lagged behind. *Think of that!* For later historians and other readers, the usual practice is to sample and shape this immediacy, tame it so it can be added to other sources and contribute to longer-term, broad and balanced stories. What happens if we shake up this order of things and keep immediacy up front? A diarist wrote to fit brazen war into her life, not to fit her life into war. So she backstopped the strange new things with familiar things (stories of new times always keep the old times nearby). She moved between the portentous and the non sequitur, from how to bear sorrow to what to wear today. She practiced writing the day and so learned what the practice of war does to time.

Reading diaries this way we do not always find the war we expect. Take death, for instance. The diarists actually wrote very little about death, especially mass death. Even the deaths of brothers or friends do not fill many pages. Diaries are not memorial texts, it turns out. Women paid their respects and voiced grief, but they wrote many more pages on routine, friends, travel, landscape, scandal, clothes. These and other old reliables were weirdly transformed by wartime, and yet they did not disappear. Even in the face of war's violence and the impossible marriage of flat-out loss with the ever-hopeful coaxing of good news from bad events, diaries still were about what to do today and what happened today and most days, and so deadly war achieved a lived-in character.

At the same time, women wrote war as something sublime. War revealed normal life as just a cover thrown over *something else*, something huge and dark. War exalted the senses and the will. War danced before the women's eyes. If we see them as they wrote, inscribing the war while in its daily path, repelled and enchanted, the women appear less certain than we are used to expecting—less sure about war's aims, violence, even loss. They are more distractible, more paradoxical and ragged and funny—just as their diaries let them be. The ladies' frankness, as the war swallowed up normal life, amounts in their pages to its own kind of achievement.

In this light, the women as writers seem open to empathy because they struggle in the present tense for a purchase on time, as we do, too, whenever we look at the past. *What does it all mean?* is their question and ours. They try to put their hands on a new narrative (so do we) and arrive at a place not always comfortable, but right there in the midst of it (a kind of place we know, too). Doing this, they make the observations and pray the prayers we expect from Confederates. "The Nation mourns and bleeds," Emily Harris wrote in late 1864. She asked—again—for the "intervention of the God of battles" on the Confederate side. A chance for empathy *here*? We have heard this before from women like Harris, and we have a ready response: you got what you deserved. The moral rightness of Confederate defeat cannot be clearer. But there is also this: many in the past who have been defeated have *not* deserved it, and we listen to them and learn much. I don't want to be too quick to be deaf to those who deserved defeat and so make it certain I will learn nothing from them. Emily Harris is not recruiting us or scamming us. Words like hers are not talking points or ploys; they arise from the naked, present-tense moments diaries collect. If wanting to understand a foreign, even alienating, subjectivity is what drives a search for empathy, I have to read through her wrongness and my alienation to get to the bones of her diary writing and what it says about the wartime she knew.[2]

So here are wartime diarists leaning on the everyday and bracing for the sublime, playing with the chaotic possibilities now served up by daily life and with the surprising, molten thing war made of time. First, war brought jaw-dropping shifts in what had been bedrock normal, making a new stage for things in what everyone called "the times now." Then the mighty war staggered in 1865, and time seemed to come to a momentary stop. War had taken things away from the diarist, but it gave something back, too, there in her pages. She held on to this mystery as everything healed over.

THE TIMES NOW

The war fascinated with its stirred-up scenes and with its softer insinuations into the ordinary. Diarists pushed themselves to see and to say how different were the times now, to find words for all kinds of change built of extremes. Her home swallowed up by the battle of Winchester, Virginia, in 1863, Cornelia McDonald heard the not-to-be-imagined "screaming of shells." She saw "balls of light go shooting over our heads." She took her children onto the porch to see, all of them "looking up at the shells as they flew over and came crashing down." Emma LeConte went out on her porch, too, in Columbia, South Carolina, as the Union army made ready to enter the city in early 1865. The sound of the artillery was fearsome and the moment heavy, "and yet there is something exciting—sublime—in a cannonade." In an altogether different kind of whirling novelty that made the impossible real, Mary Chesnut had to earn money—directly, on the barrelhead—for the first time in her life. This was beyond humiliating for a woman like Chesnut, beyond imagination really. The elite's world of refined women and provident men now stood on its head. But she went ahead and set up a neighborhood butter-and-egg business with her former slave, a woman named Mollie. As Chesnut wrote it, the unimaginable morphed into another way to have the last word with her husband; after making fun of her "peddling," he borrowed money from her anyway, and she laughed at him. Emma Holmes worked for pay for the first time, too, as a seamstress. She had vowed never to make a shirt for a man—too subservient—but she began sewing in wartime, was soon sewing shirts, and her old resolution disappeared in the face of "our sewing machines working very prettily." Making money surprised: Holmes had feared being demeaned by "yielding up my long-cherished liberty to the will of another," but on her first payday, she found something else, a "new & peculiar feeling of independence."[3]

Cannonades and personal income: writing the times now fed on the novelty but grew toward the normal. Wondrous or frightening, clamoring or bare, the war women wrote stayed attached to familiar checkpoints of feeling even as its explosions weirdly backlit the familiar. Incompatible emotions turned out to be eager bedfellows. The enemy was near, Gertrude Thomas wrote from Athens, Georgia, in the fall of 1864, and "truly the skies are gloomy." And yet, oddly, "we laugh—we smile—we talk, we jest." In Charleston in 1865, Grace Elmore was struck by "how strangely is the serious and the gay intermingling in our life. . . . One day packing boxes to send away from Yankee reach and the next night being gay over the prospect of French sugar plums at the Bazaar." The women were not easy with this mix, exactly, but they did not disparage it, either. And they were not just saying that life goes on. The play of light and dark was stranger than that, exciting because it was unforeseen *and* recognizable, like seeing God's hand in a sudden storm. It was not to be denied: the days mingled jokes and despair, flight and French plums.[4]

Such wartime things flourished in full view. Yet they might be pushed down and packed tightly into a diary so that they fit inside a woman's life. "On the whole I am a happy fortunate girl," Floride Clemson wrote on the first day of 1864. "If this year ended in peace to this land, I should have little to wish for." End this war, make me happy, says this twenty-one-year-old to her page. In this cast of mind, war was shaped to the small habits that had strung one's days together since childhood. April Fools' Day 1865? War did not toss it into the dustbin for Eliza Andrews and her friends. One of her crowd's April Fools' tricks was to cry out that the Yankees were just down the road. "We pretended to believe it," all in good fun. So one's dear life, which diaries both treasured and took for granted, grew around and over the war's novelties. Nothing was stranger for Lucy Buck, at first, than having rough soldiers suddenly appear at the door of her father's Shenandoah Valley home and ask for food or a place to sleep. But after some months of this, scarcely anything was more routine. "Soldiers in bright and early for breakfast," she began one 1864 entry, as if it were the most natural thing in the world.[5]

So women wrote the resilience of everyday life into warfare's tumbling world, and they were made resilient by writing. Diaries welcomed wonder and laughter as much as dread. I am moved by the sturdy diary's capacity for all of this and moved by how the simple order of the written page mimicked the women's faith in the (sometime) good order of the world. Decorum had not structured every antebellum day, but the ideal of it was always there, and now women held on to it as good order fell apart. I am moved by this even though I am glad for their defeat. The difference between us allows me to feel the strength of their resilience if I choose to, and to know that I am making the choice. Empathy and the understanding it brings needs this difference to push against. Historian Doris Garraway says that when we write of the past we should ask, "For whom do we remember, and whose memory do we claim to represent?" For Garraway, writing sympathetically of those who struggled for liberation in colonial Haiti, the answer was clear. For me, not so much. If I represent the memory of these planter-class women by writing about them and their diaries, it is not to say something about admiration or sympathy. I want the past to be remembered *through* them, even *with* them. But I write as a reader of their days, with a reader's distance made by the page—by the *text*, that unappeasable fragment of days—and by the women's foreignness to what I value. This distance seems right—seems necessary—as the way to breathe the air of different, past times. This air is now alien, now familiar, maybe disturbingly so, but I do not mistake it, sympathetically, for my own.[6]

And for whom do I do this? Perhaps for the dead, all of them. Which means for us, too, and for how hard it is to know the dead and their times, and for how pleasurable because it is hard. Looking for empathy with planter-class women keeps the hardness up front. For them, and for all of the dead, *we* are the ghosts. The diary helps me to know this, and weirdly, the war helps, too. The ladies wrote the war's spinning strangeness while still spinning. They could not do what they were used to doing, calculating the dimensions of good order and telling themselves they knew better than anyone else. Writing, the diarists heard but did not always heed the claims of consistency (Did I write the opposite earlier?) or proportion (How can my life be equal to this terrible war?) or self-protection (Am I being foolish?). The wartime days—"the times now"—flew past such well-ordered things. The times were dark and broken but strangely freeing, like our struggle to understand the past.

With this in mind, reading the women's war means reading for strangely mixed tones of voice and for awkward angularities of observation, all getting on the diary wagon together and bouncing along in a democracy of expression. Look for the linear if you want to, and most historians do, but know that it is a fiction, too. Women did not write wartime as a straight-line slide from peacetime confidence into wartime anxiety into exhaustion. Or, if this is how it seems to us after many decades, we can only grasp what it means by truly seeing what the diary shows: that the women slid back and forth through this same chute of feelings several times in the course of a day or two. Take two observations Kate Stone made in her diary on the same day, March 24, 1863. In one, she was thinking about the next morning, when she and her fatherless family would leave home on an unknown road, heading west—for safety, they hoped, but into exile in any case. As it turned out, she would like her new life in Tyler, Texas. But on March 24, things did not look good: "The life we are leading now is a miserable, frightened one—living in constant dread of great danger, not knowing what form it may take, and utterly helpless to protect ourselves. It is a painful present and a dark future."[7]

But Stone also wrote that day about the happiness of having her brother Johnny home for a visit with exciting news of the war beyond. He came on a Sunday, and Stone noted that "(Sunday does not seem like Sunday nowadays. It's always the time of the greatest excitement.)" She wrote this as a parenthetical truth—it went without saying, but it was still good to say it. Here was wartime change on a much smaller scale than her vision of the painful present and dark future, but change so exact and clear that it rises to the occasion to yield its meaning for the times now. The times are perfectly seen in what has happened to Sundays—they are reversed, unrecognizable!

It is hard to read the emotional weight in Stone's words, harder than the heaviness she gave to her "miserable, frightened" life. Sunday isn't Sunday anymore: she might be resigned, or saddened, or mostly matter of fact. She might be intrigued or excited, or "amused," as women of this class liked to say when they were intrigued and excited. On the same day, in the same diary, Stone may have been all of these things, possibilities pulled from the war by the thirsty page. And miserable and frightened, too. If we want to feature one meaning in the histories we write, or as readers, if we want to feel we are getting to know the diarist, we might make a choice between Stone's two March 24 remarks. My choice would be to highlight what had happened to Sundays. I like its concreteness. It stands for the tilting wartime world, better even than Stone's expression of her fear and misery. And I like how it gestures toward prewar times. Would Stone have commented on low-excitement antebellum Sundays had the war not altered them? Doubtful. So we get a bonus. I like it because, in this one aside to herself, Stone opened up her known world—of Sundays, brothers, excitement, and the times now. It reads like a hunch, or a kind of trust, that her reader would know what she meant.[8]

It is a welcome thing that diaries are not parsimonious, and a puzzle, too. I solve a puzzle if I choose to bring one quote to light and leave another obscure. And I make a puzzle: choosing sharpens vision and the desire to read on, but it freezes an on-the-move diarist and her moving war. Some diarists felt the same thing, I think, and wrote to freeze the times now and pull them back inside the rules of good order. Now new choices arise, for them and for us. Women were morality's handlers, everyone knew, who did their feminine part to shore up through good manners the rightness of upper-class rule, making a kind of ballast to offset the elite's small numbers. Good conduct was a matter of opportunity, but no less a matter of will, and wartime had plenty of both. The times now were filled with the strangeness of blood and combat far afield. Closer to home, the days were shot through with insult and indignity, and *this* a woman might directly confront. Union soldiers ransacking Mary Jones's Georgia plantation stuffed a large number of chickens into the Joneses' family carriage for easy transport back to camp and the evening's feast. The soldiers were thoughtful enough, or something, to send word that the Joneses might have the emptied carriage returned if they wished. But Mary Jones's daughter Mary Mallard did not see it as thoughtfulness. The soldiers' offer was a gratuitous "insult," she wrote, which only made worse the prior insult of "converting our carriage into a chicken-cart" to be "drawn by our own carriage horses." War changed nothing about the immorality of stealing. For the soldiers to think they were doing a good deed and expect gratitude for the returned carriage only showed how far they had strayed from the moral order.[9]

Mallard's outrage—her certainty that decorum was not her class's invention but an independent measure of moral worth—is written with the keenness of the full attention she gave to the soldiers' trespass. It *mattered*; but how do we choose to read her? Her intensity—her arrogance—is very easy to parody. The chickens make for comedy, and the whole thing can be fun, and historians often make fun of planter-class outrage in wartime. One way to do so is to use exaggerated descriptors for how something written might have been uttered. We might choose "huffed," for instance, for Mallard: "Converting our carriage into a chicken cart . . . drawn by our own horses," Mallard huffed. Or "sputtered" or "whined." Once someone sputters, huffs, or whines, we don't have to take her seriously. We don't have to listen to Mary Mallard anymore or think about what she might have been feeling and why. We don't have to think about empathy. Making fun creates the opposite of empathy; it is a moral slam dunk from modern times. And it defends us against the enemy, making her a simple villain and feckless, and certainly not one of us.[10]

Better to resist making fun and see how manners and good order distilled the times now, giving the women a rhetorical way to size up what was happening to the world. And if the women were outraged by some of it, they were other things, too; they wrote the exceptions to decorum as well as the rules. As critic Sonia Kruks observes, writing opens up the writer's subjectivity to show how she lives in her world "in modes of complicity, of resistance, or both." A diarist's hold on decorum shifted in experimental, even pleasurable ways as she tamed war for a time by admiring the resiliency of her dear life set against war's daily tampering with the rules. Engrossed in a discussion of the war at a party one evening, Emma Holmes and a group of male and female friends found themselves casually trooping through the bedroom of another woman friend ("where she was busily writing by a bright gas light"). Women's bedrooms were off-limits to partygoers, and Holmes should have disapproved, but instead she was "amused to think how war had leveled ceremony." With few servants, Lucy Buck and her sister served dinner to male friends and family. She could have felt insulted, lowered, but she was playful instead. "Nellie and I enjoyed it," mostly because the men were comically uncomfortable at being waited on by ladies.[11]

War put women in the midst of a tide of small reversals like these where the everyday world seemed to be tipping upside down, but not beyond the point of coming right again. (Men and slaves, hugely part of this world, we take up later.) War might fit inside a person's life (she had her fingers crossed) instead of breaking it open; if manners held, there was hope that she was living the right life. Every day, though, new doors to an unprecedented world kept opening. One opened onto startling, close-up contact with poorer whites—soldiers, neighbors, white refugees—whom the women treated as sheer novelty. Their men had always handled dealings with tradesmen, small farmers, and their like. Now war shuffled the social deck. "Here was a position for ladies!" Sarah Morgan wrote one day, meaning the opposite: a position ladies never would have suffered in peacetime. She and her mother (and bundles of their belongings) were aboard a schooner bound for New Orleans packed with ordinary white folks and their families. Surrounded on deck, Morgan took comedy as the high ground, depicting her mother and herself "sitting like Irish emigrants on their earthly possessions," a situation "which a year ago would have filled us with horror." Irish immigrants—alien, pitiable—and now she imagined that she looked like one. Morgan knew that the whole awkward-absurd experience on the boat would come to an end, and she cushioned the shock of this novel boat ride by making fun of herself. Arrogance waits just under the surface of her joke. At the moment, though, as she wrote it, she did not wall off the others completely. She wrote herself as if appearing in a play in a role she had not chosen. Latch on to the absurd, laugh at not having a choice. Around the edges of the joke there was maybe a ripple of fear, and maybe something oddly freeing.[12]

To say planter-class women were out of touch with poorer whites only nicks the surface of a deep ignorance. War handed ladies a new, unforeseen physical nearness to working-class white people. But blankness about poorer whites and what they felt or how they lived persisted. Diarists were curious or impatient, and then they turned away. Eliza Andrews's family gave food to some passing Confederate soldiers in May 1865, but they did not invite the men inside the house. The men got the point. Andrews heard one of them call her father "a d——d old aristocrat" who "deserved to have his house burned down." She brushed this aside as surely not a considered view. "I suppose they were drunk," she wrote. Or maybe they were conscripts, rightly ignored. More intimately, and more repelled, Emma Holmes described—and kept on describing—the dinner table of the yeoman family whose children she was being paid to teach, a nightmarish place where "the children wipe their faces & noses in the table cloth . . . {and} hogs jowls are brought on table, grinning ghastly with every tooth still projecting. Dogs & cats eat under the table, & the kids often join them. To crown the whole, Mrs. M[ickle] nurses her baby before me & any man, white or black, that happens to be by, etc."[13]

This was not the known world, and the door to it could still be slammed shut. But many diarists did not do this, or did not see how, and other scenes not in the book of manners, or even in the mind's eye before the war, pushed their way onto their pages. Scenes written as a dance of wildness and decorum, the women's ignorance of others, and their faith in manners turned into an unsteady balance of wonder and dismissal. Most intense of all were times when enemy troops came into the yard and soldiers came to the door. If they could manage it, women immediately opened a conversation with the soldiers, wrapping face-to-face danger in dialogue. Conversation: making room for moral character to come forward (theirs, certainly, and, they hoped, an occasional soldier's) and slow the pace of danger's crazy unfolding. Keep the soldiers talking, perform good manners, and talk them down. Then do it again, on the diary's page.

Mary Mallard went downstairs and met a Union soldier, an Irishman from Kentucky, as he was walking into her pantry. He looked around the room, and "the following interrogatories took place":

What's in that box?

Books.

What's in that room beyond?

Search for yourself.

What's in that press?

I do not know.

Why don't you know?

Because this is my Mother's house, and I have recently come here.

Hundreds of miles to the west, Elizabeth Ingraham encountered a Union soldier from Illinois rummaging through her belongings. He took a liking to a desk and asked if he might purchase it. Ingraham said no. "'Well, suppose I should choose to take it?' 'Do so [I replied], I can't prevent your stealing. If God's command is not obeyed, I cannot expect you to mind me.' 'But I don't want to take it that way; please sell it.' 'I can't; it is not mine; it belongs to one of my daughters.'"[14]

Mallard and Ingraham did not refuse to talk to the Yankees. There must have been some additional talk, too, as the women knew the soldiers' home states and a few other things about them, their names in some cases. Keeping silent made no sense, literally, and the diarists were eager to make sense through the decorum they knew how to manipulate. Conversation would have been tense work under the circumstances, and maybe the diary's page makes the sudden confrontation seem more orderly, more script-like, than it was. But I think Ingraham and Mallard did what ladies knew how to do and got the men talking. Conversation created space for the well-known feminine maneuver the women made here—cutting through male bluster, leading a man on with minimal answers to his questions before taking charge by shutting the dialogue down. Neither Mallard nor Ingraham pretended she could prevail except morally, though this would have been victory enough given the times now. What made decorum's moral point was allowing the soldiers to ask away for what they wanted before telling them, as you might a child (or a man, for that matter), that they have got it all wrong. Each woman said: You are asking the wrong person; you are careless and inattentive. I am not the owner of the objects you covet, and the rules of ownership still apply. Shouldn't you be thinking of that? *You can prevail, but clearly you do not deserve to.*

Conversation moved a woman to the highest ground she could occupy. Then, later, writing it down line by conversational line, she sealed the scene of standing up to outrage; she reenacted it. The scenes recall ones from novels women read and wrote. Men who threaten (or dangerously attract) women might, through the magic of dialogue, be transformed into men who aim to please. Did it work? Only up to a point. Mallard's opponent broke free from their conversation and took what he wanted anyway. Ingraham's soldier backed away from pressuring her for the desk, though later she spotted him making off with it. The diarists wrote down all of this, too, the power of their written words persisting beyond dialogue's limits.

"One cannot write a sentence until one knows who is speaking it, who authorizes it," says writer Russell Banks of the novelist's work. The diarists knew: *they* were the ones who authorized it; their trim dialogues proved it. If we follow Banks, writing makes real what we write, and at the same time shows what we think of reality at any risky moment. So Ingraham and Mallard wrenched the unimaginable reality of enemy soldiers in the house into scenes familiar to women whose mode—with men, slaves, children—was to have them be still and listen. And, on the page, the wrongdoer's ineptness and brutality could be reviewed again and again. It was a kind of capture—too late, of course, but having the last word was worth a lot. The dialogues bring wartime up close even now, and reading them lets us imagine backward from their inscription to the moment just before the actual conversation, the face-to-face moment in the pantry or the parlor. *And she: I must try it.*[15]

Locking eyes with the enemy in her home one day, a woman might be out on the road the next on a wartime errand or as a refugee. Decorum's profile grew thinner and its uses fewer. For some diarists, home itself became problematic as they took sharper turns through broader landscapes. A world turned upside down is a time-tested metaphor for revolution or war. But in diaries, war makes other moves, a spinning kind, where the world does not come to rest bottom up, but rests scarcely at all. Amazement was distilled into curiosity, and few words were 'nough said. Eliza Andrews, who was a refugee for a bit, discovered that white women on the road needed a pass to cross military lines. Such were the times now. She thought it was "funny for a white woman to have to get a pass to see her husband." It struck her that it was "just like the negro men here do when their wives live on another plantation." A white woman likened to a black man—probably the first time Andrews made such an equation, and not in outrage or with any particular end in mind, I think, but to observe just how strange the new times were. What *she* had to do is what black men had to do in days (probably) past. Funny.[16]

Other refugee women morphed into beggars or free spirits—it was hard to tell which or what to feel. Mary Chesnut hated her exile in Lincolnton, North Carolina, late in the war, staying in public houses kept by mercenary innkeepers, and yet she wrote scene after scene, eager, exasperated. Emma Holmes sat alone in her rented room in Camden, South Carolina, and felt sad or calm—sad and calm—as she stared out the window, the view from her window at home much on her mind. Pauline DeCaradeuc, hosting two refugee women, admitted she would feel relief when they finally left—exactly what Holmes imagined her Camden hosts feeling when she departed. Anxiety and curiosity joined hands. When Kate Stone and her intrepid mother traveled by wagon from Mississippi to Texas in 1863, they camped by the roadside at night. Though they had never before done such a thing, "we have read so many stories of camping it seems like an old song." Stone looked forward to setting up their shelter each night and "lying out under the shadow of a tree . . . with the lightening flashing in the North . . . and a nondescript bug attempting to creep into my ear." She was displaced, out in the windy world, and yet warmed by people who were somewhere between being in a fix and having a good time. "Everybody was animated and excited," Stone said of a train station filled with fellow travelers. "All had their own tales to tell of the Yankee insolence and oppression and their hairbreadth escapes . . . and everybody sympathized with everybody else."[17]

This was not Emily Harris's experience with the folks in her community near Spartanburg, South Carolina. The very idea of a community spun on the axis of war. Harris's husband, David, came and went on his older man's home guard errands; neighbors quarreled; slaves disappeared or said no. The neighborhood shook loose and hardened at the same time. "Everybody is calling on everybody for help and every body is too busy to help anybody," was how it seemed to Harris. Floride Clemson, back home from Maryland, took a fresh look at Pendleton, South Carolina. People were making do, but the "ladies look a little shabbyly," she thought. Was this home? Emmala Reed saw worse: her town, Anderson, South Carolina, drifting into selfishness and exhaustion in the way Harris feared. Reed went back to her Methodist church after a wartime lapse. Everything was undone: "No *deacons* scarcely—no religion no choir—no comforts . . . no stoves or salaries."[18]

Stoves, salaries, choirs—the bedrock, gone. Some days, all the lost things turned women from the busy strangeness of war to the thought that everything treasured might be gone forever. On any given day, a woman lost her grip, and losses big and small pushed her down. There would be no balancing this day's insults and gloom with good times from the past, no refreshing decorum. "The light hath risen but shineth not on me," was Lucy Breckinridge's closing thought one June day. Elizabeth Ingraham was stripped of emotion as well as possessions after Union troops quit her house. The soldiers had run like animals through the rooms. They had taken many things, "even the little red cups belonging to Mary." It may seem surprising that diarists did not write more often in Breckinridge's elegiac vein. But they were more likely to write as Ingraham did here. No Scripture to frame things. Not much framing at all. The women just stared at the alien, tipping world, talked plainly, and held up objects to view, like Ingraham's red cups. It feels deliberate, her singling them out, though it might have been accidental. The red cups: did she mean to say she missed them most of all?[19]

In the offhand (and off-center) quality of such words is another kind of opening for empathy. We can read Ingraham as resilient, but she is not taking a stand in the name of decorum. She is not delivering a lesson or making a plea. (And I choose not to hear her as huffing or sputtering.) She did not write "I am sad about the red cups." Her words are less certain than any of these things, plainer, holding possibilities. In this space made by possibility and plainness is a place for empathy—for going beyond the satisfaction of simply rising above her on morality's scale. Empathy needs such space and finds it in the airy envelope that surrounds the past, and empathy keeps this space open so the past's loss and possibility both stay alive. What was Ingraham feeling when she wrote about losing the red cups—"even" the red cups? There they are on the page, solid and plain in their absence. Maybe the cups were right on the boundary between what was imaginable about the war's destruction and what was not. The cups were just on the other side of the line of what the soldiers could possibly want, or so she had thought, and she had been wrong. These were the times now, and Ingraham recognized them. Before her feelings harden and she makes a plea for sympathy or shouts her sadness or outrage, she gives us the space described by the missing cups. We can step into that space if we choose.

The times now were made up of other moments, too, that flowed into diaries and became lodged there, moments when women acted, then wrote, to push back against or play with war's novelties and transgressions. They wrote not with the settled purpose of, say, confronting soldiers, but almost reflexively, and yet with a shot of drama or to tell of risk and absurdity. Diarists kept their eyes open and their pens unquiet—*look and see!*—even when the story to be told never quite arrived on the page. They wrote their present-tense war, where they saw themselves doing—what? War's bidding? Acts that trumped war? It was war as real as any person's war can be.

Cornelia McDonald's house had been surrounded by a Union army camp for many weeks when she found a new thing to do, a way to get back some of the coffee and sugar taken earlier by these same troops whose cooking fires she saw every night through her windows. It became a dangerous but clever routine. She waited of an evening until around midnight for a "low knock on the door" by a Union soldier who arrived with a "black camp kettle. . . . I take him to the pantry, lock the door from the inside." He had with him the coffee and sugar, for which she gave him a kettle full of flour. Then she let him out "to go his way back to the camp." McDonald did not say how she worked this out, or what it was like to stand close to the enemy man in her locked pantry. She wrote the sketch as a how-strange-the-times narrative, running along the porous line between the choice she made and *imagine my surprise.* So, too, Elizabeth Ingraham wrote of saving a pork shoulder and a side of bacon from foraging troops. Bacon in full view of the enemy was bacon lost, so, alone, she dragged the heavy meat upstairs to her bedroom closet and there spread out an oilcloth and laced up the meat for a long-term sequester. Was she outsmarting the times now or giving in to them? "Funny way of living" is what she wrote. It was as funny as Lucy Breckinridge found the time she spent worrying and waiting for her soldier fiancé who might have been taken by enemy troops, only to hear that the Yankees had missed him but had "captured" everyone at a local wedding instead. The strange turns of things did not so much flout good manners and logic as breeze by them. If you paused to look, everything was on a tangent to something else. Sarah Morgan, her "immigrant" self aboard the refugee-filled boat, sat on deck near an Irish woman crying at the foot of her son's coffin "while a strange woman sat on its head eating her bread and cheese."[20]

It was a funny way to live. The odd bundling of things, the reversals and novelties, made for diary entries electric with immediacy. "Bang, bang!" Elizabeth Ingraham wrote after soldiers shot up her parlor. "Colonel Coffey's picture has a hole through each eye!" A painting ruined, the colonel insulted, but the moment was more than that; the moment was *bang, bang!* Pistols in women's hands and hidden in their clothes? No longer beyond imagination. Accessorized with sidearms were Grace Elmore, Pauline DeCaradeuc, and Gertrude Thomas. Maybe they had fired men's hunting pieces once or twice, and doubtless they had read about off-color, armed women in novels and heard about female Confederate spies. But taking target practice in the yard was something else. Or just going outside and shooting. Hearing rumors of Yankee raiders, Thomas went into the yard and "fired off two pistol shots tonight to keep my courage up." Women slid small pistols into their corsets or tied them to the frames of their hoops. Quick draw was not a priority.[21]

Clothes, women's clothes, were stirred up in other ways by the war. Fashion was intensely public but clothes had always been intensely personal. So personal, it is interesting to hear Kate Stone state the obvious, that planter-class women did not give each other clothes that were unasked for, especially not hand-me-downs. She asked, rhetorically: "A year ago would we have thought of receiving, or of a friend offering, clothes as a present?" She compared it to arriving at someone's house unannounced. But war changed all that. "Now we are as pleased to receive a half-worn garment from a friend as the veriest beggar." Dressing well had meant finding a frisson in the proper and the dramatic, or the erotic. War's clothes and possible clothes changed this and changed fashion's balance. Women loaded their gowns with extra lace and fabric, appearing a bit overcooked but keeping these items from the hands of Yankee soldiers who would take them, like bacon, if they could. Women layered treasured items of clothing inside other clothing—hemming and basting well beyond good taste, and well past the point where appearing to have ample "flesh," as they called it, was considered attractive. Clothes were as they had never been: recombined, reworked, a blare of uses and innovations. Catherine Edmondston worked "alone all day" to turn her husband's worn overcoat inside out because he could not acquire a new one. "*Think* of it! . . . Did I ever think in former days that I would come *to sewing* on or he *wearing* a *turned* coat! . . . So we go!" This on top of the absurdity of her friend the bride wearing wedding chemises and drawers made from bedsheets.

So she went into the times handed to her by the Yankees—or taken from them. She thought that her husband's coat "looked very nice." Finding out that she had the skill to turn a coat was "one more debt I owe the Yankees!"[22]

Dress had a new politics all around. Wearing mourning dress in cities occupied by the enemy caught on quickly. So did dressing to go out on the balcony or porch to wave encouragement to Confederate troops passing by— something modest, meaning something not white or too bright; it was not good to stand out like a beacon. Women sometimes met Union officers on the street in town or at social gatherings, a weird counterpoint to soldiers' raids; meetings charged with enmity and eros. Bold women wore Confeder- ate cockades or colors; others hid a symbol of resistance somewhere in the folds of their skirts. The point of the hoop skirt had always been "you cannot come close to me." Now clothes had a new magic as statements and shields. Expecting raids, women stayed dressed in several layers all night. Pauline DeCaradeuc wore blue-tinted glasses so that Union soldiers, she hoped, would think she was an old woman. Beneath their clothes, alongside their pistols, they tied on belts of money and valuables. Was this a place of safety, or just the last place soldiers would look? The comic and the dangerous were locked in their dance. When Union troops arrived in Milledgeville, Georgia, Anna Green "ran to put on the bag of Jewelry I had made in the morning" for this very occasion. Kate Stone "had a great bag of Aunt Laura's gold around my waist" while traveling in Texas. One night the belt broke as she stepped onto the porch of a lodging house and everything "came down with a crash."[23]

Clothes were a currency of war and an incendiary. Stories of slaves, usu- ally someone else's, expropriating the wardrobes of mistresses on the lam (or worse, at home but now powerless) were inscribed by shocked and eager diarists. It was obvious—beyond question—that black women would, if they could, make a hoard of white women's clothes, sometimes given to them by Union officers seeking their favor. Cornelia McDonald's tense but manage- able relations with U.S. general Robert Milroy, the commanding officer in her neighborhood, snapped when she learned that he had received two "gor- geously dressed" black women in his quarters. Then there were the soldiers who rifled through women's closets for feminine things, toiletries and decora- tive knickknacks, as gifts for the sweetheart at home or the one yet to be met. At times it seemed random. Union troops lifted a mother-of-pearl piercer, some socks, and a few toothbrushes from Emma Holmes. But clothes were the prime target, and the thievery went beyond impulse and favor buying toward something more sinister; intimate items became trophies of war. Sol- diers did not want her chemises for their sweethearts, Pauline DeCaradeuc wrote. They "made the servants get our chemises & tear them up into pocket handkerchiefs for them." A few days after troops looted her house, a friend of Mary Jones's recognized the "large cravat upon the neck" of one soldier as the remnant of her black silk dress.[24]

Sarah Morgan had an eye for such things—underwear turned out for all to see, gowns cut to fit a man's neck. It was grotesque and dangerously erotic, like so much else previously unthinkable and now plainly said. And yet clothes still did what clothes had always done: give an occasion the style it deserved. This was wartime, the times now. Clothes, "so sacred to me," Morgan wrote, animated the very spirit of wartime, which she envisaged as enemy men driven "to pillage a whole country to procure apparel for vile negroes!" She knew she was overwrought and maybe "wicked" to think such a thought, but she "would rather have all I own burned, than in the possession of the negroes." Clothes made revolution plain to see: "Fancy my magenta organdie on a dark beauty!"[25]

And fancy Morgan dressed in her brother's trousers, a transgression much harder to think about, though she gave it a try. She wondered in her diary what a woman could do in the Confederacy's struggle when she could not bear arms. Morgan did not turn to hospital nursing or sewing coats for the men; these were practical things, and she was jumping over practical questions. The question that bothered her was about femininity: "What is the use of all these worthless women, in war times?" A half-rhetorical question, which she answered for herself in terms of clothes: "If they attack, I shall don the breeches, and join the assailants, and fight." And from here, rolling along on her diary's brave page, she asked, "How do breeches and coats feel, I wonder?" A very different sort of question. As it happened, she had made a plan to have a suit of her brother's in readiness, not to don to join in assailing the Yankees, but as a disguise should enemy soldiers come into the house and find her. Morgan thought of how afraid she would be if that happened and hoped that her "fright would give me courage" to wear the breeches. But she kept postponing a trial of putting them on. Even when urged by a friend, she was deeply embarrassed at the thought, unhinged almost. She wanted no witness; she removed her pet canary from the room so it would not see, when at last she decided to do it. The trousers lay before her on the bed. She stared at them. "I am actually afraid of them," she wrote. She put them away.[26]

Cornelia McDonald traded things with an enemy man in the closeness of her pantry; Elizabeth Ingraham wrestled bacon into her closet; Gertrude Thomas fired her spirit-lifting pistol; Sarah Morgan lay out and then refolded her brother's trousers. *Think of it.* Small stories of the war as *my* war, no end in sight, only the means: the diary making the times now. Strange days were kept spinning in multiple ways, opening to the dark or to the wondrous, and to the desperate necessity and surprising elation of getting through each one. The way women lived their days was, of course, the way they lived their war. The diary's real war: everything that happens, happens this close.

STOP-TIME

Then Gen. Robert E. Lee surrendered at Appomattox, Virginia, and the big war ended. The diarists writing their war were kicked loose from something that had been moving very fast. But their writing barreled on, fierce with inertia into a new stop-time that was not stasis, not even much of a pause, but a way to bring Appomattox into their pages and still write *their* war, too. Stop-time got a diarist to *now* when now was not recognizable anymore. Lee's surrender was a shock, no mistake, and later everyone would remember it as war's end and the Confederacy's doom. But if we just read the diarists, the end as they wrote it was elastic and personal. The wildness of war clung to their pages even as they watched it go.

Floride Clemson, not two weeks after Appomattox, carried it off sounding casual: "Well the game's up I fear." Her terseness strikes me as her usual way of not making a fuss about things, not even this; understatement made things level. Pauline DeCaradeuc, at about the same time, said more, and more along the lines of many who still stood up for the war. She felt the surge of the "terrific bewildering news," but the game was not up, not for her: "God will raise us yet." War's end in diaries was oddly flexible. Women wrote of defeat before the surrender and of surrender as if it were not defeat. Ten days or so after Appomattox, Gertrude Thomas was still hopeful that stories of the surrender were only "painful rumors." But Emily Harris pronounced the end four months before Lee signed off: "Our once proud Confederacy must sink to rise no more." For Mary Chesnut, "the grand smash" came later, in February, but still two months before Lee and Grant sat down together, and that meeting did not end it, either. She felt "shame—disgrace—misery" throughout the weeks surrounding the Appomattox moment, which made for a world "dissolved in air . . . scattered, demoralized, stunned—ruined." The Confederacy went "with one crash" for Sarah Morgan, not by way of Lee's pen but later, through the barrel of John Wilkes Booth's pistol. So the war's end was not a pen-to-paper done deal, not by Lee's hand, not by theirs. The end stretched itself out into a stop-time suspension of what life had turned into during the past four years.[27]

Just reading the diarists finds their anger and dismay and a deep, word-filled humiliation we have read many times from white Southerners who staked themselves on the Confederacy. But there also is a flatness, and a shrewdness, and Clemson's "game's up." In a way, a diarist's stop-time is hard to read because it defies the "readability" of the familiar war's-end drama: the final stacking of arms, the transfigured Lee. We expect clarity from defeat and we do not find it. Instead, the days appear as diarists now found them, stripped of the in-your-face madness of losses large and small and hinting at possibilities that escaped sure articulation but floated into each day under strange, strange skies. A diarist worked to find the words for *what just happened*. She wrote less from an urge to seal things off in judgment than a desire to keep on telling.

Even blaming someone or something for the defeat was written in this vein. Finding someone to blame was not so much a search for indictment as a set of possibilities for making a story equal to the war and war's end. Emma LeConte saw a story of heaven and earth out of joint: "Have our brave men fought so desperately and died so nobly for *this*?" Nothing for it but that the war should go on: "Let us suffer still more." Noble men were missing in Pauline DeCaradeuc's vision a month after the surrender. Their opposite was there, in fact: "Our men have behaved disgracefully, have deserted, straggled & everything else." Not men but the noble Southern people were the tale to be told, as Catherine Edmondston saw it just days before the surrender. A great people, badly served: "A noble cause & a free people well nigh sacrificed upon the altars of *Bad Government & Bad Faith with the people*." No, not bad government, said Emmala Reed, but the Southern people themselves were at fault, people like herself were to blame for losing "confidence in the *Pres't* & civil authorities."[28]

So stories were launched into a sea of mixed feelings where wishes met fear. Diarists revised themselves and then rerevised themselves. Spite was in their words, but respite, too, and a lot of thrashing around. It was far from conclusive, far even from consistent. As history's victors, we can choose to pass by this stop-time, brief as it might have been, and drive yet more nails into the Confederate coffin. Or, we can stay with these women at the very moment the war let go of them, see them taking their own existential temperature, so to say, performing self-divination, trying out possible pasts and futures in the present tense. The moment was an open question, and I think it is an empathetic move—and good historical practice—to remember how open it was each time we go back to the diaries to say something new about the war. Diarists' words are a reminder that we all write the war—and read it—at the edge of conjecture. Not knowing where to land, diarists came down in a lot of places. Pauline DeCaradeuc felt the "iron heel" of the Yankees and the ruin of her Southern home, which had become "a vile place." Stop-time: "I hate everything here." Grace Elmore moved in the opposite direction. The war had been "a long visit away from home, and {I} have just come back." Catherine Edmondston wondered at the vast quietude of her days and her muffled feelings: "I am not dejected, am not cast down," but "I sleep, sleep, sleep endlessly; if I sit in my chair for ten minutes, I doze. . . . I seem to grope after my own ideas, my own identity, & in the vain attempt to grasp it I fall asleep."[29]

Declarative and groping by turns—an unsatisfying way to write but better than a blank page. It is not what we seek, either, when we write history, but closer, maybe, to the histories we actually write. Or should write. For me, there is empathy for the women who faced each day with words and who sometimes wrote moments rich with a lack of pretention—delivering, in Marc Bloch's words, "far more of the past than the past itself had thought good to tell us." I am empathetic with a writer whose possibilities are visited by uncertainty and by the radiant opacity of the random moments that read as if they came unmediated to the page: *I hate everything here. I sleep, sleep, sleep endlessly.* War's stop-time was this immediate and blankly true.[30]

But what about the white South rising again? The women did not toss their politics away or give up their faith that good order was kept only by white people. There are times of Lost Cause sentiment and vengeance in the women's words; the urge is there and it is ugly. But a diary is too sudden a text for settled meaning, and its pages let the women pause and choose or not choose. Empathy balances briefly on such moments when defeat and the future still mingled. The women seem most alive to me—people of their own time and not figures of my need to judge them—at these moments when war's end was not something final but something with almost too many possibilities.

Gertrude Thomas went from uncertainty to relief to defiance and then back to uncertainty over a stretch of days and pages, once she acknowledged the surrender was more than rumor. On May 1 she "burst into tears and wept for joy" as it struck her that her husband and brother had survived a terrible war. She wanted to give a May Day party. "I was laughing and talking," she wrote. She heard news of a generous armistice and was thankful that it might help her gracefully accept that "the bright dream of Southern independence has not been realized—the war is over and again we become a part of the United States." She counted her cash on hand: "25 cents and one 5 cts in silver." But a week later she learned that the armistice between Generals Sherman and Johnston was void, and her joy was gone: "*Today I am more intensely opposed* to the *North* than at any period of the war—we have been imposed upon." One evening around this time, she heard two drunken men talking as they passed by her house, one declaring, "I am a rebel *now*, will be for *twenty* years, will be for *fifty years*, will be *forever*." These were drunken men, but Thomas felt the blood rush to her face and the tears come because she knew that she felt the same way. "Last week I would not have done it—Now I could not help it." The stream of her writing, her commentary, and her images, led her to this resolve. A decided rebel. Was this the end of her end-of-the-war narrative? The decision made, did time restart? It can seem so. We might like it to seem so, but Thomas was not writing for us. She went on mulling it over, and at the turn of the new year in 1866 a blank spot was still there where the war used to be: "I do not know what to think." Perhaps God had used defeat to teach Southerners a lesson, but she doubted this. She doubted whether "Providence had any thing to do with the matter."[31]

Writing, like Thomas, in early May of the war's final year, Emmala Reed, some 100 miles away in Anderson, South Carolina, followed a stream of thought about what the war's end meant or whether it was really over. Southerners' "sin & imbecility" at first explained defeat quite nicely. Unprepared Southerners had played right into the hands of the "powerful—persevering—cunning—cruel Yankee nation." Time was like a held breath and "what will the end be we *fear* to know. *All* feel *subdued*, but bear our calamities as cheerfully as possible." Cheerfulness competed with discouragement, played with it, and by the end of 1865 Reed's narrative carried her to something like Thomas's springtime relief and even happiness. Life seemed underway again. "The scenes of War all passed thank heaven—and though we are a conquered people—yet with many mercies we still exist—and now live in peace and security I hope for a long time!" She signed off on the page, inscribing herself solid and visible: "Safe in my father's home at Anderson S.C. Dec. 1865." End of the year, and the story seemed ready to reset and move time into the postwar. Yet her writing went on stirring the pot, and scarcely a month later Reed looked upon a different present, with a future altered and already set, and it was all wrong. Happiness had vanished, and so had defiance. Not the Yankees, but her sad hometown had crushed both. Anderson had become a "selfish—unsocial—sordid place" with "no spirit of improvement—amusement—or religion." People dragged through the days in a "continual *humdrum* way of living to eat and sleep—and dress a little." Anderson: "It would be better for our young family to grow up elsewhere."[32]

These streaming scenes of stop-time are as many as there were diarists keeping the days. Women writing war spilled possibilities and waded through them, and they spoke in a range of voices. So we are supplied with choices enough when we want to take up a diary and decide how to read its voice and its possibilities at war's end. Diarists' terseness is one choice, the concise words they found for the partial, the abrupt, the slate wiped clean. If women complained sometimes of being distracted from their writing by the confusion around them, they also wrote succinctly—and tellingly—when distracted. Terseness is a quality passed over in our modern wartime accounts, so it seems worth a thought. Terseness, a friend to the war weary, an ally of the diarist (and the reader of diaries), countering the profusion of words all around. Terseness, stop-time's particular gift. "Each moment I live too fast," Thomas wrote, enough said, in the week before the surrender. And Reed: "I must read & dream & *pray*." The sentence stands alone, almost conclusive, though I don't think it was meant to be; an intimation rather, written down to be let go. Small incidents, unelaborated, pointed to the present and the past, maybe to the future. Her servants gone in February of 1866, Reed now fetched the icy morning wash water herself. She had a sudden image, and wrote it down, of "menials" breaking the ice on their water, an image of long-ago peasants, it seems, but readable now as an image of people who had been enslaved by the likes of the Reeds. "Hard for us all to dress," she wrote of the cold morning. "Yet how must the *poor* and the menials have suffered at their early labors." The changed times rhymed with past times. For Catherine Edmondston, too, who once wrote with thoughts of dessert: "Puddings! What a reminiscence! . . . 'What shall I have for dessert?' seems a question of medieval times."[33]

The terseness is its own kind of insight, one that slipped past the censoring fear of embarrassment or being a bore, and one that keeps the diarist and us in the moment, like a snapshot that somehow always catches the eye. The diarist's war is still there in the impulse to put the stripped-down thought onto the page. Terseness might point to other things, too, to a hidden train of thought or buried anger. For some like Emma Holmes, wartime stayed on in the resolve to not let the finished war rest in peace but to "cherish every memory connected with it." It seems a straight line from here to becoming the town's implacable Confederate dowager, chastening to behold on her porch. It is a good story line and a comfortable one for us, but there is no need to push the diarist from the heat of war's end right into Lost Cause scar tissue. There were choices and side glances. It does not fit the big war tale we know best, but Lucy Breckinridge once imagined "bliss" waiting for her after war's end, though she would die before then, and Grace Elmore, who lamented at length the Confederacy's defeat, once saw it as "my starting out in life." Sarah Morgan had the thought that she was the great war's plaything: "I have learned to feel myself a mere puppet in the hands of a Something that takes me here, to day, to-morrow there, always unexpectedly, and generally very unwillingly, but at last lands me somewhere or other, right side up." Diary keeping—her plaything, let's say—did the same for her. Traveling through their pages but never arriving, diarists helplessly or slyly or tenderly wrote their way past conclusion and kept on going.[34]

CHAPTER FOUR

Men

When women wrote about war, they wrote about men. Men's ways had conjured up the war with well-spoken promises and undercover intentions. It followed that men's ways held the key to how the war would turn out. The war took some men away, variously husbands, brothers, lovers. It delivered others, the countryside now alive with crowds of new men—"our" common-man soldiers, brute or negotiable Yankees, possible lovers. Diarists wrote mostly of these men, the men the war brought, and the new yet old play of the sexes.

So warfare brushed up against eros and its pleasures and dangers. War shaped chances and limits for love, love shaped women's writing, and the war became love shaped in diaries. Diarists had a good time with some of this. In the mix of new men was a chance for love's promised transformations or for ordinary tenderness. There were scenes where people, funny and frustrated in love, did and said things that made the heart beat faster and the days sail on. There was a new, darkly exciting force, too. Believing in love had been a way to believe in life's goodness, which women watched over on everyone's behalf. Now the war pitted love's ways against brutality, sentiment against chaos, in a stark struggle. If men's ways had always been a little mysterious, love's promise was thought to be clear. War threatened to reverse these so that love would lose its substance, while men at war created a new reality so bluntly terrible that it became the substance of everything. Diarists wrote their small narratives of men in the face of this reversal. The young, unmarried diarists did this most often, as might be expected, although the older, married women were not outside the current of words about men. War's intensity stirred it up all around. Creation and destruction were locked together in war as in eros. Women asked in many ways, If we are to fall in love with men, *who are men really?* War would tell.

Diarists met this chance armed with the language of romance and its vision of a world alive with moments when women and men in love might become truer in spirit and nature. Men did not hold the key to everything in the ways of love, but diarists wrote of love most surely, or maybe most easily, in terms of men, and romantic sensibility supplied the momentum. There was danger in this. Romantic novels were dangerous things, as any parent of a girl knew, with their floating castles of words. Words of desire made men into words, and words fed desire but could not satisfy it. It was the novel's perfect erotic moment. Diaries might summon the language that opened up such moments, and they granted a willful privacy where they could be enjoyed. Which came first, the private diary as a place to tell of one's love, or the urge to tell of love because one was keeping a diary? Saying a secret about men in a diary's pages was sweet, and romantic phrases sweet to write. *Now I am going to tell you something, my dear friend*, a woman says to her diary just before she speaks of a lover. Saying that something is *about to be said* falls outside the diary's usual run of first thoughts. It calls on a novelist's voice, rapt and enticing in the presence of love.

The diary's own pathways for eros, though, usually had less elevation, less holding of breath. Either way, historians of the Civil War do not talk much about romantic love or look for it, though it plays a bit part in studies of war and gender. And as we have seen, some diarists, thinking to publish their journals after the war, pruned, first thing, their "silly" words about men and lovemaking. Editors remove these words, too. Trivia. Why should love talk take this hit? Maybe words of love and desire seem weightless or too intoxicated to be matched to war's big, established game, never mind that every war creates art and fiction where love and war embrace. Maybe there is uneasiness over love's peculiar emotional anarchy being even more unpredictable than war's. Maybe love talk is too close to the diary's present moment, too raw. In any case, we grow accustomed to not expecting love and the Civil War to be between the same historical covers—to be "readable" together. In the heat of war, though, before second thoughts, diarists inscribed the opposite. Men and love crowded into diaries' pages before and after the women learned that war made for broken men and worn-out women. Would love stand up to war? Would love push back against war's destruction and bitterness? Inside these questions was the question of whether *men* would stand up for love against war—stand up for the ordained, sweet, electric exchange between the sexes. Were men the creatures women thought they were?[1]

Love distracts. Diarists wrote eros in the world when it appeared, unlooked for, only partly seen, as the days rolled along and new men came into their lives. The stories of men and the chances for love, as I read the diaries, are always up front and readable. I confess that I have a hard time believing that anyone would cut them out, except maybe the diarist herself. I confess that I think eros is as serious as anything can be in war. And even if eros turns out to be just trivia, we should read it for that—for the foolishness and fantasy that burn in people's lives. Take your pick. I read the women as finding out, in their own time, with their own words, in different concentrations at different points in their lives and now in war, that there is, in novelist Tessa Hadley's nice take, "hidden inside ordinary life, the bliss of sex, running counter to everything else experience was teaching, the bustling commonsensical entropic drive." The women came to know this, I think, as they came to know men in war, and as the war countered common sense. The women wrote men and love in their own way (heavy on sugar and spirit) and they did not write at length (eros's power was self-evident *and* elusive). But their diaries say something about how women and men were alien and together. It is something that I want to read; it is something that I know, but something still so new to me.[2]

None of this was at the forefront of Lucy Buck's mind, it is safe to say, when she wrote her diary account of meeting Gen. Robert E. Lee in July 1863. But men and war and eros fill her entry even so. Lee, disengaging himself and his army from the defeat at Gettysburg, stopped by the Buck plantation in Front Royal, Virginia, for refreshment and was, of course, invited to stay awhile and rest. Buck's father brought Lucy and her sister to be introduced to the great man as he sat on the front porch. "{Lee} said to me—'won't you sit down, my daughter and let us talk some?' I laid my hand on a chair standing near in compliance but he made room for me on the seat by him and said 'No, not there, but here close by me.' When I was seated I told him how much pleasure it gave me to see our defender—the Father of our State—he replied—'Oh, No! my daughter. I only wish he were more worthy of being seen. There! Look at those young rebels (pointing to his staff) they're a great deal better worth your looking at—gallant young beaux that they are.'"[3]

Buck and her sister sang a few songs, and then Lee and his officers rose to leave, the general signing the sisters' autograph books ("at the same time protesting that he knew we would much prefer having our sweethearts' there rather than his"). His parting remark to the young women: not to "let any of those fine young Yankee officers carry us off." From beginning to end, the general's words kept eros front and center; there was no wandering away from men and women, war and love. Lee probably thought this was the way to converse with young women. He was relaxing, catching a breath. But look at what

Men

happens in his love talk. He removes himself from youth's sexual play, though he mixes the message by having Lucy sit next to him. He points to the sexual attractiveness of his officers, and he makes Yankee officers his men's decorous rivals in love. War, men, and love—of course! And Lucy Buck continued eros's work on this July afternoon by writing it all down. Everything says: love measures up to war. Wrapping up her account, she seemed delighted: "Dear old General!"[4]

The young Confederate officers taking a breather with Lucy Buck were war's new men, the interesting ones, suitable as lovers but not the neighborhood's (well-known) suitable men, and suddenly they were there on the porch. Another time, Yankee soldiers would be there, same porch, a very different kind of novel man. All these new men came under the diarist's gaze as excitingly or dangerously volatile—excitingly *and* dangerously volatile—having men's curious potential for decorum and violence. I turn toward empathy on this ground, moved by Buck straightforwardly stepping into this new, charged world at her doorstep and her delight in General Lee's refreshment of love—brutal war banished from the hour. It changed nothing else, not the Bucks' vulnerability to destruction there in the Shenandoah Valley, not the wrongness of the Confederate cause. But I reach past these things and feel Buck's instinctive move to close the door on chaos, which I think I know, too, and to believe that love matters. And just barely, Buck's scene opens up love's promise that women could reach for empathy with men. New men, uniformed and armed and Other; their foreignness made the question of empathy sharply real. Lucy Buck seems satisfied enough here with surfaces, but other diarists, as we will see, reached out further toward men to see who was there. They looked for signs, and were anxious, too.

Of course, known men—family men and men of the upper class from the neighborhood—were also in this new atmosphere, less exciting to write about but given their due by diarists. There were new possibilities here for admiration or romance. Not "known" in the same way, but familiar on the scene, were white men of the poorer classes and black men who were enslaved. These men, especially black men, women had never inscribed as anywhere near love's ground. They were not figures of desire, not even wondered about is my guess. Even the known men of their class were, as often as not, seen as simply going about their mysterious errands as men always did, doing their duty. The times now made their duties more urgent and admirable, though sometimes familiar men morphed strangely under war's pressure. Lucy Buck's neighbor Green Samuels dressed himself as a woman to evade the Yankees. Pauline DeCaradeuc's father, unable to evade the Yankees, told them he was not a South Carolinian, but French. The Reverend Robert Mallard left his wife, Mary, for the woods around their plantation, was captured anyway, and wound up preaching for the benefit of Union soldiers. Kate Stone was astonished to find that her younger brothers were carrying pistols around town when she thought they were playing marbles. War showed her "how little we can know of the heart of a boy." How little was known, too, about the hearts of Mr. Samuels, Mr. DeCaradeuc, and Reverend Mallard.[5]

The diarists did not push further into the curious moves of these familiar men. There is a hint of the women backing away from saying more, yet not wanting to let obviously odd behavior slide by unwritten. *Here is a story.* Two of the married diarists did likewise when their husbands chose to shed their active military roles. Catherine Edmondston took note in 1865 of her husband's exit from active service on a "certificate of disability." He told her everything was fine, but she puzzled through his decision on her page. She decided that the change meant not less but different service to the cause. As a gentleman, she reasoned, her husband could now "be of more service than he would be if under orders all the time." When Gertrude Thomas's husband opted out of active service and purchased a substitute, she gave her account of it a special wrapping ("I am writing confidentially to you my Journal and I will tell you exactly how I feel") and went on to say that she felt pretty mixed about his decision. Months later she was still mulling it over, saying that she had been "very proud" of his active service. Both women hinted at something going flat, the barest breath of disappointment in their men. Men's ways were men's ways but now, in war, newly seen because newly put into words.[6]

These words about men, like women's words about crazy war, were words diarists wrote wanting to settle somewhere. Instead they found their pages always doubling back and reraking the ground. Women's support for the war dried up before men's, some historians say; women were realists and bailed out, disillusioned by men's ruinous warfare madness. Other historians see women's defense of home and their hatred of Yankees as keeping them at the Confederate barricades in full strength to the end. I suppose some women did settle on a position, and we can choose to put them in one box or another. But just reading diaries tracks constant movement in the world of the sexes and war. *We* would like certainty, and the women probably did, too, but they wrote the uncertainty they found. Looking for what a woman "really" thought mixes our desire for certainty into her pages, and before we know it, we have stepped outside the circle of her experience as she lived it. So we can choose to quote Grace Elmore in December 1864: "I have lost faith in our men, I do not think they come up to the mark." But we can also find her a short time later, touched by men's need for women ("They do depend on us a great deal") and seeing not so much men's failure as one more turn of the war-seized world: "How queer the times." In their uncertainty, it was the queerness of the times that diarists reached for, again and again. And between the sexes, it was the new men, the ones the war brought, who were more likely to hold the key to the strangeness.[7]

MEN CHOSEN AND LET GO

In the midst of writing about her day, Sarah Morgan suddenly, without preface, wrote this:

> Sometimes I fancy how all will burn, until it makes me sick to think of it. Fancy a great shell in this little room! Crash! the bed posts will fall with the tester, the marble slab of the toilet table, and its ornaments will disappear in fine dust, long flames will creep in my desk and lick my letters and papers, and will turn over the pages of my books with their long red tongues quicker than my fingers can. They will swallow the washstand at one mouthful, together with all I keep in it; they will break in the armoir—they have no more respect for rosewood than pine—they will take up my dresses one by one and turn them over as though to taste them (some *are* sweet enough to eat), they will roll down the skirts and up the sleeves, eat all the lace and trimming, these wicked flames![8]

Flames wicked and full of purpose, a bedroom scene like nothing she had known or had any cause to think about before the war. War made possible the fascination of imagining her dresses on fire. It made her sick to think of it, but, writing, she found a kind of scary pleasure in each detail of her bedroom's destruction as she rode the language of romantic fiction's "wicked" play of erotic desire. It is a scene of ravishment with no injury, except to her belongings, which she sacrifices here to the dreadful delight of the vision. Two months later Morgan's home will in fact be trashed by enemy soldiers. She will hear about it only from the reports of others and write about it in her diary. It will have none of the seductive quality of the burning dresses, which burn on their own, in a leisurely way, in a scene without male figures—without human figures at all—a scene of war eating up possessions and pleasures at the pace of a daydream. So her diary hands over a piece of found eroticism from a time when romantic imagination was a struggle of wit and will against strong obstacles—a tyrannical father, a storm at sea—sensational, intense, and describable down to the last heartbeat. Now the obstacle was war, more than equal to the erotic imagination, serving and testing it.[9]

Adding the figure of a man to Morgan's scene would completely transform it. This day she wrote eros obliquely, metaphorically, but this did not blunt or deny it, as we moderns might like to think of a repressed nineteenth century. Writing around the edges of eros gave it more intensity and strength, not less, and the off-center, quiet diary was an ally in this. And when men *did* appear, the peculiar shadings of upper-class life applied: an able lover was an eligible one. He had an easy mastery of all the subtle moves of intention and inevitability known by that unfortunate term *manners*, which, again, we moderns have to think about generously, without conjuring up finger-wagging prudes. Mid-nineteenth-century courtship manners were quite up to the work of lovemaking, of intensifying the sexual frisson between women and men. It is true that manners were about surfaces, and the excitement women and men took in bouncing from surface to surface in courtship—the wordplay and parlor games just kept coming—says a lot about their erotic world. I have doubts about how much stamina I have for it and how deep my empathy might run. Love's manners seem too clogged with conquest and dependency. For the women, though, a man's manners, his *bearing* in the social world, piped erotic imagination directly into the time he spent with them. Manners were the sign and the condition of belonging to a world of desire where the play of a man's expressiveness and reserve signaled his ability to take charge but also his readiness to be thoughtful. Women looked for *attentiveness*, a man's gesture of love that was neither an act nor the anticipation of one, but somehow both together. In short, manners were sexy, and a man adept at manners (a gentleman, to use another now-creaky term) was a man who was worth getting to know because his pleasing ways promised deeper pleasures. There always had been *some* men like this in the neighborhood before the war. Having many more such men around to choose from, at a harrowingly fast pace, was wartime's surprising and problematic gift.

It was problematic because while men were not unknowable—good manners showed that—getting to know them took work. It meant, in one way or another, seeking empathy—taking the risk that one could know the world of these different creatures, men. What was the risk now that the world was aflame with war? A young Southern woman in love in a Josephine Humphreys novel about the Civil War one day realizes that "what Daddy had said might be true, that a man with his mind on fighting has little brain space left for attention to women, and war is the enemy of love. I asked myself, *Why then do men choose it?*" It is a question behind a lot of what the diarists wrote about men, and if Sarah Morgan was not asking it directly in her destructive and seductive daydream, her burning dresses were straight from the new wartime that made war's tie to men, and to women's desire for them, even more troubling and exciting.[10]

Found visions of eros like Morgan's are few in diaries, but found words of love are not. Diarists scattered vernacular words of love, words easily spoken, throughout entries where men are met and gazed upon, tested. Written down by diary-keeping chance, these ordinary words, steady in the face of war, balance the outlandishness of burning dresses. Some of it is sweet: *dear, to be dear, dear only knows what he . . . .* Some of it sizes him up: *He is right clever, right good. He is 'mazin' kind, amazing.* Words come from nature and nature's God: *pure, purest love, holy.* Yet men were strange, and it was a strange thing to be seeking them. The language speaks of unbalance, unhinging, ungood. *The devil in him, crazy on matrimony.* He was *real 'cute,* which was not like a darling child, and not even a compliment or a come-on; *acute,* that is, a little too sharp angled for his own good. The words are about movement above all, the movement of emotions, and of physical things, too. Bodies can be heard offstage. Lovers are *thrown together* by fate and now by war. Lovers *enter the field, take a fancy to.* On the flip side of success in lovemaking, more movement; she might decide to *put him on the shelf* or *send him off.* She hopes at a dance to be asked onto the floor by him and there to *dance him down.*

So diarists scooped up eros's small talk as they wrote of men, the new and eligible ones. A diary's openness to this was 'mazin', and the vernacular words of love planted prewar hopefulness in the dooryard of war, saying this: even in war, meeting men will be as it has always been, though with more to choose from and more to let go. Love will measure up to war. Even if a woman was already married, war-brought men were everywhere and worth a look. Men from away, men who came to New Orleans from Alabama, to Virginia from Georgia, single, married, or with marital status unclear. Dressed to the nines for war and touched by danger and death. The bleak antebellum field of plantation courtship—too few men of the right sort, too little variety, too many long afternoons alone mulling over the thin-soup prospects—cracked wide open. Now the pace was quick, and even the near misses meant something, women and men brushing up against each other and the nerve endings of eros. The war brought Christopher Memminger Jr. to Emma LeConte, a man special enough for her to veil him as "M" in her pages, a romantic disguise that did not hide much. She thought him "right clever" with his "wild theories and still wilder dreams." But he left Columbia just before Sherman arrived. "It is not likely we will ever be thrown together again." Pauline DeCaradeuc liked young Captain Beauregard with his "easy, finished manners" and fine singing voice. He taught her to waltz, held her about the waist, and then he was gone. "I liked him, beaucoup, but there's an end of him." She also was intrigued by Capt. Jack Milledge, just before he left Augusta for Virginia. He turned up again in South Carolina a short time later and called on her, telling her black-eyed self that "*black eyes* lured him back." But "*black eyes sent him off* for good, this time," DeCaradeuc wrote, wondering now what she had seen in him. Men washed into women's lives and washed out again. Romance had promised perfect moments when love opened and bloomed. Not now. There were too many men moving too fast and coming from all angles. Anna Green found that "I am thought pretty by some, very pretty, but not by those whom I want to think me pretty." It was "a strange and lamentable fact" for Kate Stone "that all the bald, middle-aged bachelor doctors take a fancy to me." Sarah Morgan was embarrassed, or mock embarrassed, to discover that while she and her friend Anna were singing "Wild Tremendous Irishman" with abandon, the charming Colonel Breaux was listening in from the balcony.[11]

Courtship—if that was what to call it now—headed toward the fast and loose. Lovemaking always had broken some of the rules, but now partying was partying with strangers; friends, not married aunts, were the chaperones. Even Lucy Buck, not a diarist to fill pages with emotional scenes, told of "wild" parties, including an affair where she was the one who "stirred them up and we had game after game of romps." Eliza Andrews's sister Metta was not easy meeting all the new men at all times of the day without proper introductions, "but," Andrews wrote, "I confess that I like the change and variety." And even Andrews, who worked over her diary after the war to remove the foolish times, told readers of her published volume about the trouble she took to frizz her hair for the men. Sometimes all of this was unsettling, and women worried about appearances and the incongruity of having a good time in wartime. Emma Holmes, at twenty-six, believed that partying made "all the youths of 21 or 22 . . . crazy on the matrimonial question." It was not right in wartime. Kate Stone wrote that the sexes' "mirth jars my heart" when the losses of war were so great. Still, she went to parties and was relieved to "talk nonsense again. . . . One grows callous to suffering and death. We can live only in the present, only from day to day." Emilie McKinley was tutoring children near Vicksburg, Mississippi, when, in one of the war's weird social moments, she was invited to a party thrown by a paroled Confederate officer and his Yankee captors. The Yankees were "splendid musicians," he assured her. McKinley was dubious but joined in, and it turned out that the Yankees sang very well, stayed for dinner, and "told enormous stories." Vicksburg was a besieged city of despair and death and would surrender to Union forces in less than a month, as this young woman sang with enemy officers. *It is callous.* Maybe so; but it pushed back against the war.[12]

Diaries and love thrived on *scenes*, or something even less finished—a moment or a setting, let's say, where a face is seen, a word said, a look given. Men appeared, were held briefly by the diary's light touch, then most of them moved on. The diarists were right: both playing at love and being serious about it can seem lightweight, merely comic. So I like how the poet Anne Carson writes unsparingly of what I think diarists also knew when they let passion ride over the risk of seeming foolish or being fooled in love: "To address yourself to the moment when Eros glances into your life and to grasp what is happening in your soul at that moment is to begin to understand how to live." This is as free from embarrassment as any nineteenth-century lover could wish, and there is for me a flash of empathy in how the diarists hand over small scenes of eros glancing into their lives amid war's ruin. Ghosts, still safe and eager in love. I also want to think that not everything must be told as a cold story of calculation and force, that love is as much in the world and that we should be looking for love's scenes and risk writing them. Here are some I have found.[13]

Pauline DeCaradeuc wrote eros as she discovered it in the unexpected turns of wartime travel, and in the excitement of wartime's many sudden men to be flirted with. Then, at the end of her diary, she suddenly presented her lover. The temporary men she inscribed freely, was playful and decisive with them. In the spring of 1865, the Confederacy just weeks from collapse, DeCaradeuc was traveling by train with only a woman friend, their twice-female semisecurity standing in for proper male escort. The ladies' car being full, the two women edged unnoticed into one carrying soldiers, who were "behaving shamefully smoking, drinking, &c." An eye-opening scene from men's alternate universe; a sense of *so this is how men are.* Three officers entered the car and "one very coolly pulled off his coat, then his vest, then his cravat & collar, & dear knows how much more would have come off, when he turned and saw me," DeCaradeuc wrote. She was embarrassed, thought it funny. He was "abashed." Did she look away from his body rapidly coming into view? The next day, the officers turned up at a picnic, and one asked for an introduction to DeCaradeuc and apologized for their rowdiness. The officer who had been "in dishabile," a Lieutenant Brent, was too shy to speak until "after dinner, when his heart was warmed," and then they conversed. It was a pleasant time, goodbyes were said, and he became forever on her page "Lieut. Brent (the one who undressed himself)."[14]

Another time, another train, DeCaradeuc, again with a woman friend, was thrown in with Maj. T. A. Buford from Virginia, whose pleasure it would be, he said, to escort them to their destination. He "was 'mazin' kind & attentive to us," DeCaradeuc thought. He became for a time "our Virginia major" in DeCaraduec's pages, a protector-plaything, a gentleman with the natural ease and effortless conversation that spurred eros. Then, their travel complete, he departed on his wartime mission. But this was not the end. DeCaradeuc was surprised to receive a letter from him (addressed phonetically to "Miss Pauline Colorado") a month later. Then he wrote yet again and "*respectfully opened a correspondence,* which in consideration of his courtesy & kindness . . . and of his being an entire stranger to our State, I joined." *Opening a correspondence. Joining it.* It was as physical as it sounds, and as sticky. Exchanging letters with a man left a wake of words that lingered. Implications, entanglements. Alarms went off for DeCaradeuc, and she told her father of Major Buford's request, a move which passed everything into the hands of men. Buford's "credentials" proved "first rate," but she decided it should go no further and sent him a few cold, short letters to finish the correspondence. Her dismissal of him seems oddly harsh, until—sudden revelation—she wrote that she had fallen in love with Guerard Heyward, a lieutenant recovering from the ill effects of having been a prisoner of war. Men like Brent and Buford are in her pages fully seen—imploring, undressing—but she kept Heyward under wraps as "my new summer friend" until writing him up as a consummated love story. Their "desperate flirtation . . . progressed rapidly," she admitted. Heyward was "all devotion, said everything sweet & soft in the language." He came bearing unusual gifts, such as "some pressed moss, which he fixed in prison." Pressed moss: "Dear only knows what all he don't want me to accept!" He was the lover brought by the war, her "boy" she called him, her "scamp." They were engaged by October, "God bless him." She was wide eyed at the combination that had brought it off: "Mon Dieu!! & My conspiring!"[15]

Anna Green wrote a lot about men, more than she wrote about anything else the war brought. Remaining unmarried might be all right, though she thought she was made for marriage and dreaded the "coldness and derision" faced by unmarried women. Green inscribed men in her diary in proportion to how likely they were to be the one she chose as a mate; inscribing them was part of making the choice. She had known some of the men before the war, but the war mixed them up and redealt them. In her pages, men appear in the warm light of her curiosity and frankness; she is shy but simmers gently in her shyness. Bryan Thomas was "handsome and I think a man I could admire," though writing this on the diary page was "unmaidenly." Of the attractive

Dr. Bell, she did not mind saying—the joke was on her—that all evening "I exerted myself and dressed and smiled upon Dr. B. to no purpose." She made him a tobacco pouch to take on his travels, a sure wartime token of a woman's feelings for a man.[16]

Beneath the love thoughts was a secret. Green wrote nothing about being briefly betrothed to Adlai Houston, a markedly older man with children in need of a mother after his wife, Anna's sister, died suddenly. Green wrote not a word of this, always referring to Houston as "brother," until he, too, died unexpectedly. Or as she put it with typical, sweet bluntness, he "sickened and died and I was free." Now that it was over and out on the page, she blamed herself for the "hasty act" of agreeing to the engagement and for the family tension that followed. There must have been plenty of that between the lines she wrote and the ones she did not write.[17]

When love did come, it was more than Green wanted to write alone. She twice shared her diary pages with lovers, first with the exhausting John Grieve, who flirted with both Anna and her sister. He proceeded to write himself out of Anna's life when they exchanged diaries and she found his pages "filled with distrust of me," while her diary was "teeming with affection and confidence" for him. So Grieve was let go, sent packing by his own words. With Samuel Cook, though, shared writing made love, the two of them writing lovers' dialogues in her book. Green met Cook just after the war, in one of wartime's strange chances, when he arrived in Milledgeville to be a patient at the lunatic asylum directed by Anna's physician father. Cook was no lunatic; maybe he was a recovering drinker or, more likely, just worn out by the war. In any case, he quickly was on the mend, was a gentleman, and was soon invited to dinner. Dinners led to times after dinner when he and Anna sat on the housetop under the moon. They wrote their lovemaking into her diary and so we hear the words that mattered to lovers and stood up to war. Samuel wrote that the two of them were "two in the flesh But one in the soul," and Anna wrote beneath, "Two souls with but a single thought / Two hearts that beat as one—" Samuel: "That housetop has witnessed many a pleasant hour spent upon its graveled surface—Pleasant and indeed momentous recollections." Anna: "I suppose he refers to one especial moonlight night, around which cluster most tender memories." It was play, it was serious; one person's diary in two hands said it all. And Anna was still able to take a step back and have a clear view of what the heart does. Why *this* war-brought man, Anna asked her diary (now writing singly). How did eros show itself in the form of Samuel Cook? "Does brilliant intellect attract? no—does manly beauty charm? no—does fortune seduce—no—Above all do I feel in him the power of true religion—no—and yet I love him." As it was on the page, so it was with men and love.[18]

Emmala Reed, too, had an ear for the wordy, erotic haze of war. She liked the rush of social gatherings, plentiful in late-wartime Anderson, South Carolina, and her singing and sociability drew men to her. Love's language was welcome in her pages. Yet the one man whose words she wished were there, Robert Broyles, came home from the war in 1865 and was silent. They had agreed to be engaged, Reed was certain, though it was just between the two of them; her father would have to be persuaded. Why did Broyles not come to see her when he returned? Just before the surrender, he had sent her a fourteen-page letter, "his *revelations*," she called it. She seemed a little puzzled by what he was trying to say, though she read his pages in a "happy way." Maybe she missed the point; maybe he was using all those pages to say goodbye. In any case, no further words from "Robere," no love made. But neither could there have been an end to love except in words. She sighted him on the street; he bowed. She could not go to him or be the first to speak. She thought of him physically, longed for his "*manly form*" close to her. She first believed he was "*sensitive*," then saw him as "peculiar." She portrayed him by the manners he neglected, as when he did not respond on the street to the "*calm look of wonder*" she directed at him. He ignored her friends and her invitations. At last she brought out the words for his silence: "False one!"[19]

No man was like Broyles, but other war-borne men did appear, known men and unknown, and Reed's pages gathered up the assortment. A man from town, Theodore Smith, often came by the house uninvited and helped her in the flower garden, which was odd for a man, she thought. He enthusiastically poured words of love into their small talk, comparing her to "Catherine 2nd of Russia" for her beauty and reading to her some "*pointed*" lines "from Byron, Shelly." Sitting at her feet: "You are my *queen*, my *star*, my *opiate*, my *adorable*—you *know you are*." Reed wrote it all down. But as the flood of his words rushed by, and she balanced just above their wet edge, something was missing—some intention, or even a direction. Theodore seemed only to be imitating love. It was all "*too genial* & general" for passion. The problem with him as a lover was that "he *expects* & asks *nothing*."[20]

A very different sort of man was William Henry Trescot, a man who expected and asked a great deal. A career diplomat, former member of the Buchanan administration, and now a South Carolina state legislator, Trescot had a home in Pendleton, a dozen or so miles up-country from Anderson, and likely was on wartime business of some sort when he met Reed at an Anderson party a day before Lee's army stacked its arms at Appomattox.

Reed was asked to sing, which she did—and beautifully, too, he was quick to tell her. He stood too close, she thought, polite and predatory, and was adept at joining compliment to challenge. Keep the woman off-balance, pleasured and protesting. He introduced "philosophical" questions supposed to bring out wit and character that, everyone knew, were a test of both: was it her view, Trescot wanted to know, that "mere physical & sensual" enjoyments might sometimes be superior to "intellectual and moral enjoyments"? Seductive, pressing. If she said the word "sensual" and blushed, advantage Trescot. In their half banter, half struggle, Trescot was "so quick to seize all points" that Reed responded "only from impulse—feeling every connection." He praised her "true" womanhood, but then pivoted to ask if she were not like all "placid blondes—amiable & pleasant, but not *ardent*." *Yes, I am ardent; no, I am not ardent. Which?* This sort of conversational stalking went on for a while, then Trescot let go and they said their goodbyes. He was a "rude, *worldly* man," she thought, a little breathless. She knew what was going on. He was an "old wretch with his wife & children!"[21]

Emma Holmes saw Captain Hayden (she never writes his first name), a man twenty years older than she, only a handful of times after meeting him in August 1864. They were introduced by her brother-in-law, who was in Hayden's command. She ended up disappointed by the captain, as she had been by other men. Men who seemed worthy and charming had turned out to be lax or libertine. Or drunkards. But during most of the three months she wrote of Hayden, he was an erotic ideal come to life in war, a man from afar whom Holmes had always imagined eagerly loving, "a master spirit, such a one, as *even I* should love to obey . . . one whom I could reverence as a superior, yet love devotedly." A woman freely submitting to a man never gave up the moral high ground of having made him her choice. Holmes admitted that Hayden was not physically good looking—that his "personelle," a delicately oblique word, or a bit more directly, his "outward form," was not attractive. He was "extremely" nearsighted and showed the effects of a "spinal affection" in his youth; he was "slightly deaf on one side." He also turned out to be a Roman Catholic. But all this fell away because Hayden spoke passionately to her of ideas as if it mattered what she thought, and once gently, memorably, rebuked her when she flippantly said that the world would not miss her if she were dead. Not so, said the captain, grave and caring. Everyone is dear to God and to the world, he told her, and no one's death is unremarkable because no one is without purpose. "I cannot remember all his words," but she was stirred. He talked philosophy with her not as flirtation's game but because he took pleasure in conversing with her. Their words were a physical sensation for her.

She felt carried away when Hayden's "rich streams of thought gush forth in the choicest language, fertilizing all who are happy enough to drink of them." She longed "for a draught from his ever-flowing fountain of pureness."[22]

Their few meetings and conversations were as brilliant—as memorable and inscribable—as any emotional resource Holmes could muster against the war. After Union troops had sacked the house where she was boarding, she pulled herself together by remembering what she had shared with Hayden. She paused in her diary account of the pillaging Yankees to address him directly on the page: "Capt. Haydon {sic}—should we never meet again I thank you most sincerely for all the firm trust and hope inspired by your great heart and head. You have been a beacon." Holmes could not say when she saw him last because she always expected to see him again, though she knew this was an anticipation not suited to wartime. Once, after many weeks, she heard he was nearby with an army unit repairing a road wrecked by Union troops and asked her brother-in-law to contact him. Would the captain respond, as gentlemen always did, or would "that dream of all manly virtues united, my ideal realized . . . be crushed" by his silence? Sadly, he did not reply, whether from a misplaced message or some other good intention badly served, or from the confounding vagaries of war, or because Emma Holmes was simply a young woman with whom he had spent some pleasant hours during wartime and to reply would be to transform those hours into love.[23]

"I cannot love that fellow!" Lucy Breckinridge wrote when Dr. Holloway's courtship letter arrived in the summer of 1863—another bachelor doctor, like the ones who plagued Kate Stone. But it was more than that. "I can never learn to love any man. Oh, what would I not give for a *wife*!" Her wife would be a "pure, lovely girl who would be mine and never learn to love any male." As good as this would be, Breckinridge knew that most women fell for men— "the poor, weak things will do that." Love between women and men was out of balance, desire flew off target, yet women ran into the arms of the aliens anyway. It aggravated her that women "have to unite their fates with such coarse, brutal creatures as men" even though "some of them are *right* good." Hard to parse this last thought. Was she being sly? Realistic? Was she giving in, diverted from her love for women by paradoxical eros?[24]

One right good man was Lt. Thomas Bassett, whom Breckinridge met the following fall, a cavalry officer who regularly went AWOL so that he might spend time with her. They teased each other and fought flirtation's erotic skirmishes. Neither was very good at it, pushing the other too hard, becoming angry; it left Breckinridge feeling rumpled and overheated and ready to swear him off. A man. But she tempted such times, wanted them; something in her liked to rage and threaten destructive love and love's destruction. What made Tommy "right good" among the tribe of brutish men? He was, Breckinridge wrote when she first met him, after his company had stopped near her home, "a pleasant, gentlemanly little fellow." A few days later, he turned up again. "He is so funny and smart—I am charmed with him. He has such a cute little way of saying flattering things." "Little" is a word that kept cropping up. Bassett was a boy-man, not a brute, a diverting, strange creature. But Breckinridge could fix her attention on him for only so long. "I must really try to love him better," she said after knowing him nearly a year and becoming engaged to him. "I'll make Tommy laugh next winter," she promised herself. Even so, she had misgivings about marrying him. "We won't be happy—he is too jealous and suspicious, and I too prone to play upon such feelings." Eros was much friction and little flame. With a woman as her beloved, though, all would be comfortable. "There was a mistake made about me by Mother Nature. She gave me a man's heart."[25]

Tossing about in her mixed desires, Breckinridge probably didn't need to meet Charles Kelterwell, as we might put it. As romantics would have said, though, everything fell out so they *would* meet. *To be thrown together.* It is not clear who he was or what he was doing near Grove Hill, Virginia, but the war blew Kelterwell into her life. "Mr. K. is from Baltimore," Breckinridge wrote just after meeting him. All the women loved him instantly, sympathized with his suffering from consumption, remarked on his easy, honest tears of homesickness. "He is remarkably handsome, has very polished and delightful manners, is smart and so good." Rare in Breckinridge's diary, there follows a month-long gap in her entries. The curtain drops, as the novelists say, from no design we can know. When she picked up again, her fiancé, Tommy, was still abroad at war, and Mr. Kelterwell had become "Charlie," who loved her as she wished to be loved, a "pure, holy love." He was pure, but a man, not unlike how she felt about herself, and he "has made me feel more kindly toward the male sex." He was a man, but spent a lot of time with women, intimate time, conversing with the women's circle in the parlor or in their rooms, combing their hair and telling stories. "He kissed Mary and held Annie's and my hands for ten minutes." He loved all the women as if Mother Nature had given him a woman's heart. Whatever it was, Charlie excited them to freely play eros's games. Once in a partying group, Breckinridge unpinned her hair and held a lock of it above her upper lip "like a moustache" and "burlesqued the gents," while Charlie acted the lady's part and everyone was "really very smart and funny." He was fascinating, Pan-like, and time with him passed with something like satisfied desire. It was plain: "If I had not been engaged to Tommy

I should have married Charlie." During these lovemaking days, the war rolled on at a distance, somewhere beyond Grove Hill. But that winter, 1864, the war took Mr. Kelterwell back to Baltimore. In war's way, and the diary's way, too, no reason was given, and Breckinridge wrote no more of him. She and Thomas Bassett were married less than a year later, after she had stopped writing in her diary.[26]

Diaries voiced a gentle wildness in the face of eros, their everyday soft touch paired with love's power to shake and transform—and war's power to do the same by bringing all the new men and feeding the urge to write. In one light, it is all a comic gloss on war, with parlors (or housetops) filled with fortune's fools. Young, privileged women selfishly dancing on the edges of the national tragedy! It is a limit to empathy; reading the women's love scenes can take a sudden, fatal turn into their self-absorption, which was tied to their class power and feels like arrogance. And yet. Seeing this does not erase the scenes of men and love on the page, and I hope—I can choose—to read them, as far as I can, for their generous, complicated frankness. Read the diaries as planter-class women's war diaries, yes, but deeper in, as texts of women and men and the heart. Read them for how they snag love from the hard case of war and so point to how love had been made in a time before war, a time now disappearing, but with love hanging on even so, the old, still-fresh story, love here or love gone.

Writing all this made it real, and staying with the women as writers hands over the realness as something I can know, and so empathy and understanding stay alive. Writers keeping their days and making their men on the page: Reed harbored her love and then let it go by giving entry after entry over to the silent Robert until her words had sketched the outline of the false man she discovered he was. DeCaradeuc, always delighted to tell about receiving a man or sending him off, kept Guerard under wraps until—yes!—she presented him at the end of her journal, her certain love. Green mulled over John Grieve, Samuel Cook, and other men without hinting that her brother-in-law had been her husband-to-be until she was free of him. Breckinridge chose Tommy and let Charlie go, and Holmes chose Captain Hayden and never saw him again. The women were as self-absorbed and self-privileging as their class let them be, and love thrived on this, too. But they wrote to live, and love stood up for life against war. Finding a lover in the face of death, says a character in one of Marilynne Robinson's novels, "enlarged my understanding of hope, just to know such a transformation can occur." More than that: "It has greatly sweetened my imagination of death, odd as that may seem." Writing of men and the haywire ways of love lifted the women over the encroaching darkness.[27]

This is how it was for Sarah Morgan, who, believing in love in a cranky, cranked-up sort of way, was eager to try out the new men in the storm of war, though she was not, as it happened, in search of the old, patronizing ideal of lovers' pure goodness. Morgan hoped to find more than this, and if not, she would do without. She once told the wife of a man whose lovemaking she had welcomed not to be concerned; she, Sarah, was not susceptible to falling in love. Maybe not, but her diary shows that she put herself in the thick of it anyway. She was excited but awkward in gatherings of young women and men. She was clear about lovemaking games: flirtation was made from lies and "caused many a warm hearted, confiding girl, to bestow her love where it was uncalled for and unappreciated." Erotic play in parlors was "social torment." For her it was made worse, she thought, by her unwillingness, or was it inability, to be happy as a feminine object of love who fascinated men and facilitated everyone's play. "There is Anna," Morgan wrote of a friend who could pull it off, "who can flow on in one uninterrupted stream of small talk at the top of her voice, about gloves, about shoes, and complexion, and beaux . . . without being embarrassed. I cant talk on any of those topics. . . . I am always throttling myself mentally and crying 'Fool! fool!'" Even so, Morgan was not shy, and she knew her long hair was beautiful. Her willfulness put her at the center of gatherings, where her awkwardness came across as a kind of pent-up excitement. She was particular about men, if not polished, and if a man liked frankness, she had plenty.[28]

In November 1862, Morgan's horse spooked and she was thrown from the carriage. A back injury laid her up for several months, which led to an intensive time spent with war's men and their possibilities. Her immobility sharpened her preferences in men; instead of putting everything on hold, being an invalid defined eros and choice. It also gave her more time to write, and she wrote a lot about the men carried into her circle of friends in and around Baton Rouge. She saw them at parties, where, feeling embarrassed and unique, she sat in a kind of reclining chair. Or she received them in her mother's home, sometimes with her sister Miriam. Morgan was impatient with her physical dependence and furious at men who called attention to it by helping her, which practically every man did. One of her suitors, John Halsey, insisted one evening that he help Sarah up the stairs to her room. She said no, she would send for the servants. But Halsey knew what a good man should do, and "calling the only young man left in the room . . . took up my chair, and carried me up, crimson with mortification, and feeling a ferocity and rebelliousness."[29]

John Halsey was a good man, well mannered, and such men said they were thinking of you and your desires when they were actually thinking of your *well-being*, which turned out to fit snugly with their own idea of what a woman's well-being should be. It was Morgan's prickly, cross-purposed way to resent her physical disability but use it, too, as a way of determining how "good" a man was, which is to say, how ready he was to *not* listen to her. Frank Enders was another good man, conversing pleasantly, bringing her drinks, praising her to her brother in front of her as if she were not there, saying that she looked wonderfully on the mend, bloomingly convalescent. This is how good men made her invisible. And goodness did not ignite anything, either, and while Morgan liked playing with Halsey's and Enders's attentiveness, it ultimately frightened her with a vision of marital entombment. For what was a "good" man but someone who loved by gesture, who had the bearing of a man in love, but not much else? Another suitor, Col. Isaiah Steedman, "an *unmarried* colonel," as she noted in anticipation of meeting him, turned out to be good man, too. He was "high-minded, whole souled," and she found him too easily fooled into thinking her the same. The earnest Steedman needed a mate "who could worship him ... as sweetly as an angel." Not her. The times now called for more than goodness. The realization came to her: "I cannot conceal from myself the shocking fact that it is not the *good* man I like. It is the elegant, the worldly, with a slight touch of the devil that I find myself unconsciously looking for." Good behavior in lovemaking now seemed only a pose. Something else, something sexually charged and cutting across the grain, was freshly at work in wartime's men.[30]

Writing these men into her diary kept the devil eros in play, even when Morgan wrote scenes of love where love was awkward and at loose ends. With good and bland men, she herself was the devil. In April 1863, leaving the plantation for safer territory, Morgan, her mother, and her sister Miriam, were saying their farewells to friends, including Frank Enders. Enders asked Morgan if he might kiss her goodbye. She put him off, joking that she would get around to kissing him—maybe. Enders stepped forward eagerly when he thought it was his turn: "Now, Miss Sarah!" She pulled back, serious—"Dont, please!" Shocked silence all around. The mannered moment broken, drama poured in. Friends instantly gathered around, coaxing her to change her mind and kiss Frank. "Why shame on you!" said one. "You have made him turn pale with disappointment!" Her sister told her she was being absurd. "Kiss Frank this instant!" her mother cried. But Morgan offered her hand instead: "I can't kiss you Frank, and am more than sorry I jested about it. Let us part friends."[31]

Kiss Frank and kill the devil in eros. Keep the devil alive, stir everything up, confound family, friends, and Frank, and escape in the midst of the fuss, eros in one piece. Not kissing Frank was no small matter—he stood there unkissed like a monument to her unladylike willfulness—and several diary pages flowed from the moment. Morgan compared herself to her sister (Miriam was kinder, more composed) and Frank to other men (he stood immovably among the good ones) and reflected on women and men at large. Yes, Frank was a good man, and later she would feel bad for rejecting him (though never again would Frank Enders appear in her diary), but the thing was this: "If I kiss Frank because he is good . . . why should I not kiss Mr. Halsey who is quite as good . . . ?" Eros melted away kiss by casual kiss, and "when the bridegroom comes at last, what would he say to the traces of molasses and treacle left on those ruby lips" by others? A kiss not given kept eros alive, reaching and unfulfilled, free from "the world, kisses, and other quicksands." Rereading her pages on kissing Frank, Morgan laughed at herself—"what an absurd dissertation"—but she did not razor the pages from the volume.[32]

So Morgan conjured scenes of love made and unmade when she needed them and as war provided them, and she worried about the heat even as she enjoyed it in an airily arrogant way that had its own sexual charge. Good, boring men were a safe bet, and yet writing even a good man into her pages might take unexpected turns. With John Halsey, Morgan called the tune and played all the instruments, including Halsey. He stood ready for her writing pleasure. He hovered at a party, clueless in the face of irony: "I found Mr. Halsey at my elbow, with ever so much to say." Someone told her that Halsey loves her: "I gave a scream of horror." Her friend Anna was talking in her sleep, "about either 'John' (Mr. H.) or 'bananas,' I could not understand which, but knew it was about something *green* and *soft*." Share John with her sister? What could she possibly want with "a demi-John"? Sometimes Morgan felt mild remorse, but the laughs kept coming page after page. And yet such is a diary's busy inclusiveness that it is possible to see that this good man was not always so simply played. Usually Morgan's straight man, Halsey once appeared in her pages without any staging at all—a figure, not an actor. Morgan was blue that day, mourning her girlhood killed by the war. If she could return to an earlier time, to her home and peace, "I could learn to be a woman there, and a true one, too. Who will teach me now?" Becoming a "true woman" usually appalled her. But today the war pushed her down, and on the same line, but dated the following day, she wrote without saying why, "John Halsey. Aged 30." It seems marginal, but it says *look at this*. What was Morgan up to? Rereading yesterday's entry and, maybe, being struck by something that conjured Halsey's name and age. A wistful moment, let's say, her guard down, wishing she could be a woman who was simply happy to be "true." The thought of good John Halsey sealing the wish.[33]

Then there was Col. Gustave Breaux. It is certain that in peacetime Morgan would not have spent all the exciting time she did with the one man she admits to loving, Breaux, a married man. War widened the space for unpunished trespasses, and Morgan seized it. As Breaux was married, their drama had an ending already lined up, and Mrs. Breaux did eventually step into the story. Checking up on her husband's flirtation, she looked Sarah in the eye, said "dont fall in love with my husband," kissed her, and left the room. Afterward, the colonel's visits became fewer, then stopped. Morgan did not lament, said it was for the best, but in the months spent with Breaux she was able to write about her ideal as a living man. He had the devil in him, for sure. Often Morgan could only call out his name on the page to tell what fulfilled her. "Gallant Col. Breaux!" "Charming Col. Breaux!" Breaux's fine manners stoked erotic possibility; there was always more to feel and find out. They read and played music together. He took her horseback riding and more than once "paid my hair the most extravagant compliments." In all, "the Colonel was perfection!" Yet it was their ability to talk seriously to each other about ideas, with no screen of grand, manly gestures or tense flirtation contests, that most stirred her, as it stirred Emma Holmes with her Captain Hayden. Breaux conversed instead of giving answers. He "speaks as though he believed you capable of appreciating what ever subject he is discussing." Older than she, he did not compete with her. She was eager to know what he knew. He introduced subjects, heard her out, cared for her, thought her capable. She felt freed; *this* was lovemaking. For once, Morgan was not anxious or clever or ironic: Breaux had "completely won my heart."[34]

But after leaving with his wife, Breaux did not return. She heard news about him off and on, and later in the war was surprised to see his photograph in a New Orleans studio. Frank Enders drifted away, too, in the turnings of war, as did Isaiah Steedman, though in a lingering, painful way, as he was imprisoned for some weeks, and Morgan tortured herself about whether or not to write to him and so call Yankee attention to herself and her family. John Halsey. Morgan gave John Halsey a playful, retaliatory, physical thought in the summer of 1863: "Just let me dance him down, or take a five mile walk with him, and I am revenged for that night he had to carry me up stairs." And it turned out that she saw Halsey again, in 1865 after the surrender, when men were not so much in Morgan's pages anymore. She was in New Orleans, feeling both optimistic and unsettled in war's wake, "and then who should step in a week ago, but John Halsey!!!" She wrote her pleasure at seeing him into what became the last entry—the last lines—of the year and her volume. She was delighted: "Dear John!!" She looked forward to his calling on her, would be disappointed if he did not. She wanted to see "his good, honest face."[35]

So it was John Halsey who survived in Sarah Morgan's pages, comic John Halsey, the last wartime lover standing, whose appearance in her final lines of 1865 means something, though surely not that Morgan had planned to make him the closing figure of the war years. She probably just had nothing more to say that day, and so Halsey closes the volume only by chance, a marker of the day's now-lost rhythm. A perfect fragment. We will never know if Morgan intended anything more, but we have this: John's good, honest face.

MEN UNDER ORDERS

Love seemed to hold its own in war. It was there on the page, not a small thing. If a woman thought that love would bring a worthy man under her sway, war did not erase this thought. If she wanted excitement and decorum, they were there. It was thrilling to write love and keep it from war's eviscerating power even when love took a sharp turn or faded away. The women discovered some elastic play in eros, and running to the far boundaries of love's mannered ways and finding them still there—that was pleasure. Yet at the boundaries, diarists also found that war sent men who were not partners in the making of love. It turned up men who would have been, before the war, beneath notice—a good phrase from the diarists. War's drastic move was to make these men unavoidable *as men*, plunk them down square in a lady's path. White men, ordinary ones, arriving unannounced. Common men, on the loose in large numbers. Men: now driven by destructive forces that competed with a woman's grace-note touch, her happy mission to approve a true man's decorous ways. Men were *under orders* in war, under a new order. War showed that there were forces out there at least as powerful as the form and pleasure—the manners—accorded to eros, and that some men were driven by them. Yankees, but not only Yankees, possessed purposes and pleasures so alien that they were difficult even to write. We have seen how war's sheer, crazy violence came up against the force field of manners, which in prewar times kept the unexpected from crowding in too close. In making love as in other things, privileged women and men lived their manners as proof that they were larger than life, and their peculiar arrogance was to believe that their ways and their choices marked the borders of the only world worth knowing. Men under orders threatened all this as they pushed their way onto the page.

Food served as one introduction. Hungry men on the move, refugees and soldiers, alone or in small groups, suddenly came close. Mary Chesnut, herself a refugee and traveling by train without a white man as a buffer, was approached by a soldier wanting to trade his hardtack for any food she might have. "Shaggy, scrubby, ill looking," he stepped nearer to her than any working man should have dared, except an enslaved one. She watched as he "slowly unrolled a rag—filthy! as if it had laid six months in a gutter." Inside was the hardtack he wanted to trade. Chesnut gave him her lunch, but "to touch his—oh no!" Lucy Buck was at home preparing for the next day's cooking when, startlingly, "a drunken soldier came into the kitchen from out in the rain—represented himself as one Captain Carey of the Madison Artillery—commenced swearing." She gave him something to eat. Earlier, "the long 'Reed like Alabamian' who was here yesterday and the little half demented Creole who got his luncheon here were both of them hanging around the house." She was not sure what they were up to. To be a man and appear "reedlike" to a woman was to be tall, wiry, and a little wild, an object of erotic interest; Buck was lifting the word from novels and women's love talk. But here the reedlike fellow was in the company of an unbalanced comrade, both of them—again—suddenly showing up, hungry, and getting a little too close.[36]

Women grew to expect these startling, face-to-face encounters even though they were accustomed to meeting the wider world veiled and had never been obliged to create a welcoming social atmosphere for "country" men. Such men were truly "creatures," a term women used complacently, sweetness on the edge of being snide. But now these men could not be ignored, not only because they walked in unannounced but because they were Confederate soldiers. Buck fed the "demented Creole," and Chesnut surrendered her lunch. It was patriotic. A wagonload of soldiers passed Sarah Morgan and her sister in their carriage, all of them rising to their feet and lifting their hats. "Rather queer," Morgan thought. Were they being "impertinent"? She would have thought so before the war, but now. . . . And what would be the point of resenting impertinence? The men were "Confederates fighting for us" and so were "of course privileged people." And like many other women, Morgan had the opportunity to appear on her porch or balcony and wave to the passing troops, an iconic wartime moment, though for her, that first time, it was so new that she had to get herself mentally ready for it and was careful not to wear anything too showy. Waving at men was already bizarre. It was always a slippery slope to eros whenever men were near, now even these men. Emma Holmes and her friends appeared before the ranks of men passing by, the soldiers "saluting us with 'Farewell—Goodbye ladies' and one boy called out 'goodbye gals.'" Men, lots of them, ones never dreamed of. "It was the first time I had done such a thing."[37]

Trespasses came at every turn. If not the cheeky soldiers, then the women themselves sometimes risked stepping over or redrawing the lines of good manners. In the times now, what separated a trespass from an adventure? A strange man, an ordinary country man, came near and touched you physically. This was something on the far fringe of possibility before the war, much farther out than, say, a house fire. Now it happened and women wrote it. I think they knew that physical contact with ordinary men had sexual implications if not an erotic charge, but the main thing was its outlandishness. It was hard to tell whether it was an affront, or laughable, or both. A Confederate soldier, excited to see the rapidly falling river as he talked with Metta Andrews on her plantation, took hold of her upper arm as he explained what he saw. He touched her. Her sister Eliza was quick to explain it away. "Unceremonious times," she said; the man clearly "meant no harm." Sarah Morgan, recovering from her injury, was traveling with her mother when a helpful soldier at a train station proposed lifting Sarah from the car to the platform, and although she declined, her mother told the man to go ahead and do it. "The next thing I knew, he was passing his arm around my waist," Morgan wrote. She was still thinking of it two weeks later, "that strong right arm so carefully, respectfully, delicately, yet withal so unpleasantly encircling my waist! I dont like to think of that."[38]

Even so, some chance encounters with ordinary men unexpectedly became small-scale social occasions, bringing out in the women an unlikely mix of class arrogance and a breezy override of class. Emma Holmes and her on-the-road escort, Dr. Pickett, fell into discussion with two Confederate soldiers named Crouch and Landifer about the Jefferson Davis government and the desperate state of things in 1865. The soldiers "belonged evidently to the 'yeomanry' of our land," Holmes wrote—tentatively? Archly? The men struck her as uncomfortable at first, "rather constrained," she thought, "by the society in which they found themselves," by which she meant her elevated self and Dr. Pickett. But in the end she and Crouch joined forces to argue against the doctor and Landifer and their timid views of Confederate purpose, supporting each other, late into the evening, in saying that the South should fight to the last man. Holmes spoke passionately and, she was sure, too boldly for the men, "all save Crouch." Crouch thought she was just fine.[39]

Sarah Morgan said she could do without parties, but she cruised into overheated rooms packed with invited soldiers. She danced with country men and ate cake with them. They were figures of fun, "Susceptible and Simple." They were something new, and Morgan liked the amusement. But they also were men, and if Morgan could not see them as suitors, neither did she ignore the erotic play, writing about it later in a comic vein when the sharp new taste of mixed social classes had mellowed a bit. The bodies of these men caught her eye. Lieutenant Dupres's face was not much to look at, but he had "fine form" as a dancer and "his chief merit lies in his legs." Men, dancing: One "entirely with his arms; his feet had very little to do with the time. One hopped through with a most dolorous expression of intense absorption in the arduous task. Another never changed a benign smile . . . but preserved it unimpaired through every accident." She condescended and admired; she was charmed. She did not mind at all brushing up against yeomen like Captain McClure, "who so innocently says 'I seen' & 'I done it' without the faintest suspicion of the peculiarity, and looks so sweet, and guileless, and amiable, and soft, that I cant help but wondering if he would be sticky if I touch him."[40]

Unceremonious times. But ceremony between women and men is what the diarists knew best. Ceremony *made* women and men: smart conversation, physical gestures expansive or restrained, using the eyes, having the style. All of this was missing in encounters with country men, who seemed simple, maybe childlike. Diarists were all but blind to seeing them as another angle on the male realm and empathy between the sexes. Still, for the first time, they *did* inscribe them with more than a word or two. So they wrote two things that tugged against each other: their awakened curiosity and their cramped vision of a world where not being to the manor born—to manners born— was to be in some way a plaything; or if not quite that, then a puzzle, and not a very interesting one. A country man had no future in a love story, so it was hard for diarists to say what sort of story might come out of these parties and conversations. It was *rather queer*, like entering an enchanted place of comic danger.

And in their perplexity, lacquered over by a practiced self-confidence, as I read the ladies, eros stayed around the edges of the weird pairings and odd timing that shaped their encounters with ordinary men. *What would it be like to touch him?* Even Yankee men sometimes slipped into this strange orbit. Theft and the opening moves of a flirtation were rolled into one after a Union soldier stole a volume of poetry from Emma Holmes during the sacking of her landlady's house. The next day, the book was returned with the thief's apologetic compliments, his name ("Nicholas Baird from Ohio"), and the observation that Southern women were very handsome. Holmes was outraged and amused—how could she be both at once?—shocked by Yankee

Men

"barbarity," and touched by Mr. Baird. Emmala Reed also brushed up against a young Yankee man. She had to entertain, if the word can be stretched, a Union officer whose help her father needed. She made conversation in the best style and played at a courtship parlor game with him: guess how old I am. A warped version of young women and men everywhere in the United States before wartime. Making her moves, Reed was repelled by and drawn to the red-haired New Yorker and his uncouth accent. She smiled—was careful to smile—at his too-bold appraisal of her, his "sly, mean—exultant look."[41]

Odd timing and weird pairings; men who were enemies and beau-like. This strange mix intensified women's encounters with Yankee men but also gave release, times when the war seemed to slip beneath the surface of an afternoon and leave only women and men together. Emilie McKinley didn't fool herself that the Union soldiers who rode into the yard were anything but what they appeared to be, "a very rough looking set." She was at the house of her neighbor, Mrs. Downs. The Yankees wanted corn and chickens, and one older soldier asked for some flowers. Mrs. Downs made him a bouquet. They all chatted for a while in the yard; the soldier with the flowers told McKinley he was from Iowa and had "entered the Army for his *health*." A paroled Confederate officer was in the group and in a friendly way offered the Union men some advice on getting along with the neighborhood's people. Well, where is the corn, the Yankees wanted to know. Mrs. Downs had corn in different places, and she told the Yankees which cache she would rather have them steal. They rode off to get it. Flowers, conversation, Mrs. Downs's preferences nicely followed. Not love measuring up to war, but something like it.[42]

Afternoons of small reprieves were true in their moment and dear for that, but not about to last. Yankees went from talk and bouquets to trashing homes in an instant, and men who ran off with women's underwear and liquor could only mean the worst on any afternoon. The Yankees were a *race* of men, women wrote, made grotesque by their power and making manhood unrecognizable. Union soldiers ran through the house full tilt, grunting and cursing, rifling through closets, trunks, bookshelves. They uncovered vats of fruit preserves and plunged their arms into them. They killed barnyard animals and pets as they stumbled about the yard with their bayonets fixed. They tore into the meat locker, dredging up sides of beef, eating it raw, washing it down with vinegar.[43]

If women had been asked before the war who might be capable of such acts—who would have the diabolical imagination and the fell spirit to follow through—they probably would not have said Yankees, but *men*. Some men, somewhere else. Now it was happening right here in the yard, and witnessing the lid blown off whatever repellent, terrifying thing lay deep inside men, women learned firsthand to fear the worst—rape. "Personal insult" was the term, or "personal outrage." Women wrote of it as worse than death. Floride Clemson spent a long night "dreadfully afraid of personal insults" as Union soldiers marauded through the countryside in Pendleton, South Carolina. Mary Jones heard soldiers ride up to her house just before dawn. Her servant Sue told her the men "had come upon the most dreadful intent," asking "if there were any young women" about. Jones and her pregnant daughter got out of bed and knelt on the floor to pray that God would defend "our persons and our dwelling." The Yankees did not enter the house. Pauline DeCaradeuc heard a group of Union soldiers ask her slaves "if there were any young ladies in the house, how old they were & where they slept." Later that night, hidden and disguised, she hoped, as an old woman, she heard men enter the house and go upstairs to the bedrooms. Grace Elmore resolved to take her own life if sexually attacked; would God punish her?[44]

Licentiousness. War was license, and men exulted in having it. The diarists were clear about the sexual glare surrounding the things soldiers did, and the threat of sexual violence pointed to a wider universe of ugly possibilities men might act on in war. Everything Yankee men did "taught us how impotent is the weakness and helplessness of women," Grace Elmore thought. "What horrible things men are," wrote Lucy Breckinridge after the Union soldiers had come and gone. Men, not Yankees. The sheer craziness of being physically bullied by strange men—having to face taunting aggression and physical struggle or subjugation—freed up women's responses. Some leaned on feminine gestures tested by time, others on gut-level reactions that broke new ground. "Ah," said a Yankee soldier in DeCaradeuc's house as he fingered the watch he found in her pocketbook, "does it go good?" She was seated, as many women chose to be when soldiers broke in, to show the absence of both fear and hospitality. The man put his hand on her shoulder. DeCaradeuc said nothing but looked up to meet his eyes and then "rose & stood before him, with all possible dignity & he turned away." DeCaradeuc's was a classic feminine rebuke, meeting broken decorum with silent reproof. Lucy Buck's friend Fannie LaRue, though, lit into the enemy, defying the "stripling" soldier who wanted the small valuables box she was holding. He raised his pistol and "snapped a cap right full in her face," but Fannie did not release her grip on the box. She challenged him in a "rough hand to hand scuffle" and won. Kate Stone's horse Wonka was the prey of soldiers running amok in the fenced yard at her home. Stone raced one soldier to the gate and opened it to let Wonka go free. The soldier, sweating and breathing hard, put his pistol to her head. She was still holding the lilac blooms she had been carrying when it all started. "I had just as soon kill you as a hoppergrass," he said.[45]

A lady physically threatened by men—by the *opposite sex* relied upon for protection and responsiveness or, short of that, counted on to stay at a safe distance. It seems the deepest point to which guilty brutes might fall. But what diarists wrote was not about being above men and blaming them; it was about women and men being necessarily locked together and about the dawning possibility that some hidden and deadly angle of manhood, not visible before wartime, might lie beneath men's shameful actions. Thoughts about empathy with the other sex—just touched on, maybe, in the funny breakout meetings with country men—evaporated. In war, men were under orders, as they often said—and seemed to like saying. Rampantly under orders, it was turning out. Did these orders override the masculine goodness relied upon to define the feminine, and what about men needing strength from their women, in turn? Was men's goodness, brought into the light by decorum and the legitimacy it gave to masculine power, gone forever? Were men lost? If the answer was yes, then what did it mean about the beauty of sexual difference, thought to be as natural as anything on God's earth? What would happen to the safe-haven visions of helpmate and counterpart, and if these disappeared, how were the tensions and pleasures of eros redrawn? Questions for war's blank page, which diarists circled around as they wrote men's ugly violence.

Some diarists reached again for what they knew, writing of *good* men when possible and holding on to the strength they found in praising decorum. The power of good form stood by. Catherine Edmondston was doing some reading in moral philosophy in the summer of 1864. She knew that Union troops might be on their way to Halifax County, and she was "greatly struck by a sentiment which seems applicable to our Northern neighbours.... *'Good laws without good manners are empty breath.'* They have proved the truth of it! Good laws they had & an abundance of them, but they lacked the essential *good manners*. Good manners would have kept them from intermedling with their neighbour's concerns. . . . Want of manners it is which has broken up the Government & deluged the country with a sea of blood." Good manners, always at the heart of things, now as the trigger of the war! We can laugh this off, as we can laugh at anyone's naked candor. But if we do, something of Edmondston's world falls out of reach. She is on a high horse, no doubt, there in the safety of her diary with her unquestioning trust in Confederate rightness. Because it is easy to say how wrong she was, it is easy to condescend to her and seal her off. But pause for a moment and see Edmondston making a passionate discovery about morality and warfare in her place and time. If we hold back from scoring moral points against her, we can begin to imagine war's destruction pushing into the heart of why we, too, cherish our own, different lives. For me, the sheer difference of her world and what she wanted—the "not me" of it—opens up my empathy for the fierceness of the experience that drove her to write. There was wreckage everywhere, and in a civil war, especially, a whole culture strains and cracks. Something deeper than politics fractures, deeper even than lawful order and trust in institutions and texts: all of the half-hidden, taken-for-granted gestures and restraints (manners in the deepest sense) that keep moral imagination sound and lively—these were dissolving and washing away. *Empty breath.*[46]

This is what Emilie McKinley's employer, Ellen Batchelor, wrote about in a letter to Gen. Ulysses Grant expressing her deep anger at the soldiers who had plundered her home. Though she had asked the looters face-to-face to respect "my rights of protection as a *lady*. . . . My words were to no avail. I spoke not to gentlemen but to *ruffians* and *thieves* who had no authority to act thus." This is what Lucy Buck discovered when she appealed to a Union colonel to release her cousin from arrest. "He was such a coarse kind of wretch and every time we attempted to combat his arguments he would arrest our speech by some lame attempt to act facetiously and then look around to his officers as if appealing to their admiration." This is what Gertrude Thomas heard when she asked a question of a Union officer in occupied Augusta, the first Yankee military man she had ever spoken to, and he responded, "Heigh? {Hey?}" "He did not understand my question but why make such a reply?" Thomas asked her diary. "The instinct of a gentleman should have taught him to reply 'What did you observe? What was your remark{?}'" The man's bad manners were but at the edge of the now-imploding realm of respect and self-respect, making an airless place where men barked responses to women's questions, made them the butts of jokes, lorded over them, and got in a little sly time by having them beg. Thomas, for one, pushed the point with the officer to see the extent of the damage, performing her part in how the sexes should act. At the man's "heigh?" she "slightly elevated my eyebrows and threw into my glance and {sic} expression of astonishment." The man regarded her and then rephrased his query in polite terms. Thomas was emphatically relieved: "*He understood.*"[47]

If violence and crudeness covered everything so that words between the sexes were cut short or did not avail, everything about a people would first lose brightness, then substance, then spirit. The diarists wrote sure of this and against its happening. They seized the moments in war that eros gave

Men

them not in order to teach men, nothing so calculated or plain as that, but to find out what war was doing to men, who were the face of war and the only way out. Women felt the war killing a sweetness and strength as natural to the sexes as the seasons were to nature. They felt the tension of sex and power shift to take on a new, unknown shape. Reading, I feel the heaviness in the diarists' words, and the distraction, but also the breathlessness, when it looked like men and love might be nimble enough to escape catastrophe and stay around.

So war was about the sexes, each positioned to each, in scenes diaries caught exactly—in flight, not for analysis or show, a diary's way. Did love measure up to war? The women wrote doubt and fear, and some told stories that said yes, love would last although men were startlingly new, sometimes disheveled or dangerous, and often gone. Eros, too. Cornelia McDonald wrote scenes over a few months' time that said these things, slowly, adding them up over the days. She would not agree, I am sure, that lovemaking had anything to do with her six-month aggravated acquaintance with U.S. general Robert Milroy. But eros was in play in her diary even so, in the inscription of the manners that gave women and men voice and a profile in her world. Times she spent with the Yankee general became a fragmented story of the two of them, which, in the end, suggests that eros might have survived the war through strange avenues.

McDonald and her children, living near Winchester, Virginia, were squarely in the path of the warring armies. General Milroy was an Indiana-born man in his midforties who had risen quickly from the rank of captain and who impressed McDonald as a gentleman, though a fallen one. He was one of the new men brought by war—she was curious—and one dangerously under orders. By the time she met Milroy, he had already arrived at a crude way of dealing with Southern white women who caused him trouble. Soldiers would arrive on some pretext with a wagon, take the woman aboard, and drive a mile or two down the road and into the fields, where she would be let off to walk back alone. Not the work of a gentleman. Milroy also smoked cigars in the presence of women who came to ask him for assistance or relief. It seemed that the general enjoyed doing this in the few hours every week he set aside to receive petitioning women, of whom McDonald was one. She appeared before him more than once to prevent her large and fine house from being seized for use as a hospital or officers' quarters.

So it was that McDonald arrived to see Milroy one day in early January 1863. She was shown in as the general was wrapping up a staff meeting; there would be no private conversation. It demeaned her to have to state her business before a group of men, as if selling something or serving as a messenger. Milroy must have known this. McDonald asked him to keep her house free from army use, "telling him that I came to him for protection, as he had the power." Then she played the card a lady could play by asking him to live up to the character of a gentleman; her presence before him testified that she was a lady in need. "I was sure," she told him, that he "could not want the will to protect a woman and children who were defenseless as we were." Milroy laughed at this, though not, I think, because he did not get it. He decided to string McDonald along with a rhetorical question or two, drawing her out and into his realm, playing with her, mimicking a flirtation. Or flirting; it is always hard to tell. How was it, he asked her, that she was abandoned and so in need of his protection? Where were her "natural protectors"? They are in the Confederate army, McDonald told him evenly, inscribing the contest that followed as a dialogue, with dialogue's emotional power: "'Yes,' he said, 'they leave you unprotected and expect us to take care of you.' 'We would not need your care, if we were allowed to take care of ourselves,' said I. 'It is only from the army you command that we want protection.'" So he made a jab at her men, their failure as men, but she countered it by returning the focus to him, to his command, and to the gentlemanly instinct at stake, which was his to fail. You, she says to Milroy. You are the focus here.[48]

McDonald kept her house. But in the weeks to come Union soldiers in Winchester mostly took what they wanted and broke what they left behind, and they behaved badly in other ways. War was shaking everything loose. Troops occupied the yard of her house daily with pack animals and wagons, churning up mud, "cursing and swearing, uttering oaths that make my blood curdle." Yankee soldiers had a way of sneaking up on veiled women walking along the street; they "come up by our side and sneeringly tell us how well we were beaten." In their "meanness and littleness," Yankee men were a terrible forecast of what all men might become. Responsibility rested with their leader, General Milroy, for leaders always set the tone. He was never far from her thoughts as she closed her ears to the cursing soldiers and averted her eyes from the sneaky ones. Milroy became an example of what was possible between men and women in war, a morally corrupt figure charged with passion and, in a twisted way, an object of desire.[49]

So it was that McDonald sent him a valentine in February. Some younger friends ("girls") told her that Milroy had ordered a woman of their acquaintance to leave his office while welcoming "two coloured, and gorgeously dressed ladies to be seated." Treating the women this way, the general reversed the racial order of esteem, of caring and love. Let us, the girls said, send this lover-general a valentine of his lovemaking. McDonald sketched the imagined scene and added watercolors. She made copies to circulate among her friends. The card shows Milroy, seated, with a gray beard and a puff of gray hair, receiving two well-dressed black women as a white woman heads for the door. On the wall of his office is a large painting of a fleeing black woman clothed in the U.S. flag. Milroy is saying, "Out you damned rebel, be seated ladies." McDonald's sketched scene was not a joke, but it was not an incendiary piece of work either. Milroy and the black women appear calm, or anyway self-contained, and the departing white woman seems sad rather than outraged, looking back over her shoulder at the others. But McDonald heard that Milroy was angry upon receiving the anonymous valentine. He questioned a few people in town and ordered a couple of houses searched (one, McDonald noted, where soldiers narrowly missed finding a copy). The drawing was an insult to his manhood and hit its target. It was a piece of sarcasm but also a valentine. In stirring the man and amusing her female friends, and herself, too, McDonald's valentine said what valentines say: you are mine.[50]

We might suppose Cornelia McDonald would have been happy to see General Milroy leave, not to mention his army. And so she was, but not simply, and not without a sense of an attachment being torn away. In fact, she wrote Milroy's leaving town as a scene featuring the two of them, a farewell between a woman and a man. Milroy left in a hurry four months after the valentine, in mid-June 1863, his army pretty well cut to pieces by Confederate forces retaking the Shenandoah Valley. In the midst of the three-day Union disaster, McDonald chanced to meet him on the street, mounted and heading out of town with a "pale agitated face." She "felt sorry for him," McDonald wrote, maybe a little surprised at herself. "So following my impulse of being kind I bowed to him; from pure sympathy." His troops dispersing, his command in shreds, Milroy had a golden chance to be a gentleman—maybe this is what moved McDonald, this chance for decorum to measure up to war. And this time he came through, reining in his horse, putting aside any thought that her bow was "a piece of mock respect" (as her valentine had been a piece of mock love), and "he bowed low, till his plume almost touched his horse's mane."[51]

This is how one diarist traced eros in the world, the air of attachment and release circulating among women and men at war. Writing of her days, of the war and the harshness of warring men, Cornelia McDonald pulled on many threads, not least eros's, which then lent a texture to war's events and war's men: there was an action (negotiation with a general that echoed a courtship game), a choice (to call her drawing a valentine), an emotion (the "impulse to be kind"), and a final image of true manhood alive and well (his bow, the plume). It is eros in the world, and it gives us a story line to pick up if we choose: love measured up to war but at war's pace. Men and women made what love they could on the quick and violent tide.

CHAPTER FIVE

Slaves

Enslaved people began to show up in women's diaries. Before the war, a few white women inscribed slaves now and then in letters and diaries—mostly servants who did well and those who did not. Or unnamed slaves were written as figures in the background of the main thing that needed telling. Wartime changed this. Slaves came into a diarist's pages with things to say, with words that the diarist *wrote down*. Or black people disappeared without saying anything. They acted for themselves. When diarists began writing this way, it was not always what we expect them to write, and expectations are there because slavery means so much in the big-picture history of the Civil War. Slavery defines the heart of the war's aims and passions, and we see emancipation as the first step in the struggle for racial justice that followed the war's destruction.

Slavery's crimes against humanity have made slave-owning ladies criminals in our eyes, and in the light of slavery's moral meaning, the diarists become most "readable" as characters in our narrative of evil overthrown. But here as elsewhere, diaries lose their textual abundance when they do this focused work as our historical sources. And although the narrative of evil is true and well known, it seems too self-satisfied to simply retell it. I read the women's diaries to find something more awkward and fresh, the day's slavery in the making—and unmaking. I want to read in such a way that my condemnation of slavery does not turn the diarists' world into a flat and airless place where no one could have lived.

Just reading the diaries, seeking the smallest handhold for empathy, I step around such a place, around myself and my certainties, to find the diarist amid her stories of enslaved people she knew, or thought she knew, or got to know, or did not want to know. Slaves were inseparable from *my life*, as the diarist saw it. This is how slavery had burrowed in and taken hold. And this is why women's stories of slavery coming unstuck in war are also stories of how slavery had held together, day by day, person to person. It is a simple thing and a terrible, knotted thing that is hard to grasp now, as it was hard for the diarists to let go. We have used women's diaries as sources that capture the war's "moment of truth," the slave owner's discovery as slavery disintegrated that the faithful servant was not faithful and that slavery was not God's plan after all. There *were* such times, but in the flow of the diary's present tense they do not come as a single blow: take that. Instead, the new order spools out, tangled up with the old. There were *moments* of truth. The new order of no slavery: now smothering, now aspiring, and the old order far from gone.

The master of servants, wrote George Orwell, "wears a mask, and his face grows into it." The women lived this reality, and when they became diarists, they wrote it as the old mastery fell apart. Words for enslaved people grew thickly. Diarists had written of black people, Africans, servants, Negroes, all mixed together; what were they to call them now? Behind this question, others: How do things stand between us? Who are they to me? *Servants* was the common term for enslaved people, neutral and descriptive. *Slaves* was too rough, too public, a man's term, or an abolitionist's, and saying it let disturbing things inside. *Cuffee*, a generic term for an African, had a comically exotic touch of race. *People*—as in *my people*—was a term of possession, but one that made for a soothing distance; *Negro* and *African* just created distance. In the war-changed world, all of these terms were up for reshuffling, and I have been using some of the mix as a reminder of this, and as a way of seeing the mask.[1]

SLAVES AND SILENCE

Diarists don't make seeing the mask easy. Using the thicket of terms for the enslaved, diarists hid from slaves and from themselves. Some diarists wrote about black people in nearly every entry while others wrote hardly at all—a much wider range than when they wrote about war's violence or war's men. Begin with the more close-mouthed diarists, whose reticence sets the stage for thinking about the others' words. Why would slaves *not* appear all the time in a mistress's wartime pages? Black people were everywhere, and emancipation—a wild notion at first, then a *thing*—was shocking, widespread, and undeniable. And yet Cornelia McDonald and Lucy Buck said almost nothing about their servants. McDonald only occasionally mentioned hers, mostly her maid Winnie, whose one diary-inscribed dimension is loyalty to McDonald. It has to be said, though, that McDonald also wrote sparely of her own children. Like Winnie, they were well behaved and stayed in the background. Servants and offspring: the unremarkable, fade-into-silence backdrop of one's days. When McDonald began to write about black people, they were war's Negroes, strangers, and the feeling is that she felt pressed to acknowledge them but was uncertain of how to do it. She was careful and brief. There are ironic glimpses—the two black women received by General Milroy in the valentine incident, for example—and a vision of Negroes as a doomed race, as we will see. McDonald could write temperately, handing black people the benefit of her doubt. "They do love their freedom," she finally said of the newly emancipated African Americans in Winchester in 1863, "and who can blame them if they do." Once, with a rare stab of anger—she had just seen freedwomen in town dressed up in fine clothes—she imagined Confederate artillery blowing them all away. But she turned from this thought, ashamed: "I feel wicked . . . resentful and revengeful."[2]

Lucy Buck had even fewer words for black people. Her slaves—her father's slaves—appear by allusion to their labor, then by their leaving. She awoke one morning in 1863 and went to her grandmother's room to dress. "There was no fire made, no water brought, no movement whatever below stairs." Then Buck heard her father "enter Ma's room and exclaim—'all gone horses and all.'" Poof! The servants had vanished—that's what "all" means. No movement downstairs, no sign of the usual surrounding presence, as if black people were a kind of atmosphere that had lifted and released itself. As for individuals, Buck never wrote favorably or unfavorably about any individual black person, as if all who left or stayed fell into the same zone of near invisibility.[3]

Why did these diarists write so little about the world-capsizing event of slaves freeing themselves? A dark thought comes forward in McDonald's case, a political thought. She edited her diary after the war, which would have given her the opportunity to dress up slavery in Lost Cause finery—she did not do this—or to avoid saying much at all. Maybe her silence means she chose the latter and removed black people from her pages. It would be a self-protective move, like deleting silly words about love, and politically savvy, too. For some white memoirists after the war, black people were a subject charged with possibilities for looking intolerant, intemperate, or "backward" to readers. Just stay away from it. There is no original manuscript to consult, to find out if McDonald made changes, which is true as well for the diaries of Eliza Andrews and Pauline DeCaradeuc, who also had little to say about black people. DeCaradeuc was nearly mute about all slaves and later freed people, her servants included, and though Andrews had things to say about slavery, she inscribed few black individuals. The ones who appeared exited quickly, did not cause anyone trouble, and seemed fine with being permanent servants. It all looks suspicious, and yet there is this: Lucy Buck did not rework her journal after the war, and we do have an original text. This is also the case for the diaries of Anna Green and Floride Clemson, two other women who rarely wrote about slaves. All around, the originals, too, are mostly silent about black people. So while a diarist's calculated self-censorship is worth a thought (I *am* suspicious of Andrews's smooth, even-keeled text), it is one thought among many in the bumpy saga of a diary and the uncertainty of reading ghosts.

A richer possibility: being close-mouthed about slaves in her diary was an imprint of the mask a lady wore as a mistress, a style of mastery brought to the page. Being laconic about black people was not a break with the past but a continuation of a way of living among them. Cornelia McDonald, let's say, knew surges of strong emotion in managing slaves, emotions always best handled with fewer words, not more. So that is how she wrote black people as slavery ended. Lucy Buck knew less about managing servants, being young, but she was heading toward a style of mastery that mingled primness around slaves with obliviousness of them. Either way—and it worked into the same way, really—fewer words kept things safe. A woman gained nothing by airing out personal ties to her slaves. Superfluous chat, lingering looks, self-revealing gestures—it was a style of mastery filled with danger. Don't get too close to the servants or let them see too much. Expect nothing except good service. It's a richer possibility for explaining her silence, and a more terrible one. This mistress withheld her words and learned not to expect anything truly meaningful from living among African Americans. Not about her, not about them. The war should not change this. Black people had things to do, not things to say, and their presence never *explained things*. They were part of a deep given; they are here, sure, but they are here for *us*. Fires lit, movement downstairs.

This was one style of being a mistress (available to men, too, with variations), and it led some diarists to be almost mute about slaves and war. It is a loud silence, given diarists' wordiness in other ways about the unhappy, reckless birth of a new order. Slaves, black people, were stored away behind the page—ghosts—and kept inside the covering self of the mistress; this mask makes grounds for empathy with slaveholding ladies hard to find, maybe uniquely so. But then, this was one style of mastery. There was another (opposite?) mode, embodied by the diarist who not only wrote black people, but wrote them in a compelling way, rich and unsettled, in which black people were known and unknown, enslaved and free. They were written as if they were the crazy war itself; writing them, the diarist gets a glimpse of the mask, and so do we.

Work around the house gave diarists the richest field for writing about black people and war. Richest because so well known. The household was a place for the stacking and sequencing of ordinary things. Its insistent familiarity made it easy to write without a lot of second-guessing or self-consciousness, yet with some urgency; nothing was so commonplace that it escaped the war's chaotic, liberating reach. So the household, slaves included, became something women found particularly compelling to write, as a place transfigured by wartime's weird amalgam of drudging work and breathtaking innovation.

White women's leading domestic question in wartime was, How is the work going to get done if there are no enslaved people to do it? It is a damning question in our eyes, just as it was a proudly defiant one for believers in the Lost Cause after the war. For diarists, it was practical and basic. It was the hard stare of emancipation's local face: How will we get through this day? Who is going to pick up the mop? The white women were vexed and challenged; they improvised, complained, bargained. Black people, mostly women, did the same. In the confusion, new realities stood up in front of everybody, truths about slavery's world as *my* world. Sometimes there was the personal violence, woman against woman, which ran through all of slavery's days before the war. Personal violence was slavery's bedrock, but diarists rarely wrote it down in any detail. It was embarrassing to lose control and strike a servant. It was humiliating for a Christian and a lady—and frightening, maybe, to think of slaves' retaliation, throats slit. Or for some of the diarists, moments of personal violence may have been among the ugly, trivial things quickly bottled up and put aside without words; it's over. Whatever it was, even the violence of the war did not shake personal violence loose enough to often be put on the page.

Some diarists seemed to write themselves as heroes in the new order because now they stooped to do housework, "cooking & washing without a murmur." Scorning them for this is almost a reflex, sparked by our pleasure of seeing their class privilege upended. But when diarists wrote of taking up domestic chores it was more than self-drama or self-pity. It was about grasping the slippery mix of the old order and the new without time for strategy. Prewar mistresshood had been aggravating sometimes, but this was different. Now the white women were fumbling for a handhold on the routines of their own households. They are approachable because they were frank about how disturbing this was, and when they blurt out how servants and mistresses *ought* to be, they hint at how their best days *had been* before everything started spinning.[4]

Ladies were blind to much about their servants, but they saw a lot, too. Just read and don't discount what the diary yields, even if it's from the hands of a woman who possessed human beings. Mistresses were on the lookout for signs from the Negroes in wartime and sharp eyed about how normal life had shifted and become worth writing about. Winnie, Cornelia McDonald's maid, did not leave in 1863 with other former slaves but stayed at her job. Once when Winnie was ill, McDonald had her young sons launder the clothes, and she saw that Winnie "looked sorrowfully on at the usurpation of her prerogative" as chief laundress. Catherine Edmondston watched, too, and thought that servants in her household were "demoralized" and set adrift by wartime changes in the domestic routine. These two white women were deluded, we can say. African Americans demoralized by slavery crumbling? Sorrowful about *not* doing the laundry? And yet I think Edmondston and McDonald were picking up something in the air of the shaken household, not just their fingers-crossed wishes, but something ragged and real replaying hour after hour as the cooking and the laundry waited for a plan (and now there was more than one person's plan). Everyone *was* baffled and stirred up by the strangeness of the new day. McDonald's sons doing the laundry, Winnie looking on and feeling—what? This was emancipation: What next? What will it mean for *me*?[5]

Emma LeConte decided that the less said the better about the new atmosphere in her house. Slaves were leaving one Charleston household after another in early 1865. Work had a new pace; the old don't-even-think-about-it authority staggered. It was day by day. "If Jane offers to clean up our room, all very well—if not, we do it ourselves. This afternoon I washed the dinner things and put the room to rights." Some workers seemed "quite willing" to work. As for LeConte, "this is my first experience in work of this kind and I find it is better than doing nothing." Staying calm was the way for Grace Elmore, too, but she brought everything out into the light with Jane, Cynthia, and a few other household workers. As always, Elmore took things very seriously. "'Twas time for intelligent servants to be told how matters stood," she said to the group of household workers. Union troops would arrive any day now; many workers had departed but work still needed doing. She hoped everyone would cooperate, and she wanted them to know that she was still the same person despite the war and that "I shall endeavor to discharge my duty to them." She was satisfied with the black women's response but "could not join in their laugh" when "the girls," her sisters, joked with Cynthia that *she* would play hostess to Sherman when he arrived with his new regime.[6]

It was about appearances, which kept things together after all. It was about judgment and mannered ways taking on awkward new decisions. It was about work around the house, the plainest of subjects. *Better for me to work than to do nothing.* It was about the diarist's knack for writing the plain things that showed how the new order was made by everyone making it up. And what did the black women see happening? Reading Cynthia's take on things from Grace Elmore's words risks falling into the blindness of mistresses who thought they spoke for their slaves. But Cynthia is *there* and not to be ignored on the page, and the Sherman joke scene is a gemlike moment to imagine. If Cynthia joined in the laughter of Elmore's sisters at the thought of playing hostess to Sherman, what *sort* of laugh were they having? What appearances was Cynthia keeping up or trying out? Was she—was everyone—laughing because Cynthia hosting General Sherman was an outlandish thought, or were they laughing to prepare the way for its reality? Elmore did not ask this question when she wrote Cynthia into her diary, but having Cynthia there makes it possible for us to ask.

Gertrude Thomas had never been silent about her slaves, now and again writing individual slaves into her prewar diary with an anxiously practical concern for her mistressing, and with some curiosity about her workers folded into condescension and vexation. Once the war started to be lost, black workers appeared in her diary in a stronger flood of names and images. Taking hold of whatever emancipation would mean for her meant writing black people, listening to them, and quoting them, too, trying to hold the domestic world steady. As with other subjects and scenes she chose to write, Thomas inscribed her household by writing paragraphs of lightly linked observations of people. There were times when things seemed unchanged, and the pleasure of reading Thomas is that she did not let the sheer normalcy of life dissuade her from writing it down. If anything, war made it easier to write the normal because it stood out as never before. "Every thing goes on in its regular routine," she wrote in the fall of 1864. "The children are playing in the yard. Milly nursing the baby. Patsey washing. America scouring. Nancy shelving—Tamah cooking. Frank and Wash—Hannah and Jessy playing in the yard." The mistress at work, surveying the scene. (Thomas always used servants' names, which invites the reader to try to follow them through the diary and leads to some standout sentences to modern eyes: "The children are asleep and so is America.") Three months later, at Christmastime, all was a little less calm and bright: "Tamah is sick. America has gone down to see her mother and Fanny—Patsey has gone to see some of Bobs family up town." The carriage driver, Daniel, asked Thomas for a pass to attend a party and she wrote one for him. She tried to log these events as if they were the usual Christmastime indulgence of servants. But everything was in emancipation's advancing shadow. She felt that she and the servants were straining, "trying to pass 'a merry Christmas'" when everyone knew this was no normal holiday. Would the holiday travelers return to the plantation or not? Writing Daniel's pass, "the idea occurs to me wether we shall have any servants to write tickets for when another Christmas comes around?" Emancipation's local edge: you need not write a pass for anyone because no one asks.[7]

After five months more, around the time of the surrender, Thomas wrote her household as still churning along, with her and her workers still drawing emancipation's new, gritty lines. She was paying wages now to some of the people who had been her slaves; others had left for higher wages or better promises elsewhere. Work and workers did not always match up. Work that needed doing was a sure thing; *when* and *how* (even *whose*) were not. Thomas continued to tell the days' stories, in even greater detail, as if on the page she would find the new order—or reclaim the old one. She wrote black workers as the very figure of the new world tumbling forth from the old. "This morning I sent to Tamah to do some washing. Her reply was that 'she was not able'—she is threatened with dropsy and is {of} very little account. Patsey had to go out and wash while Milly cleaned up our bedroom and Patsey attended to the baby." Some people working, some not, some reassigned; from a certain angle this was familiar enough from the days before the war. But then "Isiah came in during the morning wanting to know if I had anything for him to do," a rare request under the old order; but Isiah was working for hourly wages now. Thomas had work for him in the garden. The laundry—the task no one liked—still needed doing. With the women gone, ill, or otherwise busy, Thomas "enquired of Uncle Jim if he ever did any washing" and, recounting it, slipped into dialogue. "'What kind of washing Missis?{'} said he 'washing clothes' said I. 'Good Lord Missis' he replied 'I never wash no close.'" Thomas thought this was funny and told him he might have to learn. A few days later, back to Tamah, who seemed unusually cheerful: "Tamah has something on her mind. She has either decided to go or the prospect of being paid if she remains has put her in a very good humor."[8]

This was how it happened—Thomas gingerly took hold of emancipation by logging household routines and writing black individuals, quoting their words and hers in the friable new day. A double vision takes shape here, a layering of the old on the new, and I imagine Thomas felt it, too. Hers were the old moves of a mistress sizing up black people in servitude and looking for an advantage, maneuvers now awkwardly put to use in a time when

Slaves

Tamah had a choice and Isiah wanted his wages. The times now called for words to pin everything down. But the times now called on Thomas's curiosity, too, and frank improvisation, which also are there for us to grasp as a way of entering her world. She laughed with Jim about washing clothes—about a shape-shifting world where a man would be asked to do such a thing by his female employer—and so she wrote a moment between two people no longer quite slave and master. It might be read as the barest gesture toward empathy on her part, no less real for being still locked up in the old chains of the slavery relation. Jim is too much inside Thomas's words for us to know his take on the moment, but it is possible that he, too, felt a hint of a new day in her outlandish question. In any case, by writing this scene, Thomas wrote double: she sifted her own plans and feelings; she saw a black man.

In fact, black individuals surge onto Thomas's pages beyond any practical need to put them there. A conversation with Bob, another former slave, about work and his plans opened up a paragraph about black people she knew. "Bob was Nancy's husband," though Nancy had left him, "as she had for some time been intimate with Rinckey one of Ma's shoemakers. Bob persuaded Rhody a girl belonging to Mrs. Phinizy and Martha a girl of cousin Jane Sibley's to leave their owners." It was all worth writing down, now that she was writing. And, writing, she kept on making black people into characters, telling who was who, putting them into scenes, remembering what they said, as she did with white people. And whether she knew it or not, she put *herself* into words when she did this—her wishful hold on her slaves in the face of slavery's undoing. Written on the fly and still warm with exasperation and curiosity, sketches like Thomas's did not come to a sharp point of moral judgment—or to a moment of truth—and then shut down. Instead, the scenes are caught up in the now-normal, now-novel intensity of exchanges with black people that pushed against the good order Thomas craved. She sailed along on the richness of words into stories where everyone had speaking parts. There is a chance here to find some empathy with her willingness to write and to *see* before the lid comes down. There are intentions piling upon intentions, emancipation morphing, story layered on story.[9]

Emma Holmes wrote this play of things in May 1865:

Several days ago, Judy was so impudent to mother that she ordered her to leave the yard & Hetty soon followed. . . . {Cousin} Lila and I determined to commence at once with our household duties, so take it by turn to knead biscuits & churn & attend to the drawing room. Yesterday [May] 28th, I made my first butter, of which I felt rather proud. We succeed right well with our biscuits. Edwin White gave me my first lesson in the art, & Rutledge's Paul, the second. Ann has been sick for several weeks & Mary also, a day or two ago, so I went to work to make up my bed & sweep & dust & have been practicing washing also, preparatory to the coming emancipation. Of course it occupies a good deal of time, but the servants find we are by no means entirely dependent on them. The same time Judy left, Patty tried capers with Carrie {Holmes's sister}, who very quietly ignored her for two or three days, & ironed Sims' clothes & even Isaac's shirts, till Patty, mortified, came and begged her pardon & went to work briskly.[10]

It seems to end as a moral tale, a boost for the white woman: Patty is mortified at her bad behavior, gets back to work, and briskly, too. Maybe, maybe not. So much else springs from this passage that whatever impulsive or strategic thing Patty was doing does not give final, moral punctuation to the scene. There is no end in sight in this quiet, fierce drama of domestic struggle and détente. Holmes knew this and wrote it, showing us. The old cues are out of place or missing. In times past, Ann and Mary reporting sick would have been inseparable from the likelihood that they were feigning illness—it was axiomatic for whites. But now? It was not so certain, and it probably didn't matter anyway. Judy was impudent, and Patty tried a caper. What to do? Order Judy off the place; ignore Patty. Neither would have been much of an option under slavery. But try them now, for the old contests over work have opened wide and the work itself is flexing and re-forming in many pairs of hands.

This was a household electric with competition and experiment. There was a lot of the new order in Holmes's biscuits, mixed by more people than anyone would have thought possible. She was proud of them and her butter, too. Her sweeping? Done. Her washing? Needs practice. She knew why she was doing all of this—it was to meet head-on "the coming emancipation." But what did this mean? Right now it meant somehow getting along with the new face of household work, the bland routine cranked up. It meant wading into necessities not dreamed of and looking hard at individuals who might have, once, blurred into the mass of the other race. Holmes's passage reads as if these things were true for everyone in the household. And now that she was writing, she added a message directed to the black women who once were clearly hers: I can do without you. Patty and the other women—were they saying this, too? Room by room, slavery became an elastic thing. Imagine the laundry lesson. *Is this the way? No, do it like this, harder. Ah, I see.* Let's say that what Holmes saw was Patty biding her time, looking for emancipation, among other things. The things that matter are always "among other things." And among other things, Patty felt pride in her work and decided to hang on to that for the time being. What would happen next in this new world? No one knew. It was scary and dicey, and so *give me those clothes.*

Thomas and Holmes each possessed a kind of buoyancy as their households came unhinged. Other diarists did not. They dug in their heels, were more guarded and less curious, especially during a crisis when Union troops were on the scene, or threatened to be. Yet these women, too, wrote African American individuals into their pages, jotting down household scenes at certain moments instead of reading the Bible or collapsing on the bed. They wrote with some openness to whatever the day brought, and beneath this runs a sense of keeping track of persons and incidents. Writing to note precedent and timing, maybe with a thought of later settling scores. Writing to keep hold of their authority if only in the mental haven of their pages. Writing to say it was all for the best—or would be. From out of this bundle of mixed purposes, the diarist wrote the black people who had her attention, who were, incredibly, both essential and able to leave. The balance changed many times. With Yankee soldiers in the neighborhood, Mary Jones's cook, Kate, refused to come to the house to prepare meals. Then the servant who had been filling in for Kate left suddenly, "took herself off," in Jones's words, a former possession now self-possessed. Jones thought about leaving the place, too, but this would hand it over to the blacks—a new and terrible thought. She had no doubt: "Everything within it will be sacrificed." A few days later, war's tectonic plates shifted again, and Jones was able to write that "the house servants were all in attendance at family worship" for the first time since Sherman's arrival, and that Kate had come back to work, too, "apparently with her free consent." A servant's free consent. Jones may have been relieved, or sarcastic, or confused to write of such a thing—she does not say. I read her as straight up. Kate's consent was a fact written for the new times.[11]

Tense and tired was Elizabeth Ingraham in besieged and dying Vicksburg. Her husband, an older man, was depressed and a little out of touch, trying to accept the unimaginable, that it was somehow "God's will that the Institution {of slavery} should be wiped out." He is hardly in his wife's pages at all, but certain servants, like Maria, the cook, and Elsy, who became Ingraham's maid and informant, are active and strong characters. The husband one day ordered Maria to fix a dinner of roast turkey and turtle soup, not a plausible menu given the times. "The old thing laughed," Ingraham said of Maria, "and went off and cooked him bacon and greens, rice and green peas." Another servant,

Harriet, said that the old man "is not ready to leave his home and comforts—they must show him where to go and how to live."[12]

Ingraham, like Mary Jones, keeps close to black women's words and actions and does not conclude that she knows what they are thinking. She does not patronize the black women or roll her eyes, which puts her closer to an empathetic place for me. Like Jones, Ingraham writes to see herself and the people in her house, as I do. She has intentions and needs, and inside these are possibilities. I feel my own, different ones; empathy is not sympathy. I read wariness in her words and mine, and restraint. Ingraham frames the household moments with herself at the center, the mistress, still a rock, surrounded by a shifting and weirdly novel cast of black characters. "Elsy still faithful, feeds us, and does what she can; Ria Jane too; Bowlegs very attentive. . . . Emma beginning to tire of waiting on me, did not come up at noon; Nancy not true. . . . Martha I don't see, not Jane or Fanny either." Ingraham thought the men more willing to help than the women. She wrote a patchy sort of empiricism, a scorecard for individuals. Sometimes it was like tracking the weather; taking sightings, saying little.[13]

Her belongings disappeared daily. She was told about disputes among the workers over who should have her bedding and clothes, and over how much work to do for what pay. Blunt realities rose up in front of her: one former slave, Emma, "knows too much for me to offend her." Elsy, though, stayed close and "does not like to see me work," which was just right. Still, Elsy let her know that she wanted her husband, Jack, to "get her a home and a way of earning a living," and if he did, she would leave. And Jack was not happy with the new terms of work, not happy that his wife still "behaves just as if she was not free." Ingraham wrote herself as part of this strange trio scarcely imaginable before the war. She wrote to play on everyone in the household and to bide her time. "I do not say any thing to them one way or the other, take what they choose to do, and finish the rest myself." She observed, observed and wrote, and daily, hourly, scaled her responses and desires to the people's imagined temper. Black people became a scrim on which she wrote herself, smart mistress, biding her time.[14]

SLAVERY ENDING AND ENDING

Immediate, filled with well-worn needs and the day's chores, a diarist's household scenes took hold of things in a practical mode and flexed the new domestic order. But diarists wrote about black people in other ways, too, as slavery shuddered, which were less focused but pushed deeper into how *my life* was made by using enslaved people, using them up, and how this was fine and as it should be. Just read the diary and find these times as they come, stories with a clear direction and stories that drift; scenes sharply drawn and scenes that go dark. In the women's diaries, African American individuals come up close and then recede. They step into view and speak, fall silent, and disappear into the mass of Negroes, then return.

This is a diarist's flickering vision of what slaves meant to her, moments of truth fanned to a new brightness by the war but far from steady. And just reading the text we can choose to hold on to that unsteadiness as a gift—the diarist's first draft of writing people in bondage by trying to use them in yet another way, to take stock of war's new world and what it meant for her. She wrote her use of black people from the diary's angle of vision, imperfect and open ended, which captured something of slavery and emancipation in play as it was lived.

I choose to imagine this, and it is a struggle; I read to stay with the imperfection and not use up the stories and scenes by having them all fit into a modern narrative of justice denied or justice done. The pulses of the text revealing the diarists and black people are one of a kind. They come, let's say, from the diary's heart of darkness, the place where the mistress's mask was made in the personal moments of slave and master. The moments that had allowed bondage to work and now gave a human shape to its fall.

Such moments—of very different sorts—gave rise to a scattered range of scenes that diarists were moved to write. Scattered and wondrously diverse. One sort featured black people who appear as images of the right order of things, figures of an ideal. They are not individuals so much as a part of the diarist's personal landscape of home and things cherished. They appear and the moment is made memorable, reassuring. In April 1865, Emma Holmes was listening to a white preacher give a "practical" sermon to assembled black people—about the Yankees being devils and about balm in Gilead. She knew the Confederacy was sinking, so this was good for the people to hear. Just then an enslaved woman named Rachel came up to her and asked her how things were going in these rough times. They chatted. Holmes thought Rachel sympathized with her more than most white people did; Rachel was generous. Holmes was moved to write about the excellence of such a woman, an "old Virginia maumer" of the finest sort, graceful, caring, "respectable." She was struck now by the thought that Rachel "seemed to have taken a fancy to me the first time she saw me," and the thought pleased her. Watching her, Holmes admired the woman's sartorial style, her "becoming handkerchief turban," which made Rachel look "so homelike it did me good to see her."

Slaves should stay away from "finery" and keep to plain, traditional dress. This would be her policy, Holmes wrote, "if I ever own negroes." *If I ever own negroes.* Emma Holmes knew very well that the war would decide against slavery and probably soon. Was this a slip of the antebellum pen? Or was she holding on to the charm of possibility: the war isn't over until it's over? Is it defiance? Denial? Nostalgia? All of these, I would say. Lived-in slave owning was big enough to hold them all, made from them, in fact. In the vision of Rachel, past and present mingled. Rachel, in Holmes's admiring gaze, was a person and a wish—and how agreeable it was for a mistress to find such a figure and hold on to her with a kind of confidence. Wartime was blowing the cover from this sort of move, but Holmes wrote Rachel with the trust of a sleepwalker.[15]

Diarists wrote black exemplars like Rachel, then in the next moment turned to writing Negroes as a faceless mass. These might be warring impulses in wartime, though diarists easily wrote both, the well-seen individual and the distant group of workers passing by, and used both, at once undercutting the essentialism of race and producing it. A Rachel might rise above the dead weight of race, but only in certain lights. Around her, other indistinct slaves pass by. Kate Stone wrote black people in portable groups, taking note of times that her father's slaves were "carried" to a safe place or "brought back" or "secured" amid the movement of armies and her family. Sometimes there were names worth writing down because wartime was perilous and servants were disappearing. Lucy Breckinridge noted the different exoduses of black people from her mother's property as lists of names without personal shading: gone were "two Bookers, Mat, Peter, Willis, Jim, Jasper, Anderson, Goen." She made brief stops for individuals. Uncle Phil she found "disgusting" after he was discovered helping other workers leave the plantation. She was concerned about "dear little Josh," whom she thought coerced by other blacks into leaving. Mostly, she merely toted up the departures: "Dolly, Ferdinand, Albert, Lovelace, and Randal."[16]

Writing black people as a mass was an easy mode of possessing them, a familiar move even for the younger women who did not, strictly speaking, own servants; their parents did. Slavery had been less of a *work* for the younger women before the war (though they were apprenticing as mistresses, no mistake) and more a matter of developing a personal style around black people— being poised and not too friendly. Learning how to speak to Rachel warmly so that her warm words might come in return. Wartime pushed the younger women to grow up faster and led the older women to double down, doing what a mistress did to make servitude work: apply the moral touch, apply the sharp edge. It was a challenge filled with unpleasant faces all around and things broken or missing. So now, lumping black people together in a mass also gestured toward being done with them. Just get them out of here. Blacks in general literally performed all that was going wrong in the war. *All wrong.* Gertrude Thomas threw up her hands: "I must confess to you my journal that I do most heartily dispise Yankees, Negroes and every thing connected with them . . . a perfect abomination." She was sick of hearing about Negroes all of the time, their comings and goings, their needs, their alarming vitality. The same things shocked Emmala Reed, who wrote briefly, but often, of feeling humiliated at the sight of black people out in the streets on no one's errands but their own. It was insulting more than frightening. One's slaves—anyone's slaves—in the street, "free," was like having something personal turned outward to public view. It flaunted war's expanding field for outrage, Yankees and the "horrible disorganized state of society, *crime* on the increase—people so hardened—all *better* things done away with—shocking!"[17]

Yankees and Negroes, the duo from hell. These women had never been so roughly pushed around, with their self-confidence shaken up and self-appearance, too. Being face-to-face with an enslaved black person, a servant, had always meant coming face-to-face with how one appeared: how do I *show* mastery? Knowing how made a mistress decisive and a woman admirable. Always the focus was on the outside, on herself and her servants getting the job done, "carrying it off" smoothly, as mistresses said of a dinner party or a garden harvest. Always good manners stood by, with their premium on harmony and seeing things through with self-control. In the manipulation of surfaces, in the self-absorption it took for a mistress to mesh persuasion and force, a deeper subjectivity was an awkward thing, to be only quickly touched, and lightly. The novelist Ellen Douglas has a character, a young, twentieth-century white woman of the Southern upper class learning how to grow up in the black-and-white world, how to live, above all, as if she were "a dancer, a skier—skimming over the surface of her life as if it were a polished floor or a calm summer lake." Don't look down. So it was for a mistress of slaves, a lifetime of attentiveness to the danger of sinking into a subjectivity that might weaken what she had to do by confusing the peculiar self-absorption it took to do it. Then the war broke through the surface of this world, and diary keeping broke through from another direction, and not only her own self-absorption and subjectivity came into the light, but also, in ragged bursts, the subjectivity of black people. This was not a *moment* of truth—truths kept coming and coming.[18]

So diarists wrote amid the existential tremors of how deeply slavery had been driven into their lives. They did not write this way for very long at a stretch, but they wrote themselves beyond the black exemplars and the black mass, spinning to avoid any sharp edge, sampling voices and scenes. It was much more than seeing either "faithful" or "unfaithful" servants. It led diarists into contradictions well sunk in. It led to reaching and denial. Our struggle to understand their world is a struggle to keep these energies in play. Insights and preoccupations were not linear; they did not "develop" along predictable lines of thought. A diarist entered and reentered these places as she followed the writing moment.

Another entry point: there were black individuals in wartime who acted morally, in the women's eyes, with clarity and sureness. Not exemplars, exactly, and not simply obedient servants quick to follow orders, these individuals came forward to speak truth to wartime chaos. They are individuals, but individuals who are written as stepping out of a chorus to give a brief, center-stage commentary. They enrich the scene, then withdraw. The human lessons diarists took from them did nothing to change their inequality with whites. Far from it; black people's mix of humanity and inequality is what made their moral acts special. Emma Holmes's brother Willie, away with the army, stunned his mother and sisters by writing to announce his sudden engagement, to a widow with children no less. The mother burst into tears; consternation reigned. Writing about it, Holmes went to the heart of Willie's breach of family feeling by quoting her slave Ann, who said the moral thing that needed saying—how shocking it was "to think of Mass Willie going to be married and not even come home to see us before hand."[19]

After an encounter with Sherman's soldiers, Grace Elmore wrote in praise of Cynthia and Horace as wonderfully "smart." Cynthia did not play hostess to Sherman's men, as Elmore's sisters had joked, but did something better. "Cynthia sugared them up, as she says" with great skill, dissembling and protecting the household. And after the soldiers left, "Horace {was} so pleasant, so considerate that I feel towards him as though he were a friend more than a servant." Praising individuals was testimony to the substance of what a mistress hoped was true: the servants were servant-wise, servant-adept, and they cared. It was even more than that. Praise bridged the slavery-made gap between people and also called attention to it. It motioned toward empathy but drew a line. Elmore wrote her way toward Horace with a warm impulse, but *as though* he were a friend. When Kate Stone's soldier brother, Walter, died in Mississippi, she pictured him "dying among strangers, a Negro's face the only familiar one near him." This was "Pompey, Joe Carson's boy," who returned to tell the Stone family about Walter's deathbed. Stone was truly comforted by talking with Pompey. At the same time, Pompey's familiar face at the deathbed was "a Negro's face," not the face of the dead man's kin and friends. A *kind* of face.[20]

This writing leans toward Lost Cause portraits of beloved, one-of-a-kind slave figures. But it is not there yet, not overcooked as it will be. The black people here are not paragons; Horace, Cynthia, Ann, and Pompey are on a human scale. They speak, but the diarist does not presume to tell us what they are feeling. They do the right thing, but they are not written as if this were the only possibility. That's it: possibilities still exist, as they do not in Lost Cause makeovers. Cynthia and Ann stepped forward, and other black people did not. It was up to individuals to decide, and because this was so, there could be bursts of personal violence and times of unexplained mystery, but there could also be moments of mutual regard and surprising tenderness. Mary Mallard's servant Jack helped her through tense days of unchecked Union troops operating in the neighborhood. He scouted out open roads and possible sources of supplies. He anticipated problems and took on risky errands. Before leaving on one foray, Jack kissed his sleeping children and turned to Mallard, "charging me to tell them, 'Papa has kissed them when asleep.'" Like Ann and Pompey, Jack is inscribed as coming into the white circle briefly, without fanfare or fuss, to do the good thing. These black people, or their presence, lightly instruct.[21]

But wait. These individuals step into a diary's pages from—where, exactly? From some near periphery, from a larger black world, a world apart which the white diarists only glimpsed or guessed at, and they didn't do much of either. If the ladies wondered about wartime life in the quarters—apart from what trouble might be brewing there—they did not write about it. Instead, the black mass reemerged in the diaries. Diarists might have been pleased or pleasantly surprised by black individuals, but never by black people generally or by "Negro ways." And so, rocked by wartime events, diarists could resort with jarring suddenness to the cover—the weapon—of race. Mary Jones and her daughter Mary Mallard, after days of efficient care from Jack and a few others, wrote during a lull in Union army pressure about the widespread unrest among the workers on their plantation. Individuals like Jack recede, "the people" come forward on the page, and the diarists see black autonomy as Negroes' self-indulgence. "The people are all idle on the plantations, most of them seeking their own pleasure," Jones wrote. A smart mistress would expect nothing else. Enemy soldiers at her place, Elizabeth Ingraham came upon an officer "coolly washing his hands at my washstand and using my towel." He parried her complaints about his men stealing by telling Ingraham that her own slaves were using the general disorder to do the same thing.

He pointed to Mary, who was standing at Ingraham's side in the midst of it all, fanning her in the May heat. "That very woman," the officer said, carried off a bundle of things herself. Mary spoke up: she was saving those items for her mistress. But, ah, Ingraham wrote later, "the mistress had not seen them." And likely would not, is her sense, black people being what they are.[22]

From here, diarists flew to the recourse of taking pity on the black race, the whole body of Africans. Pity the poor servants: uplift and dismissal in one swipe. Pity them because they are being tried beyond their capacities, because they have no way to judge. Pity could be dispensed from a distance—it *made* distance—and diarists strode into it, effusive and exaggerating. "Poor darkeys," Eliza Andrews wrote, "they are the real victims of the war," what with Yankees filling their heads with impossible dreams. Yankees and Negroes again. Kate Stone heard that hapless black men fighting for the Union army were "placed by *their friends* in the forefront of the battles. . . . Poor things, I am sorry for them." Mary Jones witnessed her slaves "harassed to death" by abusive Union troops whose racism was shockingly violent. "In all my life I never heard such expressions of hatred and contempt as the Yankees heap upon our poor servants." The hatred struck her as out of proportion, but it was exactly suited to finding a lesson about race in war's catastrophe. "What hereafter is to be our social and civil status, we cannot see," Jones wrote of white Southerners. God was moving in strange ways; but for black people, there was no doubt that "the scourge falls with peculiar weight upon them: with their emancipation must come their extermination. All history, from their first existence, proves them incapable of self government." "Poor things I am truly sorry for them," Grace Elmore said about her servants. "As a class, so ignorant, so confiding, so deceived." In war, blacks "have lost the bliss of ignorance."[23]

So race came forward to give a trajectory to chaos. Race made the world as the diarists wanted it to be and had observed it to be in prewar days. A patient mistress did not take up the whip of racial disparagement unless orderly routine, the stuff of her authority and self-regard, was broken by black people's willfulness or resistance. But when this happened, race rose quickly from mental regions usually left unspoken to deliver a lashing. *Negroes are forever ——. Black people can never be ——.* Race talk rubbed out black individuals and replaced them with a force of nature. Race did its work for white women and did it well, self-affirming and self-deceiving, and, under cover, self-degrading.

The difference in wartime—a big one—was that diarists did not just use the prop of race, they put it into writing. A habitual recourse in white women's talk became an inscribed rhetoric. The race talk in diaries still carries a conversational tone, mistress to mistress, and not all of it is bleak or damning. If the worst a slave-managing woman knew about Negroes was their limitations, the best was knowing how to turn those limitations into a field for white guidance. How well the world works to supply all! Older diarists wrote narratives where they presided over a circle of black folk who needed direction, but whose neediness instructed and entertained. A storyboard for white wisdom. Catherine Edmondston sketched exasperating but funny Negro shenanigans, their earnest, indelible ignorance. Edmondston came downstairs one morning to find servants quarreling like children, breakfast in disarray. She straightened everyone out with criticism and encouragement. What a life I lead! is the story she wrote, a tale of self-admiration using "Cuffee" as her foil, the African name adopted by white people as the imagined essence of African character. And so Edmondston imagined herself—knew who she was— against a backdrop of black people who tested and complemented her with the flaws of their race. Dolly, Gatty, Owen, Vinyard—all of the household slaves partook of Cuffee, Edmondston thought. They knew it, even traded on it. One day, with Edmondston standing there, Gatty spoke at florid length to the assembled slave children about the benevolence of their wonderful mistress. Way too unctuous, Edmondston thought, but still, "Gatty understands talking to Buncombe." A blend of tones in her voice: irony, amusement, maybe admiration.[24]

If "Cuffee," for slaves as Edmondston wrote them, was something between a tactic and an identity, relying on the idea of "Cuffee" was the same thing for her. Understanding Cuffee made her a mistress and white, and it let her rise above irritation and puzzlement with the servants. It reminded her to be patient and thorough, as women of the white race were equipped and obligated to be. Cuffee highlighted blacks' familiarity if, suddenly, they seemed too exotic, and it accented their reflexive sameness if they seemed too individual. So a mistress shielded herself from too much curiosity. She could say to herself about any black person, this is the kind of thing Cuffee does, this is how Cuffee plays, or works, or thinks. Cuffee made "primitive" behavior tame and instructive. Edmondston: "Cuffee strips off the elegancies & refinements of civilization with great ease." Cuffee was her refuge, buffering the insistent clamor of individual workers, their too-close personhood.[25]

It was good practice for a mistress to be satisfied with surfaces and prune away chances for empathy in the racial tangle that slavery made. It helped make a solid identity for a white woman, solid and self-absorbed. Always the focus coming back to her and the vast, superior realm of white people, its rightness and coverage. So it would be a far fall for her when it fractured; awkwardness and fault finding would be only the beginning. Against this happening, "abolitionists" sometimes appear amid the women's talk about themselves and their slaves. The women knew well the national debate over slavery, but these abolitionists were personal, a foil, part defense, part dodge. They were conversational. Diarists called on "Mrs. Stowe" and *Uncle Tom's Cabin* when they found themselves writing strong stuff about slavery. A white adversary gave it focus. *Mrs. Stowe might suppose . . . Mrs. Stowe notwithstanding . . . .* There is a showy aggressiveness when the women write this way, like preemptive parlor repartee. Having an abolitionist or "Yankee" on hand gathered up the emotions flying around slavery, around "Cuffee," and put them at a "political" distance from the domestic world. Black people were distanced, too, as the passive objects of clueless Northern sentiment.[26]

This abolitionist maneuver was a clever one, but not easy to make. It might pry open too much, show too much. Sometimes, when a woman relied on putting distance between herself and her slaves—the distance supplied by having a handy abolitionist to mock—the same racial move revealed how closely together she and black people actually lived. Sarah Morgan was on the refugee road in 1863, and one night in cramped quarters, she shared her bed with Tiche, her maid, the two of them sleeping head-to-foot under the same blanket. Tiche was no stranger to Morgan's bedtime, but the bed sharing was something new and uneasy. Come forward, Yankees! "Tell it not in Yankee land, for it will never be credited," Morgan wrote the next day, bringing her bed onto the page. "Actually sleeping under the same bed clothes with our black, shiny negro nurse!" She scorned the Yankees for crude words too sensational for her own racial vocabulary; *she* wasn't the one who put "shiny" Tiche into the "negro nurse" box. There was a double edge to this game, though, because the racist words came easily to *her*, too, and writing them did not erase the bedtime scene. Quite the opposite—now Morgan was on the edge of writing about the races sleeping together. Wartime upheaval asked Morgan, Why *not* share a bed with Tiche? Then her Yankees step up to say, How disgusting! The crippling power of race, the black woman she knew, the *scene*—Morgan tried to somersault through all of this with help from her Yankees, and yet what remains on the page is she and Tiche sharing the covers.[27]

The proximity of whites and blacks at times like these was a closeness of sorts, and we might imagine, a vulnerable closeness for a white woman outnumbered by her servants. It seems counterintuitive to us moderns that outright fear of the large numbers of African Americans who surrounded them would be so seldom written by diarists. But so it was. There is mostly silence about personal fear in the diaries, an impressive self-confidence, or (maybe the same thing) an exercise of skim-over-the-surface denial. Gertrude Thomas wrote of her loneliness and indecision when she was managing dozens of slaves while her husband was away. Was she afraid? Of the Union army, yes. Catherine Edmondston looked at fear by writing how free she was of it. Late in the war, husband gone, her plantation surrounded by spring floodwaters, she saw herself "a kind of 'Anglo Saxon Robinson Crusoe' with Eithiopian's only for companionship. Think of it!" No other white people for miles and yet she did not feel "a single tremour" of fear. Was she whistling in the dark, pronouncing the fear to make it false? Maybe, but *think of it*. It was exciting to declare herself fearless, a shipwrecked alien in her own land.[28]

When fear did slip in, it was from around the edges of master-and-slave closeness, a sort of fear askance. The diarists seem more questioning than anything else: *should* I be afraid of my servants? Elizabeth Ingraham, embattled by Yankees on her farm near Vicksburg, also thought of herself as a Robinson Crusoe, though with less panache than Edmondston. Being Crusoe was just one more way to have trouble. Ingraham told her slaves (or former slaves, she was not sure which it was) that they could no longer take precious water from the house cistern for their use. A direct order, in slavery times not to be defied. Now there were other, disquieting possibilities. But if Ingraham felt fear, she wrote only a simple fact: "So far they have kept away." Kate Stone (after a lapse of some days) wrote a scene featuring her house servant Webster that stopped just short of voicing her fear. Webster and others were guiding her and her young brothers to the ferry as they fled from home and Yankees, only to make a play for the guns her brothers were carrying ("Webster tried every artifice to get hold of one of them"), and after failing at that, they deceived and then abandoned them at the riverside. What Stone said has some darkness, though she sounds more appraising than fearful: "All the servants behaved well enough except Webster, but you could see it was only because they knew we would soon be gone. We were only on sufferance."[29]

Maybe fear of black people blurred into the general atmosphere of wartime anxiety. Or maybe writing personal fear was like inscribing one's personal violence against slaves, too cold—or too hot—for explicit words, too out of control for the diary's page. Once Stone came closer to writing a fear of blacks, showing it more than telling it. She and a woman friend had sought safety in Stone's room during a Union raid when a "big black wretch" entered and began rifling through her dresser and wardrobe. The man threatened to kill her friend's child, laughed at Stone's shocked wordlessness, and then left the room with his "plunder," but not before coming close, "standing on the hem of my dress while he looked me slowly over." A riveting scene, written in detail, and she plainly marks the man's race. He was a soldier, a black soldier, an anomaly hard to bring into focus because it was so far outside the circle of "servants," or even "Negroes," as Stone had always thought of them. She wrote evenly. Is it a sign of fear, or not, that the story is so deliberately given up to the page?[30]

Flat-out fear of black people: if you write it, distance it. In 1865, Gertrude Thomas wrote in the months before Christmas about the rumor of a vast Christmas insurrection, but not in a way that brought it into her life among her own slaves, and Mary Chesnut observed that bloody violence had been "long desired" by blacks, but the example she turned to was the long-ago re- volt in Saint-Domingue. Or, if you write fear, write it and drop it. Just before going on at length about her pity for poor black people, Grace Elmore wrote one sentence heavier than all the rest: "All negroes are not good." And Kate Stone briefly saw it in full face: "It is only because the Negroes do not want to kill us that we are still alive."[31]

These chilling things were said—boom—and were gone. Still, writing them played with danger and a mistress's self-control—or her sense that it was *self-control* that mattered—and tempted her to look down as she flew over the surface of her life. Perhaps she felt the danger in pausing to parse her thoughts about Cuffee, the prop abolitionists, Robinson Crusoe, and sharing a bed with one's maid, which put at risk the self-absorption it took to move through all of this without a stumble. A further thought, maybe: if we need to be afraid of our slaves, then we have been living a lie. Stepping around fear avoided this thought, too, and was another way for a diarist to maneuver between the image of black people as a large mass to be wrangled—Negroes, a race—and images of black individuals, persons as sharply seen as anyone in her diary. These images were—are—hard to keep in focus at the same time, contradictory impulses growing from the contradictions of a diarist's slavery-soaked life.

To see the black person doubly: as person, as Negro. Elizabeth Ingraham thought she was being realistic when she looked around the changed world, slavery's world, and leaned heavily, like someone blind, on racial axioms ("the negroes are as idle as darkies only can be"). At the same time, her thirst to write daily life fractured the massive block of race as surely as slavery was fracturing all around her. People appeared. There was a man she called Old Dabney, for instance. He left one day on his own business, like a free man, going "to the Gulf," and while there he sent Ingraham a loaf of bread. It was "real mean Yankee stuff," but Ingraham appreciated his attentiveness and went on to write a little about him and his ways. Then she angled away from this to conclude with a nasty shot, observing how, as one would expect of a Negro skilled in feigning, Dabney's "rheumatism {is} well, now, that he is free." Soon after, when Dabney vanished for good without a word, Ingraham wrote her disappointment in him as a person mixed into the "they" of race: "I wish I had known he was going, but they do not even do that much." Even if she didn't stop to reflect on this double vision of Dabney, she did get a glimpse of emancipation's logic ("I suppose they would not think they were free if they told us where they went"), whatever her blend of sarcasm and insight. In the end though, black people's freedom was most keenly an abandonment of *her*. Her home was now "so desolate and so very dirty; no one to clear away."[32]

No one to clear away: Ingraham's epitaph for slavery. Moving between Dabney as a Negro and Dabney as a man she knew, she drew him close but not too close. She inscribed his importance and kept it at bay. White women *did* know the people who worked for them, to the extent that helped keep whites on top. Ingraham knew Dabney, his now-and-then rheumatism and his taste in bread. But she mistook this knowledge, or exchanged it, for a kind of omniscience. She jumped from knowing a man to "knowing" the race of African Americans. She could not imagine living with black people except as a race of slaves, and even as she distanced them, she could not conceive of black people living apart from her. She could not imagine them—not their solid hopes, not their plans and fears. Not really. Instead, all stories led back to her, the mistress. This is about *me*.

It is satisfying to see the diarists this way because it is harsh and they deserve harshness. It rings true but also worries me as shrugging off chances for empathy and having the mistress's living world flicker out. The trick is to see her selfishness but not push it away. See it as a way she made her mask from attachments with enslaved people who mattered to her, and stay with the rawness of what she wrote to keep alive the contradictions that she lived that day and each day. The contradictions keep coming, and if there's a chance for empathy this is where it is. For even in the midst of their blinding selfishness, diarists kept writing on and on about black individuals who, despite all odds, sometimes step out of the cloud of self-serving words to stand before us. The images are intimate, their scale everyday and solid. The diary's stories go beyond the person-Negro twosome relied on by mistresses, and are even further removed from postwar memoirs' sappiness or silence.

Take up Elizabeth Ingraham's diary again. No one black or white—no one—appeared more often in her daily entries than Elsy, the maid who figures into Ingraham's many household work scenes. Elsy seems not to have been a go-to servant before the war. But as the Union army became an every-day threat in the spring of 1863, Elsy leaped into the diary: bringing Ingraham food and reclaiming some of her clothes from the quarters ("don't ask any questions"), talking down Union soldiers ("lousy, dirty beasts") as well as fellow slaves now clearing out ("they are bad people; they are only niggers"). Elsy put herself forward with words as well as acts, Ingraham relied on her savvy, and this may describe exactly Elsy's tactic for riding out the war. She was constantly nearby in the late spring, and Ingraham wrote about her con-stantly, making her central to her wartime stories, knowing that Elsy could stay or leave as she chose. "God knows what she will do," Ingraham wrote at one moment of doubt. Wondering what a servant would do about this or that minor matter doubtless crossed Ingraham's mind many times in antebellum days. But this, this was the windy, new world. Ingraham was watching Elsy and, I think, wondering very hard.[33]

Mary Chesnut was on the refugee road that same spring and, without fanfare or commentary, began to write scenes where individual African Americans, her servants, spoke and acted. Hers are not Cuffee stories or moral exemplar stories. The scenes have voluble black people and quiet ones. Sometimes she writes them as from-the-mouths-of-babes wise, but mostly she does not write to compliment herself on her superiority or to enjoy blacks' instructive follies. Like Elizabeth Ingraham, Chesnut has moments of *seeing* the individuals who are, for now, continuing to serve her. Ellen, the woman who worked as her maid, had a great deal to say (and to joke about) when she and Chesnut searched for travel accommodations and faced down a confrontational innkeeper. Ellen, as written, had a gift for outrageous verbal comedy; she was also shrewd and observant. Just as Chesnut began to write Ellen as a type, she swung back to write her as a person, and Ellen was not a sentimental figure. She was a wartime figure, finding in war a new occupa-tion for herself somewhere between being the white woman's servant and a traveling companion.[34]

Ingraham, Chesnut, and others who inscribed their former slaves in a steady, unsentimental way were writing their personal attachment to them—or looking for one—though the emotional cast of the attachment slips in and out of focus. There is guardedness but not airlessness. The diarist did not spend time imagining the inner lives of the black people she knew, but she did not foreclose on them, either. She just wrote them acting—choosing and acting. This may not be a reach for empathy on the diarist's part, but the ground for empathy opens up a bit, and something about African American lives shows through. Clearer is what emancipation meant for her, the white woman, all the mostly unhappy realities that were about to roll over her. It came back to emancipation as a local thing made real by somebody you knew. Somebody said, yes, it's true, they are free, and each person who said it made it true again. There were more stories to write, more scenes. There was—wonderful phrase—word of mouth. Track the incidents, name the names, tell the absurdities, and while doing this, almost by accident, write meeting with black people and describe them. Quote them. They have *things to tell*.

This was a diarist's grip on emancipation, partial and self-absorbed but also aware in a way that is a step or two this side of slave-owning solipsism. And just as you think you have all the diarists' moves down, the diaries tilt and shift yet again, shading into stories with warmer emotional currents that lift and carry the diarist together with certain individuals who were—until just now—enslaved to her. Hurt feelings drive the stories, but so do gentler feelings, or the wish for them, and it is strangely welcome to read them. The mask slips, or seems to.

Catherine Edmondston was ill and depressed as the Confederacy sank in the spring of 1865. She stopped writing for three months later that year. When she took it up again, the first person she wrote about was her longtime maid, Fanny, who had cared for her during those months of despair and then had left without a word "in the night." Edmondston could not fathom how Fanny could leave this way after days spent nursing her back to health "in a most devoted & affectionate manner. . . . At times she actually wept over me & with the most earnest & tender solicitude." Everyone who had visited her in her illness had witnessed this same loving Fanny. Now Edmondston was at an emotional loss to say whether any of it had been real. The worst of it was that Fanny "actually left without bidding me good bye, altho she knew I neither would or could detain her."[35]

That was it: Fanny knew her but she hurt her anyway. It was sudden, and senseless, and Edmondston wrote it in a wondering way that lets us also wonder about the two of them, her and Fanny. A long time together, many days. Let us say that Edmondston, in her struggle to understand, at least grasped some of the emotions of her final days with Fanny. Let us say that Fanny's tears were real—not the pure tears of the Lost Cause, not the faked tears of abolitionist justice, but real—and that the care she gave to Edmondston included affection in a mixture of other feelings that we can imagine in the absence of any words from Fanny. The times now stirred up emotions with every act, and Fanny was following through on her last act for her mistress and—the bigger move—letting go of her known life. Emotion was there, let's say, which Edmondston got, and so was Fanny's decision to leave, which

Edmondston did not get. Her feelings for Fanny were cocooned in a dream where her own goodness as a mistress enclosed them both and imagined Fanny, like all black people, as not really capable of making her own decisions. And Edmondston's words point past even this, to the nakedness of what she said she wanted most of all. Not for Fanny to rethink everything and stay in servitude. Not for the opportunity to pity Fanny as doomed by her race to fail. What Edmondston wanted was Fanny's goodbye.

When Gertrude Thomas's longtime carriage driver, Daniel, left her in 1865, it was also "during the night and . . . without saying anything to anyone." Thomas was hurt, also angry, writing that she would reject him if he returned. But when he did return, she hired him. Sometime later, Daniel again left her employ, this time with notice and a recommendation from Thomas, who told her diary, "I always liked Daniel." A year or so later, the two crossed paths in town, and when Daniel seemed ready to pass by without saying anything, "I called him and said {'}why Daniel are you going away without coming to see me{?'}" He approached her, and "I extended my hand and shook hands with him, a mark of favor." It was indeed a favor, as it would have been for her to offer her hand to any man. She liked Daniel, though it took the war and emancipation for her to put it on a page. She liked him, and he had been a good driver. "And yet," she concluded, "when the Yankees came Daniel was the first one to leave us." *And yet.* Written as the new order was still coming in. Written as: what was the old order, and what is it to me now?[36]

As I read Thomas's and Edmondston's stories, I struggle to not simply use them—and use up their words—to feed the vision of slave owners' power gobbling up moment after moment spent with enslaved or newly free people. In this view, the obscene grossness of whites' power meant that when they read the Bible with their servants, or listened to their stories, or felt sad when they left, it added up to be, as critic Saidiya Hartman puts it, "a vehicle of white self-exploration." Whites imagined an "elasticity of blackness," which they then enjoyed. They lived as if they had the final word. This view is powerful because it puts power at the center of things. It points to the danger of underestimating the vast self-absorption that slave owning made possible for white people. When Edmondston wrote about Fanny, and Thomas wrote about Daniel, the old demands, the old yearnings—serve me, please me— linger in their words. And yet their words are not about final things and fatal destinies, and I do not want my words to be, either.[37]

Thomas and Edmondston did not write slavery as being *over* as it ended for them and Daniel and Fanny, but as *ending and ending and ending,* which is what happens between individuals. If slavery had any emotional field not burned over by violence and dissembling, stories like Thomas's and Edmondston's point to it, and maybe toward empathy with white women, too. In slavery's *endings*, a diarist inscribed a black person she knew, mourning her own lost life as we might mourn ours, but not giving up on a new life or claiming to know much more than what she knew today—right now. I see her looking frankly at her mixed feelings, as I hope I can look at my own and, like her, be seized by what confuses and moves me and say so.

Reading Edmondston and Thomas, I see the slavery that white people knew as having two faces, one of ownership and the other of belonging. The first was the blank and inward-looking face of power, the power to dominate bodies and wills. The face of belonging looked outward to see people, enslaved and free, in some relation, an order of things with some light and air. Slave mistresses knew both faces of slavery, but it was belonging that most shaped the diary-inscribed ways of how a mistress and her workers got down to business each day, ways that made room for everyone's habits, jokes, sulks, casts of body and eye. Even if we today cannot grasp the emotional ground covered by presuming to own people (and I doubt that we can grasp more than a little of it), we do know how it feels to belong, and this, too, might be a way toward empathy with these women. A narrow way, and risky, but one that does more than use them up. We can imagine, or try to, how it would be to have one's world of belonging spin crazily and explode. We can begin to see how, in antebellum times, too, it mattered to the diarists to be able to shade with genuine good feeling the hard line between server and served, a shading that benefited power and gave relief from it, both. *I always liked Daniel.*

IN PASSING

In the foregoing, the diarists lingered over scenes and made them into stories. Stories about slavery ending and ending, where once-enslaved people stood out in *my life*. Stories of warm feelings (*as though he were a friend*), and fear, and race clamping down on thought for a time but never, in a diary, for all time. Diarists told these stories and many more, and they are good ones, but I do not want to leave things there. Some ghost of slavery drifts through these pages not quite caught by endgame stories. I look for it as I look for other ghosts in diaries—for something openhanded and untucked. Diarists write and never quite arrive, and that is where I want to be. Possibilities, another turn in the road, even in slavery's wartime shadow. Maybe especially there.

So come back to the idea that diaries deliver the days to us raw, and what gets said on the page about slavery seems as much by the design of the diary as by the diarist's design. There are what I think of as moments that touch on enslavement and black people "in passing"—brief scenes or passages that announce themselves with an image, a sudden thought or placement of thoughts, uncrafted, even unfocused, the writer sensing something (or trying to, or seeming to) about a black person and about herself. The diarist's touch at these moments is particularly light because she is distracted or off-balance. She is not telling a tale; she is somewhere short of *telling* anything, or somewhere past it, and I am just reading. In-passing moments show the mistress making and undercutting the racial divide of slavery but not saying that this is what she's about. She shows us her face growing into its mask. It may be that these are the moments that best reveal where her chance for empathy with the black people ran into its limits, and where I feel the limits of my empathy for her.

Catherine Edmondston began talking to her foreman Henry—or maybe he was her former foreman—in the fall of 1865. He seemed "moody" but ready to talk, and Edmondston was ready, too, for she and her husband had homeplace decisions to make now that defeat had come. She had long been confident that Henry was "one of the most intelligent of his class" and had been comfortable with his "affectionate cheerful simplicity of manner & speech," which was not much in evidence now. Talking with him about work to do on the plantation, she discovered that Henry had ideas about labor and fairness, and this, in passing, is what she put on the page. Not her plans with her husband for the plantation, which were on her mind when she started her entry, and not the affectionate, cheerful Henry, but the Henry who "thinks he ought to have Land because his forefathers cleared it and he has worked it." He thought the government should see to it that land came to him and others like him. Henry had "many such Agrarian notions," she wrote, disapproving of agrarians but not doubting that Henry was one. A certain light dawned with this new Henry. Edmondston sketched him on her page, her curiosity opening just so wide but no wider, as a suddenly strange figure, opaque, opinionated, took the shape of a man from out of the fog of slavery.[38]

Away from home in 1864–65, Emma Holmes mentioned here and there a few African American women around her who were still enslaved, or seemed to be. The women were *there* as slave women always were, serving her. One of them was Liddy, a woman older than Holmes who had been loaned to her by Mrs. Mickle, the hard-mannered white woman who had somehow come up with the money to pay Holmes to be the live-in teacher of her children. Holmes disliked Mrs. Mickle and was disgusted by the children, terrible scholars who ate like animals. Liddy was the only person in the house she could talk to. This was odd enough for Holmes to put into words, though her curiosity about Liddy did not go very far. Conversing with a black woman was not as weird a departure from prewar life as teaching for a wage or living with the Mickles. Still, Liddy hangs around the edges of Holmes's entries, and just reading brings her forward. When Liddy asked Holmes to read the Bible to her and then thanked her, Holmes wrote that it was "the first word of thanks received since I've been here." When Yankee troops came by and pushed everyone around for a few hours, Liddy did her part to keep calm and noncommittal. Holmes was impressed that Liddy held herself in check until the soldiers passed on, and only then did she shake with fear and vomit "freely." Holmes had heard of soldiers assaulting black women, and "I told Liddy of this, & she said that few know what had taken place at Dr. [John] Milling's plantation, because the negroes were so ashamed they could not bear to tell." There were soldiers who "gave themselves loose rein" among the freedwomen like wild horses. Reading the Bible to a black woman was something Emma Holmes had done before the war. Talking about rape with anyone was very likely a new thing, and it happened with Liddy. Scripture and assault—crazily war-bundled stuff. Two women talking about it, in passing.[39]

Lucy Breckinridge's near silence in her pages about black individuals broke one day in December 1864 when she wrote something completely unprecedented: "I find I am a true abolitionist in heart." Unprecedented and never repeated. There had been a scene she had not been able to look away from: "Here I have been crying like a foolish child for the last half hour because I saw Jimmy chasing poor, little Preston all over the yard beating him with a great stick, and Sister not making him stop but actually encouraging him." Jimmy was Breckinridge's young nephew, her sister Mary's son; Preston was a black boy about Jimmy's age. Also in the yard was Viola, Preston's mother. "I shall never forget Viola's expression of suppressed rage—how I felt for her!" Breckinridge wrote. "My blood boiled with indignation. I never saw such a cruel-tempered and wicked child as Jimmy. I guess *my* sons had better not beat a little servant where I am! I am so thankful that all of us have been properly raised and never allowed, when we were children, to scold or strike a servant." This from a diarist who wrote little about black people and even less about slavery, and who never said anything about this incident again. The ugly, dire moment comes through, the enraged Viola not patted or "pitied" by Breckinridge, the sister fully seen enabling the abuse. One of slavery's countless moments of backyard trauma whose aggregate weight should have brought the institution down but instead kept it going. Breckinridge's words give all this over to the page. Then she pushes the whole thing out of sight by writing herself as she hoped she was, as exceptional: her antislavery feelings, her better-behaved future children (and her imagined future servants), her pride in her proper family upbringing (never mind that it was her sister who presided over the beating), and her true tears. So: a violent, vivid moment blows in. We see the people, maybe feel an emotional free fall coming on, a crack in Breckinridge's mask, and then she writes herself a haven. The stirred-up moment, and then a dead spot. I have a feeling that this is how it worked.[40]

An in-passing moment reads as coming easily to the diarist. It is on the page because, this time, she did not pause to find anything more. No flourishes, no framing, no well-liked, long-term servant. Only a flicker, or less than that, of something more—curiosity about life lived with black people, let's say. These moments would not have been written at all, I think, without wartime and diary keeping. They were too ghostly, and too awkward, to have found their way into family correspondence, though by the same token, in-passing scenes show us the prewar realities of slavery tangled up in the personal baggage every mistress carried and in the thinking she did—in *everything* personal.

The writer Alice Munro plays on the idea of writers "using up" people. Writing, she says, consumes times and places and people the writer cannot fully possess. Not like a slave mistress using up black people's labor, exactly, but maybe similar. The diary catches the diarist at this, in the act and making no excuses, in passing. And yet these moments made for her—and make for us—openings for empathy to be used or used up. I think again of how reaching for empathy is less an initiative we take than a response to another person, a wonder we risk wondering about, the simple stunning insight that other people merely and magically have lives as we do. Empathy says: we can pause in the presence of another.[41]

If there were such times between mistress and slave, and I've been saying that I think there were, in-passing moments show how they might have come about and then, just as quickly, disappear. The diarist noticed, maybe for the first time, not just a servant but a person. She wrote a bit, sometimes with an edge of curiosity, and then she stopped writing. Maybe she half realized that giving voice and shape to black individuals was a cloudy, perhaps dangerous thing to do. An admission of something, a recognition. Or perhaps—just as likely or maybe more so—she simply turned away from wondering about Henry or Viola or Liddy. Whatever was there, in passing, could not hold her; the flash of empathy guttered out. She used black people and then she used them up. This is not hard to see because we have learned to expect this of slave mistresses, and yet these expectations need not be the end of her story, or ours. It's a choice. If we are satisfied to point out the women's arrogance and abuse, we can do it. We can use them up, or not.

Read to find times, in passing, that present the choice. Four young women were in an upstairs room in Sarah Morgan's entry for January 30, 1863—she, her sister Miriam, her friend Anna, and Malvina, Anna's maid. Downstairs, an evening party was underway, and the women were excited, getting dressed, preparing their entrance. Anna anticipated meeting a desirable man she knew was waiting for her. Morgan, who loved to quote dialogue, quoted the feverish Anna: "Wait! I'm in a hurry too! Where is that pomatum? You Malvina! if you dont help me, I'll—There! take *that*, miss. Now fly around!" A flash of the young maid: "Malvina, with a faint dingy pink suddenly brought out on her pale sea green face, did fly around." Anna had slapped Malvina. The frantic party preparations, the young white women's pleasure, went up a notch with Anna's blow and then barreled on. Morgan's eye caught the faint pink emerging on Malvina's face. To see this is one thing, but to see Malvina's skin as "pale sea green" is another order of sight. Morgan writes in passing, carelessly, showing off; but she has *looked at* Malvina's face.[42]

Morgan went on with her account of the evening, which included a spiritualism session where the spirit foretold that Morgan would fall in love with a captain and foretold his name, too—Charles. Morgan scoffed at the whole thing, but she was having fun. Writing it, she came back to the slapping of Malvina. She thought Anna had been "ungrateful" to do it. Still, a burst of temper "occasionally is pardonable" in the heat of a moment charged with men and clothes. This led her to wonder how *she*, Sarah, would have acted had it been her lover, not Anna's, waiting downstairs. Yes, "wouldn't I slap Mal, and Miriam, too, in my excitement? Good Gwacious! What a row to make! Yes! after boxing my maid and pinching my sister (bless her honest eyes!) I dare say I'd skip down, and putting that same right hand in his, cry 'Dearest Charley!' with the sweetest smile on lips that had just angrily cried 'You ugly beast!'"[43]

Were those Anna's words as she slapped Malvina, or Sarah's words as she imagined slapping her? Or Sarah's words from other countless times when she lost her temper with her own maid? In passing, we do not know. In passing: this is how young white women abused, abused and included, the young black women who helped them dress and find the pomade. This is how the white women filled out their excitement, their parties, their love for men. Follow the hand, Morgan's hand, as she slaps her maid, pinches her sister, and then, all of this unsuspected by dear Charley—or maybe all of it implied in a lady—offers her hand to him. A breathtaking moment of scattershot dominance and enjoyment, written by a mistress of slaves who understood it, but did not, but *did*. Malvina's skin, in a slow-focus close-up, Morgan knew, too. And then she turned from that flash of Malvina to imagine an extraordinary moment all for herself.

Read this scene as a scene from Morgan's wartime social life, or read it as trivia that she or an editor did not delete. I read it for its surface "fun" pushing up from its underbelly of abuse and pleasure. For its language, bright and suffocating. And for this: in the hothouse of party preparation, Morgan thought that her sister and Anna were to blame for the evening's ongoing hysterical fuss; she and Malvina were the calm ones. "Mal and I should have sympathized;—only we didn't." If I knew how to fully explain Morgan *writing* this scene, and saying this, I would know how to say something about the madness of slave owning. Morgan and other diarists did not write a world where thinking about black people's feelings was impossible. They wrote a world where their lives with black people made room for this and also crushed it. *Only we didn't*. If empathy grows from a moral curiosity about other people and opens up chances for a wider social intelligence, the white women crushed these, too. What they took in exchange was a covering self-absorption, a mask and more. A mistress *kept* black people, and kept herself apart from them, by means of a long self-embrace. Despite the sharp surprise of the in-passing image of Malvina, my curiosity about Morgan starts to shut down in the face of her gleaming self-indulgence. I feel the limits of my empathy with her, start to reach for a conclusion, to judge her and be done with her.[44]

And yet. The desire to disengage wavers in the face of the diary's relentless present tense—write on! on! I read through the impulse to turn away from Morgan so that I might find something less straightforward, and less self-righteous. There is a fear, or something like a fear, that pushing Morgan away will shut me off from knowing limits of my own that I do not see or pass over as merely trivial—perhaps a kind of self-absorption, too, a blind spot in my own social intelligence about the past that I should know about, a feel for how power feasts on the casual meanness in everyone. Strange as it is, I look to diaries to keep alive the possibility of finding out about such things. My empathy is kept barely breathing by those first-draft pages and the hope they give that the diarist and I will both be surprised by discovering more than either of us knows, or even wants to know. So read on and find moments, amid all of the self-enclosed maneuvers the slave mistress made, where she moved toward a black person and there they are, both of them, on the page. The mistress might be blind, the moment might skip away, but we see a face of slavery that we cannot see without her. She can teach us about her world in the half-light that her diary gives to empathy.

The impulse to find brighter light is still strong, though, and we moderns latch on to the diarists who speak most clearly as historical sources about *our* concerns. We redeem a diarist here and there—Gertrude Thomas is one of them—whose moral take on slavery seems to edge toward ours. Thomas sees abuses and has doubts about slavery being right. But, read closely, she writes circles around the moves we have made to redeem her. Her text is too unplotted and at odds with itself, and this is something that cannot be gotten around although Thomas herself tried a way to get around it. Intent and oblivious, in passing, she made a move to step around how slavery's end had stunned her, only to be outmaneuvered by her own diary keeping.

Thomas has been quoted many times for questioning slavery in ways that sound like ours. She wrote on September 17, 1864, that "I have some times doubted on the subject of slavery. I have seen so many of its evils chiefly among which is the terribly demoralizing influence upon our men and boys." And a few days later, on September 23: "What troubles me more than any thing is that I am not certain that *slavery* is *right*" and that, perhaps, "to hold men and women in *perpetual* bondage is wrong." She seems to lean toward us in her doubt and moral misgiving. Yet what she says here seems straightforward only if we remove it from diary writing—that is, read it as a "position" instead of open-ended thinking. When read within the daily flow of pages, her doubts seem less certain—and much more compelling.[45]

The diary's flow: Thomas's 1864 doubts about slavery appear in the final pages of her diary volume in the midst of a cascade of images and thoughts. Thomas disliked coming to the end of a physical volume—goodbye to a good friend—and she was moved to write a field of things that needed saying, to cram them into the last page or two. The entry from September 17 is a long and cluttered one, with thoughts about the advancing Yankees, her husband, her reading, the Confederate spy Belle Boyd. Sheer Thomas, leaping from one train of thought onto the next one. Her doubts about slavery follow some commentary on the politics of the war, and they come just before long, loving portraits of her children. That is, her doubts, though serious, were not written to command the page as they have commanded our quotation of them. When we privilege them, we should know that highlighting Thomas the doubter comes at the expense of Thomas the diarist. So, too, with the entry of the 23rd, when she doubted that "*slavery* is *right*." This is strong stuff, but so is her follow-up hope that slavery *will* prove right, and that the novel she was reading, *Nellie Norton*, "will convince me that it is right." A week later, in fact,

Nellie Norton seemed to be doing the job. In a passage not frequently quoted by historians, Thomas stepped away from her doubts. She was embarrassed and thought that she had been "provoked" by a bad mood to express them. She jokingly likened her doubting self to a punished slave or a defeated army: "I think *I* must have been 'badly whipped' when I wrote the preceding pages." Since then "I have been reading Nellie Norton with a good deal of interest." Her questions are still there, but answers are at hand; her doubt was not a fixed insight but a moment in a back-and-forth struggle.[46]

Thomas wrote in another way, too, about slavery, where she tried to put an end to her doubts. In her diary after the war she created a very different patch of writing, a kind of memoir of her doubt that cooled the diary's warmth and confusion, or anyway worked in that direction. She did not write to redeem herself by our lights, but to make a grave for her misgivings. She first made this memorial spot in her pages by revisiting her September 1864 doubts a year later, the Confederacy gone and emancipation a reality. She recalled her doubts not as inscribed in a volume-ending rush, but as a *scene* morphing into a story, with herself as actor and critic: "About one year ago I came up the avenue & selecting a seat in the pine woods I leaned against a tree and read 'Nelly Norton' and tried to solve the vexed problem of 'wether Slavery was right?' I came with my Bible in my hand to consult and refer to." Now religion swells the story. She recalled believing that if "the *Bible* was right then slavery *must be*," and yet, devastatingly, "slavery was done away with and my faith in Gods Holy book was terribly shaken. For a time I doubted God." From here she slipped into a broader stream of thought about faith and death, took a sharp turn to attack the Freedmen's Bureau, and moved away into other thoughts. Then, as in 1864, she reread her entry a few days later and diluted the pungency of her remembered dismay. "I have just read over what I wrote last Sunday. It appears very contradictory but I will not attempt to analyse it." Both matter: the persistence of her moral misgiving and her impulse to cool it down by fitting everything into a story about herself: the pine-woods walk, the gravity of her faith, her sincerity. In 1865, she was looking to write herself as the heroine of her journal by turning this niche in her diary into memoir.[47]

Thomas did not revisit the scene in 1866 during the stretch of mid-September days (she was busy with staging—and describing—a wedding ceremony for an African American woman, Martha, who worked for her). There is no extant journal for 1867. But in 1868, she again wrote of her slavery-troubled walk, and now her story seemed to have gathered enough memorial force to relieve her of the weight of doubt. The fall weather was stirring and fresh, as it had been four years earlier. She stays with it a moment.

"It was upon just such a day" when the "wind was high and the crisp air invigorating" that she took her novel and her Bible and "went up the avenue and seating myself read, studied and compared." As was now her way to recall it, "I seated myself by a large pine tree & listened to the rustling of the wind among the pines, saw the waving of the grass, the varied lights and shadows." And now, in 1868, there was no contradiction, no bad mood. "I took heart and learned a lesson. I remembered that wether slavery was right or wrong it had been done away with—and that if it was Gods will that Grant should be elected he would be." This time, with the presidential election elbowing in, "with a shrug of the shoulders which I am afraid bordered upon French fatalism I thought 'what is the use of my being worried. What is to be will be.'" Feel her relief. Her memorial pages, a kind of antidiary within the diary, made a sweet refuge from troubling doubt. By 1868, whatever *is* might as well be right, and though she was a little uneasy coming this close to fatalism (and a French fatalism at that), Gertrude Thomas welcomed the neatness of a settled memory. She let herself shrug.[48]

But her diary did not give up on her. *What is to be will be*, and yet diary keeping always surprises. As Thomas penned her serene words in 1868, she noticed an ink blot on the page, and wrote, "(That blot was caused by my hat falling from my head) and not by tears." A falling hat, a blotted page, and a wonderful diary-writing moment, this pointing to the page. *Let us be clear: there are no tears being shed here over slavery and doubt.* She saw the ink blot and she thought of tears, or thought that somebody might think of tears, and that move, for me, pushes against her endgame shrug. It is *not* clear and it is *not* over, so Thomas the diarist shows. And her diary moved on, scooping up the days. She wrote that year, and for years after, in the curious-anxious Thomasonian way, about her husband, children, reading, work, anxiety, God. And she wrote about African Americans she knew, spirited or troubled passages where she talks with them of weather, work, and politics, and they call her "Miss Trudy" and vote Republican. These passages lightly and messily rolled far beyond her small, self-absolving memorial.[49]

CHAPTER SIX

Herself

Always at hand for diarists was the question, What sort of person am I? At hand, but not often asked. Most of the women did not face the question head-on for more than a few sentences at a time. As writers, it's clear, they did not have the inward gaze of Puritans or psychologists, and we have seen them a little leery of outbreaks of subjectivity on the page. If a diarist did pause for a close look, her self was a curiosity, part riddle, part amusement. A lot of toggling between eagerness and chagrin, with self-indulgence colored by regret, and some searching for the backlight of romance. Mostly, she took up her self like an old dress from the wardrobe or like the diary itself. Seen but not seen, familiar fit, no questions, and on to writing the times now.

Self *is* there to be found, though. As a modern reader, I want to find it, or its tracks. Self shows through the diarist's words even when she's not telling about it. It appears when she fought for the right words and against silence, and when she was sure, then unsure, of what she was doing. Meaning she got glimpses of herself—and gave them out—when the diary did its work of mixing surfaces and depths to make, let's say, stations for the self, stopping places in the flow of words and days. The war's violent strangeness, the war's men, the not-to-be-imagined ruins of slavery: have these made me someone new? She hardly ever asked it off the top; she was always asking it underneath. The self is the most elusive of everything I've been saying diarists wrote about. We arrive at self's stations and yet keep on going. This says something about the women and their cultural moment, about diaries and their plain open-endedness, about keeping war open ended through the realness of a writer's words. And about me and my choices. I am the one who made "herself" the last chapter.

Reading a diary on the lookout for self is like reading a travel book, only it's about self instead of travel. You roll along, the days give up their vistas. A lot of it is mysterious, brilliant, indecisive. A lot of it lies half-seen and disappears, food for later curiosity and imagination. Even in war, a lot of it is flat—and the same as yesterday. You roll along, looking among her words for her self, glad to be free from the bane, or whatever it is, of "readability." There is no high hill of final judgment—not for the diarist, not for me, not yet. And this is where I want us both to be. At this ground level, the diarist's self still wanders through the hours she gave to writing. She never quite arrives, and I put off arriving. So there is the feeling of some greater reality, a deep and uneven wonder of a reality, underneath both of us, writer and reader. It lies underneath her self-absorption and her abusive power, and it is underneath my censure of these and my lack of sympathy for her. It's like a place familiar and renewable, where there is always someone Other to encounter, if not to be (really) known, and to stay with for a while in a place we make for each other.

"We live permanently in the recurrence of our own stories, whatever stories we tell," says the novelist Michael Ondaatje. So women's self-stories in war branched out to find older, and other, selves and stories. War was the great dislodger of these, war and writing both. As with other things in wartime, writing put self-stories onto the page for keeping even as the diary kept everything moving, kept her *self* moving. We do the same if we read to find her on the move but keep close to her words. Whatever the war changed for her, or reveals to us, becomes over time a dream. Only her writing and our reading make it real.[1]

A SELF IN FAITH

Christianity, mostly the Protestant kind, was one station of the self in diaries. The way Protestant Christianity favored stories spoke forcefully to many diarists about who they were and what the war was doing to them. It did not speak to all of them. Some of the women thought they did not have the heart or the courage for Christian faith; others said almost nothing about religion. But for those who took hold of it, personal faith in a Christian God spoke with almost instinctual power about the self as a quest and a witness, a self not led into temptation, or, if it was, given a way out. It was a faith that linked the *now* of wartime (and the *now* of diary keeping) to the transformations their faith was always asking of them *now*. Keeping faith happened moment by moment. Whether or not they believed, women knew the moves of faith, the logic of it. It was everywhere around them in public speech, casual speech, and in the folds of the community's hopefulness. The essayist Marilynne Robinson writes of this ordinary, atmospheric Christian faith as alive in the "burdened silences" of everyday life, holding more than anyone can say but letting people take for granted "an intimacy with the thoughts of those around" them. I do not share such a faith, or even feel a need for it, but seeing it in diaries, up front or between the lines, I wonder about the space it opens up for empathy with the woman herself. It is like the space made by art—fulfilling, unnerving, the presence of *something* that brings you closer to someone else. Absent the war, probably, the women would not have had much reason to put this quotidian faith into writing, but wartime pulled it to the surface. Women rested in their faith and they wielded it; the self would follow.[2]

One logic of Christian faith in war led to Judgment—to punishment and glory—and the scale of it was as large as the failing Confederacy. The war gave the Christian romance of falling and being raised up a terribly new scope and intensity. Before the war, sinners were chased down by God—at most, a whole congregation was shaken up—but the Christian South itself was beyond doubt. But by midwar it was not possible for white Christians to deny that, as Southerners, they seemed to be in the field of God's wrath. Defeat in battle, the deaths of friends and family, political confusion, free Africans all spelled the end of days. Diarists gave the enemy names straight from the Bible and antiquity: Yankees were Pharisees, Vandals, Pharaoh's hosts, the legions of pagan Rome. Emmala Reed thought that her personal faith was holding up, but she was dismayed at the general coarsening of the Southern people who were not heeding God's word as they should. Every day made worse the enormity of their failed devotion. She looked around one morning at church and saw the fatal ruins: "Not a half dozen *males* & these so *worthless* . . . nobody being brought into the church—the old falling off—till we are broken up." Corruption, humiliation; this was not a test. Or it *was* a test of another sort, the run-up to Judgment. Others were calmer than Reed, but it was the calm before the punishing hand. "God will deal with us according to his mercy, & justice," Floride Clemson wrote, and the only part now for the faithful was to find the "strength to bear whatever chastenings he has in store for us with a proper spirit."[3]

Still, Clemson and Reed were not preachers on a doctrinal mission. Writing faith in diaries made for some wiggle room. Faith was in the Word, and faith was in words, and though the wartime world grew dark, it was not beyond rewording. In their pages, diarists talked their way into righteous punishment, but also through it and out the other side. They made space for themselves (the diary a vessel with plenty of room) to implore and bargain.

They obeyed but not quietly; with an edge, in fact. Some even enacted their faith in the open, imperiled and brave as their Christian heroes had been. Faith's readability was clarified by times of dread and then softened by the diary's native hunger for yet another moment when things turned a corner. So the diarist filled out the person she thought she was, and reading, I look for her in the loose ends among the promises of faith, because nothing about the self was final, not in war, not in a diary.

In her prewar diary, Grace Elmore had written often about her troubled mind and her relation to God. She was cast away. She was agitated and unsure. She was not *able*. As she wrote herself into the war, the war overtook her yearning for personal peace and carried it into a collective doom. The stage was huge, but her words clear. "We are Carolinians that is our crime" she thought was God's wartime message. "Our present situation is darkly, terribly, strange." She looked for relief and found that "God does press very near to us in sorrow," which, if not exactly relief, was better than emptiness. Faith gave the resolve not to "murmur," as the phrase had it, so that God's will would take shape in the stillness of one's obedience. "Be strong in faith," Elmore instructed herself, and wait. But it was not easy to wait or be quiet in war. Complaining would do no good, but she had questions that she did not write as questions (no question marks), and so her words on the page suggest an imperative tone taken with God: "Will he never hear us, will he never consider," she wrote. Was she asking, or was she making a statement on the brink of desperate impatience? Surely God must know that Southerners' weaknesses were a plea for mercy. Stay in step with God in the times now, do not look down: "Think not the Lord has forsaken you or he will give you up."[4]

Fear mixed with hope in their words, desperation and pride looking for spiritual traction. Anxiety for self and the Southern people drew on Scripture, especially the psalmist's imploring voice. Diarists reminded God, they pointed to his page: "Year after year has our cry gone forth, how long oh Lord, how long," Elmore asked or stated. These particular words in the mouth of a mistress of enslaved people come to our ears with the worst sort of irony. But the emotional charge goes past irony with abandon. Were they abandoned by God? "How long, O Lord, how long is our probation through this fearful furnace of affliction and sacrifice to last!" wrote Emma Holmes, also not dressing it up as a question. A historical balance sheet for God's consideration suggested itself to her: "Certainly the horrors of a slave ship have been out-rivaled by the sufferings of our heroic Southerners." The war as payback time for the Middle Passage—it's a little surprising, this global-historical turn on slavery, though Holmes executes it only to point out that suffering's account book *must* be balanced by now. The rub, as Catherine Edmondston saw it, was not God's accounting, but the manner in which the punishment came, by way of murderous Yankee soldiers and the scum, tricksters, and unspeakable hangers-on who would profit from a Union victory. Why did it have to be this way? She accepted God's chastisement; much harder was "to look beyond the human instrument" chosen by God to deliver it. Reminding God and leaning on the rock of decorum, diarists wrote their Christian selves by protesting their obedience, teaching the lesson back to God.[5]

Doubts kept pushing forward, though, and the aggrieved self was tested. Prayers popped onto the diary page, impulsive and fresh, with the intensity of the writing moment: "Help and revive us all Oh God!" "Grant me a renewal of thy spirit oh God—and increase in me the wish to do thy will." "Stir up thy strength, O Lord! and come and help us." "Increase my *faith* O God! Increase my faith! Thou seest this wickedness & in thine own good time Thou wilt punish it!" The one-line prayers are faith's vernacular, and they punctuate almost any scene. So the women shored up faith as they voiced frustration, rehearsing their desires as the Deity's obligations. God *must* do these things, the women say. For us, for *me*. It was a Christian's line to walk, the one between self-abasement and self-glorification; preachers walked it all the time. With prayer, put stark need into words heavy with formulaic power yet deeply personal—and wait for the sign. Times when a sign appeared were electrifying and doubt dissolving. Gertrude Thomas's God heard her when she turned to him fearing that her husband was in battle: "On my knees I prayed 'Oh God save my husband. Take all else but save him. Save him Oh God! Save him' and lo! my prayer is answered!" Prayer's power was now at hand, and it surprised even a devout and practiced Christian. Mary Jones, long a minister's wife, and you would think long used to praying, observed after days spent under the gun of enemy troops that "I never knew before the power or calming influence of prayer. From the presence of our Heavenly Father we feared not to meet the face of man. We must have died but for prayer." The self humbled and exalted—the Protestant dream. "When I pray most I feel best," Thomas wrote.[6]

It took a strong person to keep up with her faith, which was always rushing ahead of her and pointing the way to a new lookout. Faith never took no for an answer. If the view is bad, seek a better place, and see! Find the words to keep up with faith's quick pace, words giving war its due but making it fit inside one's even larger life. Scriptural words of faith covered everything, *positioned* the self in war's awful expanse. "Everything seems dark and threatening, yet I will not despair but commit our cause to His hand who 'out of

Herself

chaos' brings forth order," Lucy Buck believed. Bad news from the battlefield was "a knell to our peace," Catherine Edmondston admitted. But remember: "He that keepeth Israel shall neither slumber nor sleep." It was not simply that war recalled Scripture; the times were again scriptural. "The days of the Israelites are returning," Elmore thought early in the war. Cornelia McDonald saw the continuity of death across the ages erasing the gap between biblical times and now: "Alas! now as then our precious sons, the pride and flower of our land must be daily given to the devouring sword." Emily Harris felt her faith slipping but wanted to believe that the Confederate nation "stood like the land of Goshen amid the plagues of Egypt" and so would revive. On this stage, a woman's life contained multitudes. Find the highest place, and catastrophe will fit into your hand.[7]

Women made this move in the very face of the enemy. *Fear not to meet the face of man.* When enemy soldiers rode up to the house, a Christian hoped to become large in her faith and equipped for the moment. The story—the real story—was not her fear or the looting and yelling, but God's will and the strength it gave to the faithful heart. Elizabeth Ingraham pointed out the obvious to the Union soldier who wanted to steal her desk that she was powerless to stop him. But then she stepped to one side and introduced God into the room: "If God's command is not obeyed, I cannot expect you to mind me." A Yankee soldier stealing a bucket of eggs from Mary Mallard and her mother "stumbled and fell as he went down the steps and broke them all." It was precisely "Psalms 27:2. When the wicked, even mine enemies and my foes, came upon me to eat up my flesh they stumbled and fell." So the meanest thievery was nothing less than a timeless lesson drawn from the Word. See! The enemy will stumble and fall, and the victim will stand revealed as God's witness.[8]

A writer closing the scene here at God's side in a postwar memoir, say, might come off as merely self-righteous. But the diary's play-by-play frankness slid past epiphany into other ground, comic and ironic, like the day, like life. Rolling on through the scene, the diarist did not stop with her triumph, so we see the loose ends of those biblical moments in the parlor and the dooryard. Jones's thief, for instance, may have lost all the eggs in the bucket, as Scripture promised, but she went on to note that the soldier nonetheless "carried off the bucket." And the troops sacking Ingraham's house put a weird spin on the stand she took with God by stealing several Bibles ("what such rascals want with Bibles I can't tell"). Irony, or bathos, in full view, women wrote on without fear of diminishing the moment lit up from within by faith.[9]

Another such moment at home and on the page came for Mary Jones, this one life threatening, when yet another body of Union troops arrived at the house with questions about what the women knew and what they were hiding. Jones's daughter wrote it all down. What about rebels nearby, the soldiers wanted to know. And where were the valuables? They told Jones they would kill her if she answered their questions with lies. This time, Jones "stepped out upon the little porch" to face the mounted men at eye level. She told them, "In the beginning of this war one passage of Scripture was impressed upon my mind and it now abides with me, 'Fear not them which kill the body and after that have no more that they can do, but fear Him who, after he hath killed, hath power to cast into hell.' I have spoken the truth and do you remember that you will stand with me at the Judgment Bar of God!" There was a pause, God having once more joined the group, and then one of the soldiers said, "Madam, if that is your faith, it is a good one." And Jones rose above the encounter as if from the grave. I think she was lucky that the men shared enough of her faith to listen to her rather than (as she thought she heard one of them say) blow her brains out. But for her, it was faith that handed her a pure, blessed moment. Then the diary passage pushes past this moment, putting Jones's feet back on the ground, with the anticlimax that diaries are so good at not refusing: the soldiers did not harm her, but they did not ride away in awe of her, either. Baffled by her faith, they took a parting shot that her daughter faithfully recorded. They called her "an old devil and applied some other dreadful epithets such as are used by the lowest and most profane."[10]

Even so, I see Mary Jones blazing fully in body and mind when she took her stand on the porch. Faith's story was so strong that the diarist could write herself past the moment, past the times now. Faith was in the present moment, and faith abided. It shone from the extraordinary encounter and the ordinary afternoon, and it is not, as it would be in a memoir, under suspicion as self-serving hindsight. Jones—and Ingraham, too—called upon their faith at the very moment they locked eyes with the enemy and so said to him, What you are doing does not end here; what is done here is not its sole meaning. They stand in the moment and they stand outside it. Reading, the first thing I see is the pillaging, and the women losing their Bibles and their eggs. Then I see irony in the diary's eagerness to move on to the next scene. Then I see women transcending all normal fear.

I wonder at this and can go only a step or two into what it opens up, the idea of timeless faith and its power. I am glad—relieved, or something—that the diary keeps everything day-to-day personal and through a glass darkly. A person's faith was her own and needed her tending, because whatever happened next happened on her watch. "Forenoon. No enemy thus far," Mary

Herself

Jones wrote some days later. "God be praised for His goodness and mercy. Our nights have been free from intrusion. A keen north wester is sweeping over the lawn and whistling among the trees." *God be praised.* What do these words add to the restless January day? They gesture toward something, and they are something. They give a sign and make a space. They say that everything at this moment is for the best, and that a new moment will soon be here. They speak against the fear that life might be only the wind in the trees. The words strengthen the self but also mark time, and they have a kind of magic that is not otherworldly, exactly, but keeps the self keyed up. She is tending to her faith as she should. The diary lets her do it with unforced ease, as her faith itself should be, always ready for her touch. Ready, too, for the sharp tug when faith is again tested. Even Mary Jones, as determined a seeker of God in the ruins of war as any of the diarists, still had questions about herself after the soldiers had gone. She still doubted that she had proven to be the person she should be. At every point with the enemy, "I never failed to let them know that before high Heaven I believed our cause was just and right." And yet, raids over, Jones was moved to ask her daughter and her friend who had passed the harrowing time with her—and ask them more than once—"Tell me girls, did I act like a coward?"[11]

Faith might fail after all and the self be lost. Pauline DeCaradeuc felt that "things are rushing along at so terrible a rate, to some fearful climax" that she would break. Maybe she had broken already. She tried to pray but could not, "altho, sometimes I'm over an hour on my knees trying to turn to God as I used to." Her gesture at prayer was "like my spirits, empty." Over an hour—she was keeping track. It was spontaneous to write it, this minute-counting moment, and so push past faith's good behavior on its knees and reach out from her time to ours. Writing her self, DeCaradeuc went over the top of compliant faith into ever-ready doubt and found some words for it. It would be an awkward moment for others to see, so I feel I am coming across a half-hidden truth—a truth about faith and also about her Christian face, and so about self and deserving a place to stand. For Gertrude Thomas, it was not only the fear that her faith was in free fall, it was also the fear that God might fail *her*, a near-blasphemous, bottomless thought. Thomas felt its pressure when the Confederacy surrendered. She was astonished at God's silence in the face of Southerners' need, and she matched the silence with her own. She was unable to write in her diary. She later explained why. "Our cause was lost. Good men had had faith in that cause. Earnest prayers had ascended from honest hearts. Was so much faith to be lost?" If the sheer bulk of faith counted for so little, and heartfelt prayers went nowhere, then faith itself was suspect, maybe a long time hollow, long before the war. Thomas fell into a gloom so deep that she felt herself "mocked" when she tried to read the Bible, and "when I prayed my voice appeared to rise no higher than my head."[12]

How small the self, and how large. I get a glimpse of it and wonder at it, the war made legible in the image of Thomas's baffled prayers hovering in the space above her head. Then it all might be rewritten and the space filled with a faith large enough to swallow up the war after all. Diarists inscribed it from both directions and so slipped away from a final knell by capturing faith in the present tense, as it eroded and as it was remade. That's it: we read and see faith in practice. And everything, in practice, had nicks and seams. Attention wandered, even for the devout, and the play of the self on the page moved in and out of the Christian romance. Faith written in this way did not require sustained self-reflection or end with a clear resolution. Diary-kept faith was more like being open to surprise and then finding the words to circle back to the familiar. Words find a way. Thomas recovered herself and returned to her Bible reading without any fanfare in her pages. Emma Holmes went to church, but more often wrote to review ministers' intellectual gifts rather than her personal faith. Floride Clemson joined a church for the first time in her life during the war, yet she said nothing about it in her journal. A woman's self absorbed a lot of things that needed tending, and it was a writer's agile choice to inscribe both faith and self in the opportunity of the moment.

FEMININITY'S CHARM

"Why record gloomy & despondant doubts," Edmondston asked her diary. There were men around to do that. A woman's way was light and her strength limber. "Thank God for my elasticity, the best personal boon he has given me!" A sure-handed and ready hopefulness belonged to the race of females. Theirs was a flexible cast of self, moving with, never against, the strong currents of the world until the moment came (there would be many in life) for a woman lightly to take charge and teach others how to do the right thing and be happy. This crowning femininity, sweet, ordained, and relentless, is gone now. But it was there for the diarists, a known station for the self and a treasure of womanly means and maneuvers. She was ever aloft.[13]

Edmondston was able to call upon the charm of her femininity after the war had crashed into it, but other diarists were not so sure. Feminine elasticity seemed to be hardening, or becoming only a reflex. There were war's attractive men, true, and partying and playing with them. There was falling in love. But none of this made femininity or even defined what made it real.

Femininity was a woman's spark clean and clear, a spark, like her religious faith, that would always fly upward. If it died, all the rest would vanish. Stifled by terrible war news every day late in the war, Emily Harris's womanly light degraded into mere persistence: "There is no pleasure in life and yet we are not willing to die." Grace Elmore felt this deadlock as her self having "lost all elasticity, all buoyancy of temper" under the war's constant grinding. Was she just becalmed for the moment—emotions blew in and out, womanhood was constant—or was she actually changing as a person, a woman? Elmore was afraid that she was "settling into a hard, strong willed, go-ahead" sort of woman, somewhat like a man. She was becoming selfish, calculating petty advantages at every turn of the day—with men, the servants, even family. Gone was femininity's illuminating calm. Seventeen-year-old Emma LeConte felt something feminine slip away and sink when she realized that she had been at war since she was thirteen. "We girls, whose lot it is to grow up in these times, are unfortunate! . . . I have seen little of the light-heartedness and exuberant joy that people talk about as the natural heritage of youth. It is a hard school to be bred up in." The light heart of a girl guttered in Lucy Breckinridge now that the war was forcing her to "reconcile myself to a life of hardship and sorrow." Sad days ahead, and maybe her spiritual undoing, too, for "sorrows are too apt to harden my heart against God."[14]

So it played out, especially for the younger women, whom we can read with many grains of salt if we want to—they were sheltered, they were spoiled, they knew little about life's challenges, and the like. All true, all very finger-wagging—and so? They were young, yes, and who better to say how the war was working itself into the lives of the young? It hardened young women, coarsened them; they lost a happy flexibility at the heart of being feminine. "What is happening to me?" was a question that youth made it freer and more urgent to ask, a frank question without an agenda and maybe without an answer, and so a portal for empathy. It also was the kind of question that occurred to a *writer*. Emma LeConte knew what she had lost because she believed in the feminine world of joy and goodness, and she knew her loss because she had been writing it. She read the story of her femininity slipping away each time she returned to her pages. A volatile and real self all the more dear as she saw it morphing into who knew what—the war's casualty or its trophy. *A hard school.* Women could be unsexed with shocking quickness by self-preoccupation or crude scheming, and war invited both. As a diarist, LeConte wrote herself into the midst of war's risks and attractions, watched herself do it, and sometimes when she reached for her girl's light heart it was not there.

Do we hear the women's words as a kind of wondering or as a kind of whining? If they are whining about their lot as fallen elites, they are easily put away and we can move on, sure once more about justice done. But if I hear them as wondering about themselves, I listen and wonder, too. I wonder about the war as something that raked over the self and femininity's promise about the sparks always flying upward. I read diarists dismayed at finding femininity emptied out and coming to find, by writing, that *I scarcely know myself*. I can make a guess or two about how this felt and what it means about the hollowing-out power of wartime, and I think, again, that empathy is about making the best guess I can about a life I do not admire. Grace Elmore lived the good life by standing on enslaved people's work and lives. She had the comforts and the license that were a rich, white woman's to enjoy until the Civil War brought it all up short. I know this like I know other things I have studied about this place and time—well enough to find the historical sources (Elmore's diary for one), size them up, and make an argument about the fall of the slave system. But as Elmore writes of herself changing in fearful ways in a falling-down world, she writes things that I must feel to understand. Things alive in the text, now hidden, now in your face. Things that stray from what we usually think of as *the point*. She wondered why she did not love John Rhett, the man who loved her even in the craziness of war. She feared that she was leaving unattended her faith in God and in her own feminine spirit, and that this was the surest sign that her self was draining away. She loved her sisters and mother, but she could not deny that the war had shown them to be naïve and frivolous. She was a person who did not like surprises, war was full of them, and it all added up to wondering if she was becoming less herself. The monster war was doing an impossible thing: making her someone "so different . . . from what I was by nature," the feminine nature which gave her the ability "to soften or to brighten life . . . to encourage sensibility or freedom of expression." The war was a vast realm all its own. And there she had learned to do something too terrible to have imagined—to repress herself: "To repress, till that has become stronger than nature."[15]

This was war becoming larger than life, swallowing up a life, Grace Elmore's. As war broke the charm of femininity in the pages of her own diary, she reached further inside herself to an older self, which, doubling back, she also wrote—write on! She found a melancholy girl who had felt most alive cherishing her own special sadness. "Sorrow was mine, and I could feel, tho' there were often sorrows, twas not like unto my sorrow. . . . There was even a charm in the feeling I was a mourner, all unknown" to the rest of the world. She had held her sorrows close—"not even my best loved guessed; there was a subtle pleasure that I was worthy to suffer, and that suffering brought me nearer to God." The war snuffed out this dear melancholy and with it the spirit she knew as herself. "Now, the fullness of heart has gone, and words are faint to express the utter deadness of life within me. And where is the use of words, when I've but to look in the face of my neighbor and see there the shadow that rests upon mine." I can take up these words with the idea of keeping Elmore away from me. I can say, from on high: Grace Elmore at last grew up and found out, as we all must, that our sorrows are like the sorrows of others. It's as easy for me to say this as it was hard for the women to find it out. Nothing sticks to me if I say it. I condescend, and I go free. But if I stay, *the fullness of heart has gone* are sticking words: the war and the self in one naked sentence. They are words that come as Elmore's hold on herself and her writing wavers. If I stay with her, I can know something of what she felt because all writers know it—where *is* the use of words? A sinking time for Elmore or any writer to doubt that words mattered in the times now, to see everyone speaking in the same way into the same emptiness. So Elmore wrote and found a changed self. A year later, she was more aphoristic about what had happened, but in a way more sad. Women's elastic spirit had toughened, and "suffering makes one very selfish. One is apt to be so taken up with their own woes, that they are more than apt to overlook the troubles of others." She was clear that she was speaking of herself.[16]

A lot of women did not doubt as much as Elmore doubted, or fall as hard. No diarist was Everywoman or even Everydiarist. Even so, Grace Elmore lived within a femininity that embraced all women of her class, more or less, and what she endured or enjoyed about herself, and what she feared losing, belonged in some measure to all of them, young and old. The war was making her selfish, she wrote, and it was not the old, self-absorbed pleasures planter-class women enjoyed without thinking (and without calling it self-ishness). The new selfishness came from "the world" breaking into this, into femininity's charmed realm. Femininity had promised: your sex is special (apart, above, pure) in the wide world; you live outside the world's common schemes. War stripped that promise and broke its spell: you have your mean interests and you know it. A charmless world without spirit, and Elmore was not liberated by any part of it. She did not even seem curious about it. She felt it as a dead loss of something dear and deep. Maybe we know, or can imagine, something of this feeling, too. We may know or fear or risk the shock of famil-iar comforts and lively joys sucked into the world's glare and gloom and see it again or anew in Grace Elmore. A former life vanishes with no consoling secret, only longing. We hold on to a new, poor self: *selfish.*

The naked emotions of war—times when tides of feeling took a woman's breath away—did these push back against the war or draw her into it? The question was another stopping place for the self in diaries, and diarists answered both ways and wondered. War's emotions were not something measured by loss or gain, like faith or femininity. Emotions were wildly inconstant, and they seduced. Was a diarist writing her way into self-knowledge or into blind self-preoccupation? A dilemma for a heroine in a novel; but unlike their heroines, diarists did not love their contradictions. Mary Chesnut took opiates when her heart beat too fast; many others took at least a lot of time to recover from a day's emotional ride. *Boisterous* was the word for what fascinated and frightened a diarist about the ride and the self it revealed. A string of numb days, then surging emotion rough and full of itself. Women wrote wanting less of it, and more.

"I *cannot make* myself feel anything," Pauline DeCaradeuc wrote late in 1864 after many days of feeling too much. Her diary entries seem to follow extremes of feeling, warm for days in a row, then cool. But now she thought the war was deadening her emotions, and it was more than that. Once upon a time, "I could never be lonely with my desk, my Bible & *my* copy of Tennyson." But in war she became lonely in company and lonely solo; she could do nothing right because she could not stir up any feeling. "I'm so slow, I can't flirt or affect, or be witty or amusing, or in fact *anything* like anybody else." The war might shrink in size through writing it, or it might grow larger. DeCaradeuc would face either, if she could only *feel*.[17]

Lucy Buck thought she felt too much, though she never wrote her emotions line by line as they played out. She let them roll on by and wrote about them later. So, wild emotions appear in placid paragraphs, one of the diary's neatest tricks. It was during a thunderstorm, that great world metaphor for stirred-up feelings, that Buck one day realized she had what it took to withstand war's exploding emotional world. She calmly quieted the small children in the thunder and lightning. She was pretty sure: "My nerves are growing stronger and I am, I hope wiser now." Buck had often looked to her pages for emotional lessons learned, and she can seem a little prim, quick to tie up her feelings and sell them short. She loved her friend Maggie Mohler because Maggie was at ease with her feelings, an amusing, conversational person with whom Buck was content to feel inferior. The love between them was a natural thing, "the influence of a stronger, brighter nature over a weaker, dimmer one." So she told it. But dressed up in calm words are some scenes where Buck was anything but dim. She now and again went "crazy" with war news, and when she went "upstairs to take a cry," she needed to be put together again by friends like Fannie who "danced me in her arms" until she came around. There were parties at two o'clock in the morning ("a wild time we have had of it") and a boisterous outing in a rowboat ("firing a salute from Dick's revolver to the party on shore"). Instead of dousing her crazy times, Buck's even voice was precisely the way for her to put emotions on the page for safekeeping. For display, even. That placid Lucy Buck was a young woman who could say "heigh-ho" to life in the midst of war does not seem likely on first reading her. But here she is: "My birthday—twenty-one years old today—free, white, and twenty-one! Heigh-ho!" A "dim" self? Maybe when she stood to one side and gave herself a sober look, or stood next to Maggie Mohler. But here was a woman who liked blasting away—read it!—with Dick's revolver.[18]

Buck was made wiser by war and by how she managed to write it, but Anna Green, reading her pages and looking for herself, believed the opposite was happening to her: "I am growing older, without growing wiser or happier or better. That is it. I am not growing wiser or better." The page did not lie. Green wondered aloud on the page more than Buck, and her thoughts rolled out through her pen with, it seems, little screening. Her emotions circled the strangeness of being herself, and how strange it was to realize, as she had in wartime, and in the course of her diary, that although "there is little variety in life . . . each ones life is new to himself." The wonderful pull of the self. Yet it might be a trap for the vain, this supposed novelty of each person. Self-absorbed and false. So Green sized up herself with a deliberate lack of vanity that seems to be a willful young writer's, but also something war-won and a kind of wisdom after all: "I am now twenty, tolerably good looking moderately intelligent and altogether mediocre." She marveled that this plain self could sometimes hold so "much pride and strong feeling." The war had brought dangers large and small, and writing had sharpened the dangers into truths. One truth was about herself and her family. Green loved them, and they had stayed together during the wild swings of the conflict. And yet she had discovered something false about them, "a thin mask of concord and happiness concealing our family feelings," and she came to see "how little real unity of feeling exists" among her closest kin. War had exposed fraught emotions, and her family's very survival brought their weaknesses to the surface, just as her own flaws were revealed when she wrote. Was she asking too much of her family? Was she worrying it too much by writing about it? Was the "want of harmony at home . . . the secret spring of all my unhappiness—Or is it selfishness—." The war might have created this puzzle for Green; she does not quite say so. It is just as likely that writing the war had shaken it free from an older corner of her mind.[19]

Anna Green wanted to be certain about the person she was, and it's easy for us to want this, too, from any diarist. We want reliable "sources" for our historical ventures because we take our cues from them. We know where we stand because *she* does. But no diarist was at peace with her emotions in war, and no diary kept pace with them. Writing furiously toward certainty, then away from it, is what we have. The self caught up in the rush of words, the self *as* a rush of words. It is the best we can know, and it is exactly right. The words race along the stolid page—the page that always wins when matched against the writer's struggling vision. The self we find will not be one the diarist was sure of, but the one she needed *now* for the hungry page. At the same time, her choices were not random, and the variety she chose from was not limitless: the first-draft selves *do* yield a woman we can know over time. Be patient. She embraces, denies, circles back, renews. In this, because of this, she is there.

Sarah Morgan sounded confident about her Confederate self one day in early 1863, and the strong, bell-like tones of her declaration have made it a favorite to quote: "I confess myself a rebel, body and soul. *Confess?* I glory in it!" She pronounced herself satisfied that Southerners and Northerners were "two distinct tribes," irreconcilable, and that "if I cant fight, being unfortunately a woman, which I now regret for the first time in my life, at least I can help in other ways" like sewing and giving men "words of encouragement." Passionate words, as if she were a patriotic woman in a pro-Confederate text, or the loving sister of a novel's citizen soldier. Which is to say, the sort of woman Morgan usually scorned or made fun of, the assertive, war-enhancing woman who talked politics loudly at dinners, the syrupy ingénue whose soft voice urged the boys toward death. The diary passage is oddly pumped up, too, when read in light of surrounding entries where Morgan, if not quite losing stamina for the war, was not writing with patriotic verve either. Her rebel-and-glory words are quotable in our hands, but in her pages they read as sheer experiment. She was chasing down some self, some place to land, and she was trying, for the space of those lines, to seem as if she had arrived. We latch onto her emphatic self because *we* want her to arrive.[20]

Most days, most pages, Morgan just lets the chase happen, and the driving power of her words is the closest she comes to an emotional destination. We ride along with her in the trip toward herself. Not long after the "rebel" passage are pages where Morgan, complaining and unsure, faces once again her nemesis—her intense emotional discomfort at being a lady in wartime who presided over parlor gatherings, smiled at the men, smiled through battlefield catastrophes, and worst of all, had to come up with *words of en-couragement*. True, sometimes she carried it off. But more often she froze up. Why? She struggled to say why, many times, and this time came up with the thought that "I can never rid myself of the feeling that I am made like glass." Literally transparent and breakable. She was not "speaking exaggeratingly, or figuratively. I feel as though made of clear transparent material." When this self emerged in company, as it always seemed to, she fell silent. Then she was further baffled when others took her to be a fascinating woman of mystery. They would not think so if they looked at her "fixedly, with their eyes on mine," for then they would easily see "all the workings of my brain." She was silent only because it was "useless to repeat what they must already see." If there was a mystery, it was the comic-bitter one of why so many people kept finding her "deep, O *so* deep!"[21]

Morgan lived the struggle with her glass-like self through the different pressures and temperatures of wartime, and she made it real—made it a matter of *self*—in the arms of her diary. Content with neither the diary's surfaces nor its depths but loving the play between them, saying that she wanted a peaceful mind, but all the time writing her way past it or around it: this was Sarah Morgan, exactly right. A religious scent wafts in from time to time, at least once with the intensity of prayer. She imagined herself a Catholic, someone able to "make a vow" in a public, showy way. One "wild, tempest beaten night" she did pray to God—to "help me be good!" and to no longer fight against life's great truth: "'What Will be, Will be' & 'What ever Is, is right.'" Maybe surfaces were enough. She made a kind of vow to embrace *whatever is, is right* by telling her diary self (her "soul") to note well "if I still cling to this faith in the darkness and trouble" of the life that awaited her. And a future self answered her on the same page in 1896 to affirm (a little somberly) that she had kept her vow: "Thank God! I have! through such Joy—through such sorrow as that poor little girl never dreamed of!" A good editor, this older Morgan, speaking as the soul of the younger one, alive to the moment thirty years before, answering, annotating, erasing nothing.[22]

Morgan went to New Orleans in late 1863, where Union forces were in charge. Her brother was there, a Unionist who knew his way among Yankees. She was deeply tired of wartime travels and ready to have a firm routine. She thought she could figure out the city's social dangers and political risks. It might even prove satisfying, another chance for whatever is to be right. "Kismet! it is destiny!" was her happy thought as she circled back to that place in her philosophy, or temper, or both. "What ever is, is right. And it is a dear, jolly old life, if one only knew how to take it."[23]

It was a devout wish, with some whistling in the wind, and it worked, though not for long. Life might be jolly, but she still had to learn the hard part—how to take it—and Morgan never cozied up to kismet. She was too restless, busy inside her diary (time and again, whatever was, was *not* right), pushing and pulling at the woman she might be. She denounced herself for being selfish, a diarist's try for a moment of refreshing penance, but when she again popped to the surface of her words and looked out at her pages, she was shocked at their lurid expanse. Instead of shaping the war to the scale of her life, her pages inflated her life into a vanity beyond all proportion. "I am so sick of me, me, everlasting Me! Cant I find a new subject? What an egotist! Poor Sarah! fighting against self-contempt and that of others, raging at her own deficiencies." It was the worst thing to see, page after page. She did not fit into jolly old life at all, and instead "I seem to pet myself, pamper myself, and stick Me up on a high altar above everybody else." She was a figure in her own religion, comic, glorious, "where I dress myself in rain-bow hues, burn incense and sing hymns of praise to my idol." A religion of herself, the writer, alone "with no one to disturb my devotions at my shrine, or to swell the chorus either." Too much emotion, too many moments of the self—it was the diary's trick on her, and for us readers it's the way in. Words come to the page always in play and make a self for the time being. It is never quite there, it is always there. Exactly right.[24]

LOOSENED SELVES

This is how it seems sometimes: outside of the diary's stations for the self, the hard and fleeting moments spent with faith and femininity and crazy emotion, the self simply drops into plain view on the page. Time after time, the good diary takes the woman away from berating herself, or preening herself, and away from the questions she half asked herself and even from those she pressed with all her might, and leads her back into the flow of days where we are, too, reading. Then, for writer and reader, the act of writing loosens up the self, and there it is.

It happened any day, any entry. A woman stood surrounded by her most ordinary words, and, surprise, the self came calling. It may be, as the writer William Maxwell said with gentle understatement, that "too many conflicting emotional interests are involved for life ever to be wholly acceptable." The writer keeps on writing because she wants to find a way out of this fix. Write, stay in the worded field, and look for ways to find, as Gertrude Thomas wrote, "what all lives are—a Romance." Some diarists found this in wartime by finding past selves. Women wrote the times *now*, thought about the times *then*, and folded them back into the *now*. Kate Stone spent a rainy day talking with her mother, escaping from wartime but really making the war fit inside her self. She listened to her mother's "tales of my babyhood" and for the first time learned that she had been the "delight of my Father, who thought me a wonderful little creature." She had always thought of herself as the misfit, "the ugly duckling of the whole family." Instead, "I was my Father's favorite," and now it could be told on the wartime page. Prewar selves were there in prewar letters and diaries, too, ghosts of their own kind, reread and taken to heart even as war put them at risk, many women destroying their writings rather than having them delivered up to the enemy. Catherine Edmondston was going through her old papers, came across some she thought she had already burned, and stopped to read them. She had changed so much in a dozen years! "My religious life does not cost me the struggles, the pangs, the unhappiness, it used {to}. . . . I do not smite and accuse myself as I then did." Emma Holmes took time to read, too, and was moved by "what treasures old letters are and my old journals," which let her "enjoy the society of my friends in hours of darkness and pain." An older self, brought into wartime and finding new life there. Women read from past pages and thought: so this is the way I am.[25]

Other times the loosened self comes to the page without this old-days destination, without any destination at all, and it feels like brushing up against something big, like the whole diary text itself and its way of not arriving. Readers make these times as much as the writer does. For the reader, it's like a found object, this self. The diarist did not hand it over; it might not have even appeared except for the reader. So a reader's diary, made from patience, crosses paths with a writer's diary, made from the distractions of getting from one place to another, or to nowhere in particular, and the self is in the merging of these two diaries. It might appear as she struggles to find the words the reader also is struggling to know; or as she inscribes words that come easily to her but are a reader's surprise. Or the diarist's self appears when her thoughts—and the reader's, too—take a certain shape from *right this minute* and come down at a sharp angle to what was just now said, or to what seems in need of saying. We are both rummaging around, so to say, and suddenly the self turns up. A straight up textual moment, the ragged text stepping through the familiar historical source to show itself. If you love the diary as a text, a forever first draft, this is what you love.

These moments fill this book, and many more have slipped away from me. Two more to close, then, and so make the diary's loosened selves a reader's stopping place but not an ending. One from Grace Elmore, young, single, and Christian, announcing herself amid layers of selves, and the other from Gertrude Thomas, busy as an anxious bee in northeast Georgia, flying from one station of the self to another. Elmore wrote a raw sort of self, because any one thing she decided to tell (God's silence, Cynthia's goodness, her own suicide if raped) was likely to be stripped away and followed by an equally painful doubt about it all, or by taking up a different thread altogether. She mourned her failed country. She burrowed into layers of possible futures, almost disappearing from sight. Or she flailed about, and the chips falling where they may were worked into the next day's revision. But then we read, in the dead aftermath of Sherman, without preface, "I believe I've lost all cowardice, & have become a brave woman." One of the plainest sentences Elmore ever wrote and one of the most certain. It seems to rise from the page to give it shape, and for the duration of this sentence Elmore's self flares up like nothing else around it. It holds the moment, and the jumbled stuff of the war, her war and mine, seems to settle around the clear thing it has to say.[26]

Gertrude Thomas wrote something similar, though it came to rest at a different angle. She traveled to Macon, Georgia, more than a year after the war's end, though wartime stayed at the front of Thomas's life well after April 1865. She made the trip alone, with no man accompanying her. She was "wonderfully strengthened from the trip." While traveling, she thought about what the still-fresh war added up to, and one thought was about herself: "My life has been a happy one.... I feel that my nature has expanded, my life has been ennobled and that today I am a matured woman.... I think and think boldly, I act—and act boldly." A new self, swept clean. Yet as she told of her travels with a wild branching out of details, driven and generous (as she almost always told things), Thomas loosened up a former self, the old blunt and embarrassing self, the woman who did crass things like blurting out in company her pleasure at the sudden pop of a champagne cork. How could she be so vulgar! Her bold Macon trip unspools on the page in the old eager-regretful style: she had once again embarrassed herself by asking too many questions of everyone; she was annoyed by ill-mannered men, including the mayor of Macon, but was unable to hide her annoyance as she should; she worried too much about her husband and children, and she worried about worrying. She admired people whose thoughtfulness and ease "added some trimming" to social affairs, and was again disappointed to find that she had not the talent. So as she told the story of her new self, her old self stayed in step, in fact swinging out into the lead. It was not *war over, new self*. The self was cannier than that, and more comfortable, too, with not arriving.[27]

So was her diary, or any diary. So the reader of diaries can choose to be. Thomas and Elmore found war-changed selves and said so. Told to the page one day: I am a new woman. And both diarists showed other familiar things about themselves as they wrote, so that we hear the new women speak in older voices from their well-known, unkempt pages. The diary holds both, but see: coming upon their self-stories, I put them into my story—my reader's story of Grace Elmore, Gertrude Thomas, and wartime selves. I read Elmore's new, courageous self as coming out of Sherman's wreckage, passing through the surrender, visible despite it all. There is a fresh light on her. But I see Thomas's new, active self coupled to a tenacious older one, and the light turns mellow. Telling the women this way is my best call, my best move toward empathy and their world, though I know it is possible to come up with different lightings. So it was for a diarist, too. Thomas kept her diary, she once said, "for my own consolation and the benefit of others." I can say pretty much the same thing about why I read diaries and want to write about them. Writing and reading are in the same world of guesswork, and it's a choice to stay with the text and not arrive, and so live with all the ends untucked. She wrote and I read as we both must—on, on!—wanting to tell, in need and in blindness, what diaries will faithfully show.[28]

When the big-picture war holds sway, the loosened moments of the diarist's self are among the easiest to skip over, to toss out as "trivial" or as against "readability." The moments read as non sequiturs or false starts, or missed opportunities. They often *are* these things, and though too much might be made of them, it is far easier to make not enough. Diaries gather and hold their power from all such finally unparsable moments, reminding us that while the war put them forward to be written, the diary kept them and so created them. War fades away, writing not as much. That is what makes lives larger than the war, and gives us the war not as it was but as we need to remember it. Don't lose the diary's text—or any text—in the happy din of historical sources. Don't shake it awake, and it will answer for all that it can and give us a woman as real as we are. The diarist comes close to herself, flees the scene, then returns, and we readers do the same. As real as that.

A Guide to the Diaries and Diarists

This is a brief guide for the curious to the outlines of each diarist's life and to basic information about her diary: dates covered, publication highlights, status of the original manuscript. The guide also serves as a bibliography of the twenty diaries that make up the primary sources of this book. As noted in the preface, nearly all of the diarists are well known to students of the Civil War and have been much cited in histories. All but one are represented here by the most often used scholarly published edition of their diaries. The exception is Gertrude Thomas, whose published diary is a fraction of the original; I used a typescript of the whole manuscript instead.

ELIZA FRANCES ANDREWS
(August 10, 1840–January 21, 1931)

Home and whereabouts during war: Washington, Wilkes County, Georgia. She moved between home and staying with kin in the southwest part of the state.

Single or married: Never married.

Notable: Her father was a prominent Unionist. She is the only diarist here to publish her own war diary; she kept a postwar diary, 1870–72, since published as well. She also published fiction and a student textbook on botany after the war.

Dates covered by diary: December 24, 1864–August 29, 1865. Daily, uniform entries.

Original manuscript: Probably destroyed after she edited it for publication in 1908.

Volume used here: *The Wartime Journal of a Georgia Girl, 1864–1865*, introduction by Jean V. Berlin (Lincoln: University of Nebraska Press, 1997). This is a reprint of *The War-time Journal of a Georgia Girl, 1864–1865* (New York: D. Appleton, 1908).

Percent of diary published: All of it, but with some close editing, according to Andrews, so that a Civil War story larger than her personal life takes center stage.

Diary's prior, partial, or other forms: Andrews's 1908 volume was first reprinted in 1960, with an introduction by Spencer King, who added an index. The introduction and index have been removed in the 1997 volume.

LUCY BRECKINRIDGE
(February 1, 1843–June 16, 1865)

Home and whereabouts during war: Grove Hill plantation, near Fincastle, Virginia.

Single or married: Married Thomas Jefferson Bassett in 1865.

Notable: She became ill ("typhoid") and died in 1865, six months after her diary ends.

Dates covered by diary: August 1862–December 1864. Short, consistent entries.

Original manuscript: It survives and is in the possession of her descendants.

Volume used here: *Lucy Breckinridge of Grove Hill: The Journal of a Virginia Girl, 1862–1864*, ed. Mary D. Robertson (Columbia: University of South Carolina Press, 1994).

Percent of diary published: All.

Diary's prior, partial, or other forms: The 1994 volume is the diary's first publication.

LUCY BUCK
(September 25, 1842–August 20, 1918)

Home and whereabouts during war: Bel Air plantation, near Front Royal, Virginia.

Single or married: Never married.

Notable: Like Cornelia McDonald's, Buck's home in the Shenandoah Valley often put her in the path of battle. She wrote letters to her brothers in the Confederate army that mirror some scenes in her diary.

Dates covered by diary: December 1861–April 1865 (she stopped writing between September 1864 and February 1865). Regular, medium-length entries.

Original manuscript: Most of the manuscript is in the possession of a descendant, but it has been winnowed. Pages from the original were given away to some of the recipients of a much-edited, privately published typescript in 1940. Another part of the manuscript, dated from May 28 to July 8, 1862, and catalogued as the "Diary of Lucy Buck of Front Royal, Va.," was a gift from other Buck descendants in 1953 to the Albert and Shirley Small Special Collections Library, University of Virginia, Charlottesville.

Volume used here: *Shadows on My Heart: The Civil War Diary of Lucy Rebecca Buck of Virginia*, ed. Elizabeth R. Baer (Athens: University of Georgia Press, 1997).

Percent of diary published: About 90 percent.

Diary's prior, partial, or other forms: There are two other print versions of the diary in circulation. Like the 1997 volume used here, they are incomplete, but in different ways. The first is the privately published volume mentioned above: *Diary of Lucy R. Buck, 1861–1865*, ed. L. Neville Buck (n.p.: privately printed, 1940). The other is *Sad Earth, Sweet Heaven: The Diary of Lucy Rebecca Buck during the War between the States*, ed. William Pettus Buck (Birmingham, Ala.: Cornerstone, 1973). This editor restored some passages cut from the 1940 version but deleted others. The editor of the volume used here pieced her version together from these two texts, plus what remains of the original.

MARY BOYKIN CHESNUT
(March 31, 1823–November 22, 1886)

Home and whereabouts during war: Mulberry plantation, near Camden, South Carolina. She spent some days in Chester, South Carolina, and Lincolnton, North Carolina.

Single or married: Married James Chesnut Jr. in 1840; no children.

Notable: Probably the best known of the diarists here, connected through her husband to the Confederacy's political elite. She was kin by marriage to diarist Grace Brown Elmore.

Dates covered by diary: February 18–December 8, 1861; late January–February 23 and early May–June 26, 1865. Scattered entries, with days sometimes filled in retrospectively.

Original manuscript: Mary Boykin Miller Chesnut Diary, Mary Boykin
     Miller Chesnut Papers, 1838–1981, South Caroliniana Library,
     University of South Carolina, Columbia.
Volume used here: *The Private Mary Chesnut: The Unpublished Civil War
     Diaries*, ed. C. Vann Woodward and Elisabeth Muhlenfeld (New York:
     Oxford University Press, 1984).
Percent of diary published: All.
Diary's prior, partial, or other forms: Chesnut revised and greatly added to
     her diary after the war, staying with the diary form. An edited, notably
     altered version of this text was published after her death by a friend
     and her associate: Isabella D. Martin and Myrta Lockett Avary, eds.,
     *A Diary from Dixie, as Written by Mary Boykin Chesnut, Wife of James
     B. Chesnut, Jr.* [. . .] (New York: D. Appleton, 1905). This volume
     became the basis for another, differently altered volume, Ben Ames
     Williams, ed., *A Diary from Dixie, by Mary Boykin Chesnut* (Boston:
     Houghton Mifflin, 1949). These volumes are discussed and Chesnut's
     expanded postwar text is recovered and published in full in *Mary
     Chesnut's Civil War*, ed. C. Vann Woodward (New Haven, Conn.: Yale
     University Press, 1981).

FLORIDE CLEMSON
(December 29, 1842–July 23, 1871)

Home and whereabouts during war: Pendleton, South Carolina, with travels
     to Bladensburg and Beltsville, Maryland.
Single or married: Married Gideon Lee in 1869.
Notable: She was the granddaughter of John C. Calhoun and the daughter
     of another prominent South Carolinian, Thomas Green Clemson.
Dates covered by diary: January 1863–October 1866. Sporadic entries,
     sometimes with gaps of weeks or months.
Original manuscript: Floride Clemson Diary, 1863–1866, Special Collections
     and Archives, Clemson University Libraries.
Volume used here: *A Rebel Come Home: The Diary and Letters of Floride
     Clemson, 1863–1866*, ed. Charles M. McGee Jr. and Ernest M. Lander Jr.,
     rev. ed. (Columbia: University of South Carolina Press, 1989).
Percent of diary published: All.
Diary's prior, partial, and other forms: First published in 1961. The 1989
     edition has a new introduction and includes some letters exchanged
     between Clemson and her mother.

PAULINE DeCARADEUC
(October 31, 1843–January 29, 1914)

Home and whereabouts during war: Montmorenci plantation, near Aiken, South Carolina.

Single or married: Married Jacob Guerard Heyward in 1866.

Notable: She was Roman Catholic and conscious of being outside the Protestant mainstream.

Dates covered by diary: June 1863–March 1867 and March 1875–March 1888. Sparse, intermittent entries, most falling between 1863 and 1867.

Original manuscript: Lost or destroyed.

Volume used here: A Confederate Lady Comes of Age: The Journal of Pauline DeCaradeuc Heyward, 1863–1888, ed. Mary D. Robertson (Columbia: University of South Carolina Press, 1992).

Percent of diary published: All.

Diary's prior, partial, or other forms: Around 1928, DeCaradeuc's daughter Maude Heyward transcribed the manuscript diary and had it privately printed for a targeted readership as *Journals of Pauline DeCaradeuc (Mrs. J. Guerard Heyward): 1863–1867, 1875–1888* (Savannah, Ga.: Braid & Hutton, [1928?]). This text became the basis for the 1992 volume, and a copy of it is at the Georgia Historical Society in Savannah.

CATHERINE ANN DEVEREUX EDMONDSTON
(October 10, 1823–January 3, 1875)

Home and whereabouts during war: Looking Glass plantation, Halifax County, North Carolina.

Single or married: Married Patrick Muir Edmondston in 1846; no children.

Notable: She stayed close to home throughout the war, managing the plantation; an eager reader of newspapers and an interrogator of wartime morality and politics.

Dates covered by diary: June 1860–January 1866. Regular, conversational entries.

Original manuscript: Catherine Ann Edmondston Diaries, North Carolina State Archives, Raleigh.

Volume used here: "Journal of a Secesh Lady": The Diary of Catherine Ann Devereux Edmondston, 1860–1866, ed. Beth G. Crabtree and James W. Patton (Raleigh, N.C., Division of Archives and History, 1979).

Percent of diary published: All.

Diary's prior, partial, or other forms: There is an earlier, greatly abridged volume, *The Journal of Catherine Devereux Edmondston*, ed. Margaret Mackay Jones (Mebane, N.C.: privately printed, [1955?]).

GRACE BROWN ELMORE
(November 19, 1839–June 3, 1912)

Home and whereabouts during war: Columbia, South Carolina.

Single or married: Never married.

Notable: After the war she taught students at a female academy, drafted a war novel, and wrote brief reminiscences, a few of which were published. She was related by marriage to Mary Chesnut.

Dates covered by diary: September 1861–September 1868, with entries dropping off rapidly after 1865. Long, introspective passages, though often days pass with nothing written.

Original manuscript: Grace Brown Elmore Diary, in the Grace Brown Elmore Papers, 1861–1872, Southern Historical Collection, University of North Carolina, Chapel Hill. For a time, and for unknown reasons, she made entries in two books, with overlapping dates: Book One, September 1861–January 1867 (only two entries after 1864: one each in 1866 and 1867); Book Two, September 1864–September 1868 (no entries in 1866).

Volume used here: *A Heritage of Woe: The Civil War Diary of Grace Brown Elmore, 1861–1868*, ed. Marli F. Weiner (Athens: University of Georgia Press, 1997).

Percent of diary published: All.

Diary's prior, partial, or other forms: The 1997 volume is the diary's first publication. Long after the war, Elmore rewrote parts of her diary in a "literary" style, probably with the aim of publishing it. Two slightly different versions of this text are in the Grace Brown Elmore Papers at the Southern Historical Collection and in the Grace Brown Elmore Diary Collection, South Caroliniana Library, University of South Carolina, Columbia.

ANNA MARIA GREEN
(September 26, 1844–February 9, 1936)

Home and whereabouts during war: Milledgeville, Georgia.

Single or married: Married Samuel Austin Cook in 1869.

Notable: After the war, she wrote and published a history of Baldwin County, Georgia. She lived longest into the twentieth century of all the diarists here.

Dates covered by diary: January 1861–December 1867; concentrated in 1864 and 1865. Episodic entries, some of them long, with gaps of weeks or months.

Original manuscript: Anna Maria Green Cook Diary, Anna Maria Green Cook Family Papers, 1845–1934, Hargrett Rare Book and Manuscript Library, University of Georgia, Athens.

Volume used here: *The Journal of a Milledgeville Girl, 1861–1867*, ed. James C. Bonner (Athens: University of Georgia Press, 1964).

Percent of diary published: About two-thirds. Most deletions are of poetry and letters Green had copied into her pages, but the editor also deleted conversations with her fiancé and some introspective moments.

Diary's prior, partial, or other forms: A typescript of the entire diary, made before editorial changes, is in the Anna Maria Green Cook Papers.

EMILY JANE LILES HARRIS
(June 6, 1827–March 26, 1899)

Home and whereabouts during war: Spartanburg District, South Carolina.

Single or married: Married David Golightly Harris in 1845; seven children.

Notable: She and her husband shared the work and management of their farm and its enslaved workers. Her entries are contained within a diary begun and continued by him.

Dates covered by diary: Emily's entries are between November 1862 and March 1865; David's extend from 1855 to 1870. Hers are brief, informative, sometimes reflective.

Original manuscript: Emily Liles Harris Journals, Manuscript Collection, Louise Pettus Archives and Special Collections, Winthrop University, Rock Hill, S.C. When the combined diaries were given to Winthrop, David's entries from 1855 to May 1859 were not included and are missing. All of Emily's entries are intact.

Volume used here: *Piedmont Farmer: The Journals of David Golightly Harris, 1855–1870*, ed. Philip N. Racine (Knoxville: University of Tennessee Press, 1990).

Percent of diary published: All.

Diary's prior, partial, or other forms: A microfilm of the manuscript diary, including the parts by David now missing, is at the Southern Historical Collection, University of North Carolina, Chapel Hill.

EMMA HOLMES
(December 17, 1838–January 22, 1910)

Home and whereabouts during war: Charleston, South Carolina, with some
nearby refugeeing.

Single or married: Never married.

Notable: She lived in a female household with her widowed mother and
sisters and was a reader of newspapers and an avid commentator on the
fortunes of war.

Dates covered by diary: February 1861–April 1866. Long entries, with gaps
filled in retrospectively, usually within a few days.

Original manuscript: The diary's three manuscript volumes are held by
two different libraries. Volume 1 (February 13–August 19, 1861) and
volume 2 (August 20, 1861–April 2, 1862): Emma Edwards Holmes
Diaries, 1861–1862, David M. Rubenstein Library, Duke University,
Durham, N.C. Volume 3 (April 3, 1862–April 7, 1866): Emma Holmes
Journal, in the Emma Holmes Papers, 1861–1971, South Caroliniana
Library, University of South Carolina, Columbia.

Volume used here: *The Diary of Miss Emma Holmes, 1861–1866*, ed. John
F. Marszalek (Baton Rouge: Louisiana State University Press, 1979).

Percent of diary published: About three-quarters.

Diary's prior, partial, and other forms: There are typescripts of the complete
diary, before editorial cuts, at the South Caroliniana Library and at
the Southern Historical Collection, University of North Carolina,
Chapel Hill.

ELIZABETH INGRAHAM
(September 14, 1805–September 12, 1872)

Home and whereabouts during war: Ashwood plantation, Claiborne County,
Mississippi, about thirty miles south of Vicksburg.

Single or married: Married Alfred Ingraham in 1827; six children.

Notable: Born in Cadiz, Spain, she was a sister of U.S. general George
Meade. She is the oldest diarist here, and probably the least known to
readers today.

Dates covered by diary: May 2–June 13, 1863. Long, daily entries, undertaken
as a record to inform the Ingrahams' three daughters who had been
sent out of harm's way when the Union army threatened.

Original manuscript: Unknown.

Volume used here: Elizabeth Ingraham, "The Vicksburg Diary of Mrs. Alfred Ingraham (May 2–June 13, 1863)," ed. W. Maury Darst, *Journal of Mississippi History* 44 (May 1982): 148–79.

Percent of diary published: Not clear. Darst, the editor, was not working from an original manuscript, but from a previously published text, noted below. He presented all of it, but calls the text a "portion" of the diary, which could imply that there is (or might be) more to it.

Diary's prior, partial, or other forms: First published as "Leaves from the Journal of a Lady, near Port Gibson, Mississippi, kept during Grant's march upon Vicksburg, via Grand Gulf and Port Gibson," in Sarah A. Dorsey, *Recollections of Henry Watkins Allen, Brigadier-General Confederate States Army, Ex-governor of Louisiana* (New York: M. Doolady, 1866), 397–420. Darst's 1982 version follows the Dorsey text, except for two one-word deletions. A subsequent volume restores the deletions and adds many new paragraph breaks: Elizabeth Meade Ingraham, Rebecca Blackwell Drake, Sue Burns Moore, and Sarah A. Dorsey, *Leaves: The Diary of Elizabeth Meade Ingraham: The Rebel Sister of General George Meade* ([Raymond, Miss.?]: Champion Hill Heritage Foundation, 2010).

MARY JONES
(September 24, 1808–April 23, 1869)
and
MARY SHARPE JONES MALLARD
(June 12, 1835–August 31, 1889)

Home and whereabouts during war: Mother and daughter, living at Montevideo plantation, Liberty County, Georgia.

Single or married: Mary married Charles Colcock Jones in 1830. Her daughter Mary, the youngest of three children, married Robert Quarterman Mallard in 1857; she gave birth to the fourth of their five children during the days recounted in the diary.

Notable: The Joneses owned three plantations in Georgia. Charles Colcock Jones was a Presbyterian clergyman widely known for advocating conscientious treatment of slaves. The diary is quoted in the memoir of Mallard's husband, Robert, *Plantation Life before Emancipation* (Richmond, Va.: Whittet and Shepperson, 1892).

Dates covered by diary: December 13, 1864–January 27, 1865. Closely seen, often dramatic entries.

Original manuscript: Missing or partially missing; it's unclear. There are two surviving manuscripts, one in the handwriting of Mary Jones and the other in Mary Mallard's. Jones's is the one that supplies the text used here, and it is clearly a copy; she incorporates her daughter's diary into hers. The extant diary in Mallard's handwriting covers only a week (December 13–20), and while it might be original, it can be inferred from internal evidence that there was also another, perhaps earlier, text. All surviving manuscripts are in the Charles Colcock Jones Papers, Louisiana Research Collection, Tulane University.

Volume used here: *The Children of Pride: A True Story of Georgia and the Civil War*, ed. Robert Manson Myers (New Haven, Conn.: Yale University Press, 1972), 1220–48. This much-used volume is primarily a collection of 1,200 wartime letters exchanged by the Joneses. The editor put the women's diary in its chronological place among the letters.

Percent of diary published: All.

Diary's prior, partial, and other forms: *Yankees A'Coming; One Month's Experience during the Invasion of Liberty County, Georgia, 1864–1865*, ed. Haskell Monroe (Tuscaloosa, Ala.: Confederate, 1959). This is the complete Jones diary, with some slight differences from the Myers version. Unlike Myers, Monroe fails to acknowledge the Mallard manuscript. A typescript apparently made for the publication of the Monroe volume, and consulted by Myers, is in the Jones papers at Tulane.

EMMA LeCONTE
(December 10, 1847–March 2, 1932)

Home and whereabouts during war: Columbia, South Carolina.

Single or married: Married Farish Carter Furman in 1869.

Notable: Youngest of the diarists here, she was fourteen years old when the war began. She kept a diary in later life, from 1900 until the year of her death.

Dates covered by diary: December 31, 1864–August 10, 1865; regular entries, descriptive and incisive.

Original manuscript: Lost or destroyed. There is a surviving manuscript in the diarist's handwriting, but it is a copy: Emma LeConte Diary, 1864–1865, Southern Historical Collection, University of North Carolina, Chapel Hill.

Volume used here: *When the World Ended: The Diary of Emma LeConte*, ed. Earl Schenck Miers, foreword by Anne Firor Scott (Lincoln: University of Nebraska Press, 1987).

Percent of diary published: All.

Diary's prior, partial, and other forms: The Works Progress Administration prepared a typescript of LeConte's handwritten copy in 1938, which was the basis for Miers's volume, first published in 1957. A new typescript of the diary, created in 1998 from the manuscript, is available electronically at "Documenting the American South," University Library, University of North Carolina, Chapel Hill: docsouth.unc.edu /fpn/leconteemma/leconte.html/.

CORNELIA PEAKE McDONALD
(June 14, 1822–March 11, 1909)

Home and whereabouts during war: Winchester, Virginia.

Single or married: Married Angus W. McDonald III in 1847; nine children.

Notable: Like Lucy Buck, she lived in the midst of the Shenandoah Valley campaigns, and more than any other diarist here, lived with Union troops on her property for weeks at a time.

Dates covered by diary: 1861–65, with most of the text focused on 1862–64. Detailed, narrative accounts.

Original manuscript: The original was either lost or destroyed. There is a manuscript, however, that is a composite text, as the diarist frankly acknowledges. She began her original diary in March 1862. In July 1863, fleeing Winchester, she lost portions of the 1862 diary. Not long afterward, she rewrote these months from memory in diary form. It is often hard to tell, but actual diary entries mainly cover days from late 1862 to the summer of 1863. In 1875, she wrote and included recollections of years both before and after those covered by the diary. Eight copies of this composite text were given to kin, and her modern editor worked from one of these, made available to her by the diarist's descendants.

Volume used here: *A Woman's Civil War: A Diary, with Reminiscences of the War, from March 1862*, ed. Minrose C. Gwin (New York: Gramercy Books, 2003).

Percent of diary published: All.

Diary's prior, partial, and other forms: *A Diary with Reminiscences of the War and Refugee Life in the Shenandoah Valley, 1860–1865, [by] Mrs. Cornelia*

McDonald, Louisville, Kentucky, 1875. Annotated and Supplemented by Hunter McDonald, Nashville, Tenn. (Nashville: Cullom & Ghertner, 1934). This is a version of the diarist's composite text, edited by her son, with many unflagged interventions.

EMILIE RILEY McKINLEY
(November [?], 1836–July [1?], 1864)

Home and whereabouts during war: Living (and working) at Mount Alban, Mississippi, about five miles east of Vicksburg.

Single or married: Apparently never married. Less is known about her than about any of the diarists here. She was working in a plantation neighborhood as a teacher of children, particularly in the family of Ellen Batchelor of Hoboken plantation.

Notable: She was born in Pennsylvania. Her diary entries come to a close in March 1864, and she died just four months later, probably in Connecticut where she is buried.

Dates covered by diary: May 18, 1863–March 18, 1864. Consistent entries, often long and filled with people and conversations.

Original manuscript: Emilie R. McKinley Diary, Missouri History Museum Archives, St. Louis.

Volume used here: *From the Pen of a She-Rebel: The Civil War Diary of Emilie Riley McKinley*, ed. Gordon A. Cotton (Columbia: University of South Carolina Press, 2001).

Percent of diary published: All.

Diary's prior, partial, and other forms: The 2001 volume is the diary's first publication.

SARAH MORGAN
(February 28, 1842–May 5, 1909)

Home and whereabouts during war: Baton Rouge and New Orleans, Louisiana.

Single or married: Married Francis Warrington Dawson in 1874.

Notable: She wrote and published essays and journalism after the war. More than most diarists' here, her diary has captured the interest of Civil War buffs. Various abridged versions of a 1913 edition prepared by her son are in circulation.

Dates covered: January 1862–June 1865. Five manuscript volumes; regular entries, often lengthy. She sometimes recaps a week or so. There is a sixth volume covering some weeks in 1865, but it is more a travel diary than a war diary and is not included in the current published volume.

Original manuscript: Sarah Morgan Dawson Diaries, 1862–1865, in the Francis Warrington Dawson Family Papers, David M. Rubenstein Library, Duke University, Durham, N.C.

Volume used here: *Sarah Morgan: The Civil War Diary of a Southern Woman*, ed. Charles East (Athens: University of Georgia Press, 1991).

Percent of diary published: All (manuscript vols. 1–5).

Diary's prior, partial, and other forms: Morgan read through her diary in the late nineteenth century, making some marginal notes. Her son intrusively edited a version after her death: Warrington Dawson, ed., *A Confederate Girl's Diary [by] Sarah Morgan Dawson* (Boston: Houghton Mifflin, 1913). This flawed volume was republished in 1960, with a new foreword and contextualizing notes by James I. Robertson Jr. as part of the Civil War Centennial Series from Indiana University Press. East's volume returned to the original manuscript, with new notes and an index.

EMMALA REED
(June 11, 1839–January 27, 1893)

Home and whereabouts during war: Anderson, South Carolina.

Single or married: Married George William Miller in 1867.

Notable: Her father was a locally prominent businessman, lawyer, and judge. She was locally renowned for her singing voice.

Dates covered by diary: March [?], 1865–April 7, 1866. Detailed, conversational entries.

Original manuscript: Emmala Reed journals, 1861–1866, Anderson County Museum, Anderson, S.C. The diaries before 1865 are brief and episodic.

Volume used here: *A Faithful Heart: The Journals of Emmala Reed, 1865 and 1866*, ed. Robert T. Oliver (Columbia: University of South Carolina Press, 2004).

Percent of diary published: All.

Diary's prior, partial, and other forms: There are microfilms of portions of manuscript diaries for 1851–52 and 1864, plus the years here, in the Emmala Thompson Reed Diaries, South Caroliniana Library, University of South Carolina, Columbia.

KATE STONE (SARAH KATHERINE)
(January 8, 1841–December 28, 1907)

Home and whereabouts during war: Brokenburn plantation, thirty miles
northwest of Vicksburg, Mississippi.

Single or married: Married Henry Bry Holmes in 1869.

Notable: Her widowed mother managed a large plantation herself. Of the
diarists here, Stone is the one who traveled farthest from her home
during the war, from Mississippi to Texas.

Dates covered by diary: May 1861–September 1868. Brief, regular entries.

Original manuscript: Lost or destroyed. There is a copied manuscript in
the diarist's handwriting, made in 1900: Kate Stone Diary, 1861–1868,
in the William Waller Carson Family Papers, Hill Memorial Library,
Louisiana State University, Baton Rouge; there also is a typescript.

Volume used here: *Brokenburn: The Journal of Kate Stone, 1861–1868*, ed. John
Q. Anderson, new introduction by Drew Gilpin Faust (Baton Rouge:
Louisiana State University Press, 1995).

Percent of diary published: All, or nearly all, of the diarist's handwritten copy;
Anderson, the editor, is not specific.

Diary's prior, partial, and other forms: The copied manuscript was out of
public view for years, with whereabouts unknown as late as 1995. It was
the text for the first published volume, *Brokenburn: The Journal of Kate
Stone, 1861–1868*, ed. John Q. Anderson (Baton Rouge: Louisiana State
University Press, 1955). This volume was reprinted in 1972, with a new
foreword by Anderson, and again in 1995 with Faust's new introduction.

ELLA GERTRUDE CLANTON THOMAS
(April 4, 1834–May 11, 1907)

Home and whereabouts during war: Augusta, Georgia.

Single or married: Married J. Jefferson Thomas in 1852; nine children.

Notable: The most persistent diarist here, with journals spanning forty-one
years, from privileged schoolgirl to advocate for women's suffrage.

Dates covered by diary: 1848–49, 1851–52, 1855–59, 1861–66, 1868–71, 1878–89.
Regular entries, often long and discursive, sometimes recapping a week
or so, in the volumes before 1870. Afterward, entries are infrequent.

Original manuscript: Ella Gertrude Clanton Thomas Diary, Ella Gertrude
Clanton Thomas Papers, David M. Rubenstein Library, Duke
University, Durham, N.C.

Volumes used here: Ella Gertrude Clanton Thomas Diaries, 1861–1868 (typescripts), Ella Gertrude Clanton Thomas Papers, David M. Rubenstein Library, Duke University, Durham, N.C.

Percent of diary published: The full text of the diary has never been published. The typescripts are complete and usually reliable but should be checked against the manuscript.

Diary's prior, partial, and other forms: About 30 percent of the complete diary was published as *The Secret Eye: The Journal of Ella Gertrude Clanton Thomas, 1848–1889*, ed. Virginia Ingraham Burr, introduction by Nell Irvin Painter (Chapel Hill: University of North Carolina Press, 1990).

A NOTE ON READING

A lot of reading over many years has inspired and provoked my thinking about slave-owning white women, the South, and keeping diaries. If I tried to write a true essay on reading there would be no end in sight. So I include here a few works by fellow historians that got me going or kept me going.

Anne Firor Scott's *The Southern Lady: From Pedestal to Politics, 1830–1930* (1970) was a new book when I first read it. It started me thinking about planter-class women who rethought themselves after the war, and it made me curious to know more about their world before it. Catherine Clinton's *The Plantation Mistress: Woman's World in the Old South* (1982) and Jane Turner Censer's *North Carolina Planters and Their Children, 1800–1860* (1984) showed how the antebellum years were more than a pedestal where elite women languished; they were years with work to do, and with satisfactions, too. In *James Henry Hammond and the Old South: A Design for Mastery* (1982), Drew Gilpin Faust brought the careers of planter-class men into the picture, and in *Mothers of Invention: Women of the Slaveholding South and the American Civil War* (1996), she saw slave-owning white women pushing back against the war before their men did. The debate was then joined by historians who see mistresses as having been more militant and less changed in wartime, including Jacqueline Glass Campbell, *When Sherman Marched North from the Sea: Resistance on the Confederate Homefront* (2003), Victoria Ott, *Confederate Daughters: Coming of Age during the Civil War* (2008), and Lisa Tendrich Frank, *The Civilian War: Confederate Women and Union Soldiers during Sherman's March* (2015).

Two histories in the front of my mind for seeing black and white women entangled in slavery, then in the war, are Laura F. Edwards, *Scarlett Doesn't Live Here Anymore: Southern Women in the Civil War Era* (2004), and Thavolia

Glymph, *Out of the House of Bondage: The Transformation of the Plantation Household* (2008). In both there is a keen sense of how race shaped personal life and how war shifted all the old horizons. White women off-balance and finding ways to plant their feet are also in LeeAnn Whites, *The Civil War as a Crisis in Gender: Augusta, Georgia, 1860–1890* (1995), and Jane Turner Censer, *The Reconstruction of White Southern Womanhood, 1865–1895* (2003). The emotional world of slavery and emancipation, and the moral atmosphere that surrounded the lives of women and men, before and during wartime, are in Stephen Berry, *All That Makes a Man: Love and Ambition in the Civil War South* (2003), Stephanie M. H. Camp, *Closer to Freedom: Enslaved Women and Everyday Resistance in the Plantation South* (2004), and Anya Jabour, *Scarlett's Sisters: Young Women in the Old South* (2007). In various ways, and from different places on the intellectual map, this interior world is in Franny Nudelman, *John Brown's Body: Slavery, Violence, and the Culture of War* (2004), Mark Noll, *The Civil War as a Theological Crisis* (2006), Jason Phillips, *Diehard Rebels: The Confederate Culture of Invincibility* (2007), and Michael E. Woods, *Emotional and Sectional Conflict in the Antebellum United States* (2014).

Then there are books on the era's diaries, writing and reading them. Diaries are pretty much captives of well-established literary genres in Edmund Wilson's *Patriotic Gore: Studies in the Literature of the American Civil War* (1962), where what diarists wrote overwhelms the fact that they wrote it in diaries, and in Daniel Aaron's *The Unwritten War: American Writers and the Civil War* (1973), where diaries are treated as embryonic memoirs or not quite novels. Both of these authors, though, got me thinking early on about diaries and where they belong in an intellectual world.

Some of the most thoughtful writing on the Civil War's female diarists is in the introductory remarks by the editors of the diaries here, including C. Vann Woodward on Mary Chesnut, Charles East on Sarah Morgan, Robert T. Oliver on Emmala Reed, Elizabeth Baer on Lucy Buck, and Minrose Gwin on Cornelia McDonald. Nell Irvin Painter's introduction to *The Secret Eye: The Journal of Ella Gertrude Clanton Thomas, 1848–1889* (1990) has a close hold on Thomas's diary keeping. But the diarist's kinswoman, Virginia Ingraham Burr, in her preface and editor's note, is not ready to let go; Painter and Burr should be read together. Kimberly Harrison, in *The Rhetoric of Rebel Women: Civil War Diaries and Confederate Persuasion* (2013), relies on most of the diarists in my pages here to argue how the rhetoric of diaries captured the Confederate cause. Clara Juncker, in *Through Random Doors We Wandered: Women Writing the South* (2002), reads diaries as a compelling kind of informal autobiography, which, in the Civil War, overcame some of the century's restraints on female self-expression; Juncker takes up Gertrude Thomas, Kate Stone, Mary Chesnut, and Sarah Morgan.

Jack P. Greene's introductory essay to his *Landon Carter: An Inquiry into the Personal Values and Social Imperatives of the Eighteenth-Century Virginia Gentry* (1965) mostly looks through the diary form instead of at it. Still, for me, this essay shook the diary free from the literary criticism that privileged fine arts writing, so the diary could breathe on its own. Two other essays that are introductions to published diaries do this and more. In *An Evening When Alone: Four Journals of Single Women in the South, 1827–1867* (1993), Michael O'Brien sees diaries as ranging through intellectual life and collecting fragments of it, perfect fragments not inferior to more finished sorts of texts. In *Princes of Cotton: Four Diaries of Young Men in the South* (2007), Stephen Berry prompted me to think about a diary as standing for the persistence of impermanent things, because it is so unabashedly alive in its moment. In *The Accidental Diarist: A History of the Daily Planner in America* (2013), Molly McCarthy writes about generations of Americans who crowded experimental feelings and cryptic observations into the tiny pages of their daily planners. Maybe they longed for more space, but maybe not.

NOTES

PREFACE

1. Margaret Atwood, *Negotiating with the Dead: A Writer on Writing* (Cambridge: Cambridge University Press, 2002), 178–79.

CHAPTER 1

1. The idea of broadcasting as distinct from dialogue as a way of communicating I borrow from John Durham Peters, *Speaking into the Air: A History of the Idea of Communication* (Chicago: University of Chicago Press, 1999). Thanks to Mickey Stamm for bringing this book to my attention.

2. Grace Brown Elmore, *A Heritage of Woe: The Civil War Diary of Grace Brown Elmore, 1861–1868*, ed. Marli F. Weiner (Athens: University of Georgia Press, 1997), [March?] 27, 1864, 59; David Golightly Harris [and Emily Liles Harris], *Piedmont Farmer: The Journals of David Golightly Harris, 1855–1870*, ed. Philip N. Racine (Knoxville: University of Tennessee Press, 1990), February 20, 1865, 364; Floride Clemson, *A Rebel Come Home: The Diary and Letters of Floride Clemson, 1863–1866*, ed. Charles M. McGee Jr. and Ernest M. Lander Jr., rev. ed. (Columbia: University of South Carolina Press, 1989), October 29, 1863, 44.

3. Sharon Marcus, *Between Women: Friendship, Desire, and Marriage in Victorian England* (Princeton, N.J.: Princeton University Press, 2007), 75.

4. Still the best place to start on empathy is Edith Stein, *On the Problem of Empathy*, trans. Waltraut Stein, 3rd ed. (Washington, D.C.: ICS Publications, 1889). Also helpful are Michael Slote, *Moral Sentimentalism* (New York: Oxford University Press, 2010); Margaret Urban Walker, "Ineluctable Feelings and Moral Recognition," *Midwest Studies in Philosophy* 22 (1998): 62–81; Nancy Sherman, "Empathy, Respect, and Humanitarian Intervention," *Ethics and International Affairs* 12 (1998): 103–19; Dominick LaCapra, *Writing History, Writing Trauma* (Baltimore: Johns Hopkins University Press, 2014), esp. 37–42; and Patricia Yaeger, "Consuming Trauma; or, the Pleasures of Merely Circulating," *Journal x* 1 (Spring 1997): 225–51.

5. Mary Boykin Chesnut, *The Private Mary Chesnut: The Unpublished Civil War Diaries*, ed. C. Vann Woodward and Elisabeth Muhlenfeld (New York: Oxford University Press, 1984), 33 (hereafter cited as Chesnut).

6. A good case for this point of view is in G. Thomas Couser, *Altered Egos: Authority in American Autobiography* (New York: Oxford University Press, 1989), esp. 159–62, 179–86.

7. Annie Dillard, *Encounters with Chinese Writers* (Middletown, Conn.: Wesleyan University Press, 1984), 4.

8. Michael Holroyd, *Basil Street Blues* (New York: W. W. Norton, 2000), 143.

9. As an editor of a diary myself, I know the tough decisions editors have to think about, though I had the relief of being able to publish an original text, uncut.

10. See the editorial comments in Ben Ames Williams, ed., *A Diary from Dixie, by Mary Boykin Chesnut* (Boston: Houghton Mifflin, 1949) (hereafter cited as Williams), and Warrington Dawson, ed., *A Confederate Girl's Diary [by] Sarah Morgan Dawson* (Boston: Houghton Mifflin, 1913) (hereafter cited as Dawson). Williams relied much on, and changed much in, Isabella D. Martin and Myrta Lockett Avary, eds., *A Diary from Dixie, as Written by Mary Boykin Chesnut, Wife of James Chesnut, Jr.* [...] (New York: D. Appleton, 1905). Dawson's volume was reprinted in James I. Robertson, ed., *A Confederate Girl's Diary [by] Sarah Morgan Dawson* (Bloomington: Indiana University Press, 1960), with Robertson supplying endnotes and a foreword but having no criticism of the Dawson volume's flaws.

My discussion is guided by the editorial notes of the two diarists' most recent editors, who worked with the original manuscripts and so were able to reconstruct the patterns of manipulations. For Chesnut, see Chesnut; and Mary Boykin Chesnut, *Mary Chesnut's Civil War*, ed. C. Vann Woodward (New Haven, Conn.: Yale University Press, 1981). For Sarah Morgan, see Sarah Morgan, *Sarah Morgan: The Civil War Diary of a Southern Woman*, ed. Charles East (Athens: University of Georgia Press, 1991) (hereafter cited as Morgan).

11. Williams, viii, ix, x; Dawson, xxxi.

12. Morgan, 5; Dawson, 1.

13. Williams, 1; Chesnut, February 18, 1861, 3. In the latter volume, Chesnut's editors call attention to (instead of obscuring) the uncertainty of the diary's opening date. They note that the February 18 date is the earliest one Chesnut inscribed, though given the entry's summary quality and comparatively neat appearance, it might have been written later, as a lead-in to the February 19 entry. This latter entry strikes them in its scrawling haste as the first of the "continuous entries" of the diary; see Chesnut, 7.

14. Anne Carson, *Decreation: Poetry, Essays, Opera* (New York: Alfred A. Knopf, 2005), 45.

15. Virginia Ingraham Burr, editor's note in *The Secret Eye: The Journal of Ella Gertrude Clanton Thomas, 1848–1889*, by Ella Gertrude Clanton Thomas (Chapel Hill: University of North Carolina Press, 1990), xi.

16. Emma Holmes, *The Diary of Miss Emma Holmes, 1861–1866*, ed. John F. Marszalek (Baton Rouge: Louisiana State University Press, 1979), xxxii, xxxiii.

17. Anna Maria Green, *The Journal of a Milledgeville Girl, 1861–1867*, ed. James C. Bonner (Athens: University of Georgia Press, 1964), 6 (hereafter cited as Green); Anna Green (Cook) Diary (typescript), January 30, 1864, MS pp. 67–68, Hargrett Rare Book and Manuscript Library, University of Georgia, Athens; Green, January 30, 1864, 46–47.

Gender plays a role here—a male editor is taking charge of a young female diarist. Green's editor calls her "Anna Maria" throughout his introduction. Kate Stone's first editor also stays on a first-name basis. Andrews's first editor seems unsure what to call her: she is sometimes "Miss Andrews" and other times "Fannie."

18. See Elizabeth Ingraham, "The Vicksburg Diary of Mrs. Alfred Ingraham (May 2–June 13, 1863," ed. W. Maury Darst, *Journal of Mississippi History* 44 (May 1982): 148–79. The diary appears as an appendix in Sarah A. Dorsey, *Recollections of Henry Watkins Allen, Brigadier-General Confederate States Army, Ex-governor of Louisiana* (New York: M. Doolady, 1866), 397–420. Dorsey writes that "as a favor" she has been "permitted to extract these pages," suggesting that there might be more (397).

19. Pauline DeCaradeuc Heyward, *A Confederate Lady Comes of Age: The Journal of Pauline DeCaradeuc Heyward, 1863–1888*, ed. Mary D. Robertson (Columbia: University of South Carolina Press, 1992), xiii–xiv.

20. My description of the various texts draws on the archival notes for the Mary Jones and Mary Sharpe Jones Mallard Diary, Charles Colcock Jones Collection, Manuscripts Department, Howard-Tilton Library, Tulane University.

21. Haskell Monroe, ed., *Yankees A'Coming: One Month's Experience during the Invasion of Liberty County, Georgia, 1864–1865* (Tuscaloosa, Ala.: Confederate, 1959), 11.

22. Emma LeConte, *When the World Ended: The Diary of Emma LeConte*, ed. Earl Schenck Miers, foreword by Anne Firor Scott (Lincoln: University of Nebraska Press, 1987); this volume was originally published by Miers in 1957 with the same title by Oxford University Press. LeConte's comment on her copying is quoted by Scott in her 1987 foreword (viii). Miers's remarks are from his introduction (xxxi, xxx). For the deleted passage where LeConte notes trimming her January 2 entry, see Emma LeConte, "A Journal, Kept by Emma Florence LeConte, from Dec. 31, 1864 to Aug. 6, 1865 [*sic*; the final entry is August 10], Written in Her Seventeenth Year and Containing a Detailed Account of the Burning of Columbia, by One Who Was an Eyewitness," typed transcript prepared by the Historical Records Survey of the Works Progress Administration, May 1938, 3, accessed March 9, 2016, http://docsouth.unc.edu/fpn /leconteemma/leconte.html.

23. Eliza Frances Andrews, *The War-time Journal of a Georgia Girl, 1864–1865* (Lincoln: University of Nebraska Press, 1997), 6; the "hateful old striped rag" quote is on p. 219. For introductory remarks, see Jean V. Berlin, introduction to Andrews, *War-time Journal*, vi, and see Eliza Frances Andrews, *The War-time Journal of a Georgia Girl, 1864–1865*, introduction by Spencer Bidwell King (Macon, Ga.: Ardivan Press, 1960), viii.

24. See editor Minrose Gwin's introduction to Cornelia Peake McDonald, *A Woman's Civil War: A Diary, with Reminiscences of the War, from March 1862*, ed. Minrose C. Gwin (New York: Gramercy Books, 2003), and the diarist's own brief account of her editing, where she says that she tried to make the pages she rewrote seem "as nearly as possible like the original" (21).

25. [Cornelia Peake McDonald], *A Diary with Reminiscences of the War and Refugee Life in the Shenandoah Valley, 1860–1865, [by] Mrs. Cornelia McDonald, Louisville, Kentucky, 1875. Annotated and Supplemented by Hunter McDonald, Nashville, Tenn.* (Nashville: Cullom & Ghertner, 1934), ix.

26. Alice Munro, *The View from Castle Rock* (New York: Alfred A. Knopf, 2006), 347.

1. Emma Holmes, *The Diary of Miss Emma Holmes, 1861–1866*, ed. John F. Marszalek (Baton Rouge: Louisiana State University Press, 1979), June 3, 1861, 53 (hereafter cited as Holmes); Pauline DeCaradeuc Heyward, *A Confederate Lady Comes of Age: The Journal of Pauline DeCaradeuc Heyward, 1863–1888*, ed. Mary D. Robertson (Columbia: University of South Carolina Press, 1992), June 18, 1864, 50 (hereafter cited as DeCaradeuc).

2. Holmes, March 4, 1865, 398–412; Ella Gertrude Clanton Thomas Diaries, 1861–1868 (typescripts), Ella Gertrude Clanton Thomas Papers, David M. Rubenstein Rare Books and Manuscript Library, Duke University, Durham, N.C., September 23 and 30, 1864, 3–6 (hereafter cited as Thomas).

3. Thomas, September 22, 1864, 4, and November 1, 1868, 18; Sarah Morgan, *Sarah Morgan: The Civil War Diary of a Southern Woman*, ed. Charles East (Athens: University of Georgia Press, 1991), May 24, 1863, 494 (hereafter cited as Morgan); Floride Clemson, *A Rebel Come Home: The Diary and Letters of Floride Clemson, 1863–1866*, ed. Charles M. McGee Jr. and Ernest M. Lander Jr., rev. ed. (Columbia: University of South Carolina Press, 1989), May 1, 1865, 83 (hereafter cited as Clemson); Mary Boykin Chesnut, *The Private Mary Chesnut: The Unpublished Civil War Diaries*, ed. C. Vann Woodward and Elisabeth Muhlenfeld (New York: Oxford University Press, 1984), March 11, 1861, 34 (hereafter cited as Chesnut).

4. George Steiner, *Real Presences: Is There Anything in What We Say?* (London: Faber and Faber, 1989), 40; Thomas, December 31, 1863, 125.

5. Catherine Ann Devereux Edmondston, *"Journal of a Secesh Lady": The Diary of Catherine Ann Devereux Edmondston, 1860–1866*, ed. Beth G. Crabtree and James W. Patton (Raleigh, N.C.: Division of Archives and History, 1979), headnote entry "1860," 1 (hereafter cited as Edmondston); Anna Maria Green, *The Journal of a Milledgeville Girl, 1861–1867*, ed. James C. Bonner (Athens: University of Georgia Press, 1964), January 10, 1863, 28 (hereafter cited as Green); Eliza Frances Andrews, *The War-time Journal of a Georgia Girl, 1864–1865*, introduction by Jean V. Berlin (Lincoln: University of Nebraska Press, 1997), 4 (hereafter cited as Andrews); Lucy Breckinridge, *Lucy Breckinridge of Grove Hill: The Journal of a Virginia Girl, 1862–1864*, ed. Mary D. Robertson (Columbia: University of South Carolina Press, 1994), August 11, 1862, 25 (hereafter cited as Breckinridge); Edmondston, headnote entry "1860," 1. In addition to Edmondston, several of the women in this study had kept diaries on and off before the war: Reed, Thomas, Elmore, Holmes, perhaps others.

6. Edmondston, July 8, 1863, 424; Holmes, July 9, 1863, 277–78.

7. Edmondston, July 7, 1863, 423; Thomas, September 17, 1864, 195–96; Edmondston, May 25, 1864, 566, and June 11, 1864, 574; Thomas, September 17, 1864, 196.

8. Andrews, May 7, 1865, 227; Thomas, October 22, 1864, 8; Emmala Reed, *A Faithful Heart: The Journals of Emmala Reed, 1865 and 1866*, ed. Robert T. Oliver (Columbia: University of South Carolina Press, 2004), "March 1865," 3 (hereafter cited as Reed).

9. Lucy Rebecca Buck, *Shadows on My Heart: The Civil War Diary of Lucy Rebecca Buck of Virginia*, ed. Elizabeth R. Baer (Athens: University of Georgia Press, 1997), February 13, 1865, 310 (hereafter cited as Buck); DeCaradeuc, June 18, 1864, 50; Grace Brown Elmore, *A*

Heritage of Woe: The Civil War Diary of Grace Brown Elmore, 1861–1868, ed. Marli F. Weiner (Athens: University of Georgia Press, 1997), March 22, 1867, 138 (hereafter cited as Elmore).

10. Thomas, December 31, 1865, 98.

11. Breckinridge, August 11, 1862, 25; Thomas, June 28, 1864, 155; Edmondston, October 11, 1862, 272.

12. David Golightly Harris [and Emily Liles Harris], *Piedmont Farmer: The Journals of David Golightly Harris, 1855–1870*, ed. Philip N. Racine (Knoxville: University of Tennessee Press, 1990), February 21, 1863, 277 (hereafter cited as Harris). "Superfine" was a top grade of cotton.

13. Thomas, September 17, 1864, 201; Green, December 31, 1867, 128; Clemson, October 24, 1866, 116.

14. Elmore, September 30, 1864, 74; Reed, January 16, 1866, 156; Holmes, June 18, 1864, 355.

15. Thomas, December 27, 1864, 32; Edmondston, January 23, 1863, 348.

16. Edmondston's manuscript volume 3, beginning in February 1863, is embossed "P. M. Edmondston" (see Edmondston, 349), and Thomas's manuscript volume 9, beginning in September 1863, is inscribed "Account Book of J. Jefferson Thomas" (see Thomas, September 22, 1863, 2).

17. Cornelia Peake McDonald, *A Woman's Civil War: A Diary, with Reminiscences of the War, from March 1862*, ed. Minrose C. Gwin (New York: Gramercy Books, 2003), May 15, 1863, 149 (hereafter cited as McDonald).

18. Holmes, April 7, 1865, 432; Edmondston, April 11, 1865, 692.

19. Edmondston, April 11, 1865, 692.

20. Thomas, December 31, 1863, 129; Anna Green (Cook) Diary (typescript), January 30, 1864, MS p. 68, Hargrett Rare Book and Manuscript Library, University of Georgia, Athens.

21. McDonald, September 27, 1862, 76; Buck, October 29, 1863, 251.

22. Thomas, August 27, 1864, 186; Holmes, January 23, 1865, 393; Morgan, June 26, 1863, 513; Thomas, March 29, 1865, 53; Emma LeConte, *When the World Ended: The Diary of Emma LeConte*, ed. Earl Schenck Miers, foreword by Anne Firor Scott (Lincoln: University of Nebraska Press, 1987), May 17, 1865, 99 (hereafter cited as LeConte); Reed, February 13, 1866, 204; Sarah Katherine Stone, *Brokenburn: The Journal of Kate Stone, 1861–1868*, ed. John Q. Anderson, new introduction by Drew Gilpin Faust (Baton Rouge: Louisiana State University Press, 1995), August 25, 1862, 140, and April 25, 1863, 199 (hereafter cited as Stone).

23. Holmes, October 18, 1865, 474–75.

24. Edmondston, May 7, 1865, 708; LeConte, May 28, 1865, 105; DeCaradeuc, January 30, 1864, 35, and August 19, 1866, 105.

25. Chesnut, March 6, 1861, 25.

26. Stone, September 28, 1868, 378; Clemson, October 24, 1866, 116; Andrews, August 29, 1865, 384 (manuscript page torn from book at this point); Breckinridge, December 25, 1864, 221; Buck, April 15, 1865, 320; DeCaradeuc, March 28, 1867, 116; Harris, March 12, 1865, 367; Holmes, April 7, 1866, 489; Mary Jones and Mary Sharpe Jones Mallard Diary, in *The Children of Pride: A True Story of Georgia and the Civil War*, ed. Robert Manson Myers (New Haven, Conn.: Yale University Press, 1972), 1220–48, January 27, 1865, 1248; Elizabeth Ingraham, "The Vicksburg Diary of Mrs. Alfred Ingraham (May 2–June 13,

1863)," ed. W. Maury Darst, *Journal of Mississippi History* 44 (May 1982): 148–79, June 13, 1863, 179.

27. Green, June 16, 1865, 84; Holmes, August 15, 1865, 466; Mary Boykin Chesnut, *Mary Chesnut's Civil War*, ed. C. Vann Woodward (New Haven, Conn.: Yale University Press, 1981), June 3, 1862, 359; Holmes, August 15, 1865, 466. For Elmore, see Elmore, June 15, 1867, 150–54. Chesnut's fiction ultimately was published as *Two Novels by Mary Chesnut*, ed. Elisabeth Muhlenfeld (Charlottesville: University Press of Virginia, 2002).

28. Holmes, October 31, 1863, 319; Chesnut, February 23, 1865, 233.

29. Clemson, May 1, 1865, 83.

30. Morgan, May 24, 1863, 495 (see 455–60 for the account of her Madisonville stay); Green, April 13, 1863, 33; Edmondston, June 26, 1862, 201; Morgan, May 24, 1863, 494.

31. Annie Dillard, *The Writing Life* (New York: Harper & Row, 1989), 56–57.

32. Morgan, May 24, 1863, 494, and August 7, 1863, 532–33.

33. Thomas, December 31, 1865, 98.

34. Breckinridge, December 21, 1864, 220.

CHAPTER 3

1. Catherine Ann Devereux Edmondston, *"Journal of a Secesh Lady": The Diary of Catherine Ann Devereux Edmondston, 1860–1866*, ed. Beth G. Crabtree and James W. Patton (Raleigh, N.C.: Division of Archives and History, 1979), May 1, 1863, 385 (hereafter cited as Edmondston).

2. David Golightly Harris [and Emily Liles Harris], *Piedmont Farmer: The Journals of David Golightly Harris, 1855–1870*, ed. Philip N. Racine (Knoxville: University of Tennessee Press, 1990), December 31, 1864, 355 (hereafter cited as Harris). On empathy being a response to foreignness, see Edith Stein, *On the Problem of Empathy*, trans. Waltraut Stein, 3rd ed. (Washington, D.C.: ICS Publications, 1889), xviii, 10–12.

3. Cornelia Peake McDonald, *A Woman's Civil War: A Diary, with Reminiscences of the War, from March 1862*, ed. Minrose C. Gwin (New York: Gramercy Books, 2003), June 14, 1863, 158 (hereafter cited as McDonald); Emma LeConte, *When the World Ended: The Diary of Emma LeConte*, ed. Earl Schenck Miers, foreword by Anne Firor Scott (Lincoln: University of Nebraska Press, 1987), February 15, 1865, 32 (hereafter cited as LeConte); Mary Boykin Chesnut, *The Private Mary Chesnut: The Unpublished Civil War Diaries*, ed. C. Vann Woodward and Elisabeth Muhlenfeld (New York: Oxford University Press, 1984), early May 1865, 237 (hereafter cited as Chesnut); Emma Holmes, *The Diary of Miss Emma Holmes, 1861–1866*, ed. John F. Marszalek (Baton Rouge: Louisiana State University Press, 1979), April 7, 1866, 488; October 17, 1863, 314; and November 21, 1863, 325 (hereafter cited as Holmes).

4. Ella Gertrude Clanton Thomas Diaries, 1861–1868 (typescripts), Ella Gertrude Clanton Thomas Papers, David M. Rubenstein Rare Books and Manuscript Library, Duke University, Durham, N.C., September 22, 1864, 3 (hereafter cited as Thomas); Grace Brown Elmore, *A Heritage of Woe: The Civil War Diary of Grace Brown Elmore, 1861–1868*, ed. Marli F. Weiner (Athens: University of Georgia Press, 1997), January 4, 1865, 88 (hereafter cited as Elmore).

5. Floride Clemson, *A Rebel Come Home: The Diary and Letters of Floride Clemson, 1863–1866*, ed. Charles M. McGee Jr. and Ernest M. Lander Jr., rev. ed. (Columbia: University of South Carolina Press, 1989), January 1, 1864, 47 (hereafter cited as Clemson); Eliza Frances Andrews, *The War-time Journal of a Georgia Girl, 1864–1865*, introduction by Jean V. Berlin (Lincoln: University of Nebraska Press, 1997), April 1, 1865, 124 (hereafter cited as Andrews); Lucy Rebecca Buck, *Shadows on My Heart: The Civil War Diary of Lucy Rebecca Buck of Virginia*, ed. Elizabeth R. Baer (Athens: University of Georgia Press, 1997), July 18, 1864, 291 (hereafter cited as Buck).

6. Doris Garraway, *The Libertine Colony: Creolization in the Early French Caribbean* (Durham, N.C.: Duke University Press, 2005), 293.

7. Sarah Katherine Stone, *Brokenburn: The Journal of Kate Stone, 1861–1868*, ed. John Q. Anderson, new introduction by Drew Gilpin Faust (Baton Rouge: Louisiana State University Press, 1995), March 24, 1863, 185 (hereafter cited as Stone).

8. Stone, March 24, 1863, 184–85.

9. Mary Jones and Mary Sharpe Jones Mallard Diary, in *The Children of Pride: A True Story of Georgia and the Civil War*, ed. Robert Manson Myers (New Haven, Conn.: Yale University Press, 1972), 1220–48, December 17, 1864, 1229 (hereafter cited as Jones/Mallard).

10. Examples of this are legion. Here are two, not to pillory these historians for something commonly done: "'I am not willing for her to stay on her terms,' Matthews huffed in his diary." Stephen V. Ash, *Middle Tennessee Society Transformed, 1860–1870: War and Peace in the Upper South* (Baton Rouge: Louisiana State University Press, 1988), 129. "Hissing, as one planter did, that they would rather see their slaves dead." Susan Eva O'Donovan, *Becoming Free in the Cotton South* (Cambridge, Mass.: Harvard University Press, 2007), 114. (She also uses "sputter" on p. 114 and "fume" on p. 104.)

11. Sonia Kruks, *Retrieving Experience: Subjectivity and Recognition in Feminist Politics* (Ithaca, N.Y.: Cornell University Press, 2001), 57; Holmes, July 18, 1863, 284; Buck, June 12, 1863, 213.

12. Sarah Morgan, *Sarah Morgan: The Civil War Diary of a Southern Woman*, ed. Charles East (Athens: University of Georgia Press, 1991), April 22, 1863, 487 (hereafter cited as Morgan).

13. Andrews, May 3, 1865, 200; Holmes, March 4, 1865, 411.

14. Jones/Mallard, December 15, 1864, 1223; Elizabeth Ingraham, "The Vicksburg Diary of Mrs. Alfred Ingraham (May 2–June 13, 1863)," ed. W. Maury Darst, *Journal of Mississippi History* 44 (May 1982): 148–79, May [5?], 1863, 152 (hereafter cited as Ingraham).

15. Russell Banks, "In Response to James McPherson's Reading of *Cloudsplitter*," in *Novel History: Historians and Novelists Confront America's Past (and Each Other)*, ed. Mark Carnes (New York: Simon & Schuster, 2001), 67–76, 72.

16. Andrews, March 8, 1865, 111.

17. Stone, June 19, 1863, 222, and April 21, 1863, 191. For Chesnut, see Chesnut, February 16–23, 1865, 227–35. For DeCaradeuc, see Pauline DeCaradeuc Heyward, *A Confederate Lady Comes of Age: The Journal of Pauline DeCaradeuc Heyward, 1863–1888*, ed. Mary D. Robertson (Columbia: University of South Carolina Press, 1992), October 15, 1864, 59–60 (hereafter cited as DeCaradeuc). For Holmes, see Holmes, January 31, 1863, 228.

18. Harris, January 16, 1865, 360; Clemson, January 8, 1865, 74; Emmala Reed, *A Faithful Heart: The Journals of Emmala Reed, 1865 and 1866*, ed. Robert T. Oliver (Columbia: University of South Carolina Press, 2004), January 14, 1866, 151 (hereafter cited as Reed).

19. Lucy Breckinridge, *Lucy Breckinridge of Grove Hill: The Journal of a Virginia Girl, 1862–1864*, ed. Mary D. Robertson (Columbia: University of South Carolina Press, 1994), June 5, 1864, 191 (hereafter cited as Breckinridge); Ingraham, May 8, 1863, 160.

20. McDonald, February 20, 1863, 123; Ingraham, June 5, 1863, 176; Breckinridge, December 19, 1863, 167; Morgan, April 22, 1863, 483.

21. Ingraham, May 8, 1863, 160; Thomas, July 30, 1864, 178.

22. Stone, April 15, 1863, 189; Edmondston, February 25, 1865, 671–72. For an example of the lace and trimmings, see Morgan, August 13, 1862, 213.

23. Anna Maria Green, *The Journal of a Milledgeville Girl, 1861–1867*, ed. James C. Bonner (Athens: University of Georgia Press, 1964), November 25, 1864, 62; Stone, April 27, 1863, 202. For DeCaradeuc's blue glasses, see DeCaradeuc, February 18, 1865, 68.

24. McDonald, February 19, 1863, 122; Holmes, March 4, 1865, 403; DeCaradeuc, February 18, 1865, 67; Jones/Mallard, December 21, 1864, 1232.

25. Morgan, August 13, 1862, 213, and August 17, 1862, 215.

26. Morgan, July 20, 1862, 166–67.

27. Clemson, April 21, 1865, 81; DeCaradeuc, April 26, 1865, 74; Thomas, April 20, 1865, 56; Harris, December 31, 1864, 355; Chesnut, February 23, 1865, 234, and May 15, 1865, 246; Morgan, June 15, 1865, 611.

28. LeConte, April [20?], 1865, 90; DeCaradeuc, May 15, 1865, 76; Edmondston, April 6, 1865, 689; Reed, May 3, 1865, 72.

29. DeCaradeuc, May 15, 1865, 76; Elmore, March 1, 1865, 106; Edmondston, April 16, 1865, 695.

30. Marc Bloch, *The Historian's Craft* (New York: Vintage, 1953), 64.

31. Thomas, May 1, 1865, 57–60; May 8, 1865, 67–69; and December 31, 1865, 98.

32. Reed, May 3, 1865, 72; December 1865, 305; and January 1, 1866, 134.

33. Thomas, March 29, 1865, 50; Reed, April 20, 1865, 45, and February 16, 1866, 204; Edmondston, May 1, 1863, 385.

34. Holmes, October 30, 1865, 478; Breckinridge, July 23, 1864, 200; Elmore, October 27, 1867, 158; Morgan, February 23, 1863, 430–31.

CHAPTER 4

1. Emma LeConte and Eliza Andrews both say they removed love talk from their diaries. Emma Holmes implies that she did, and Sarah Morgan thought that she should.

2. Tessa Hadley, *The Master Bedroom* (London: Jonathan Cape, 2007), 187.

3. Lucy Rebecca Buck, *Shadows on My Heart: The Civil War Diary of Lucy Rebecca Buck of Virginia*, ed. Elizabeth R. Baer (Athens: University of Georgia Press, 1997), July 22, 1863, 236 (hereafter cited as Buck).

4. Buck, July 22, 1863, 236.

5. Sarah Katherine Stone, *Brokenburn: The Journal of Kate Stone, 1861–1868*, ed. John Q. Anderson, new introduction by Drew Gilpin Faust (Baton Rouge: Louisiana State University Press, 1995), October 30, 1863, 251 (hereafter cited as Stone). For the others,

see Buck, January 3, 1864, 262; Pauline DeCaradeuc Heyward, *A Confederate Lady Comes of Age: The Journal of Pauline DeCaradeuc Heyward, 1863–1888*, ed. Mary D. Robertson (Columbia: University of South Carolina Press, 1992), February 18, 1865, 68 (hereafter cited as DeCaradeuc); Mary Jones and Mary Sharpe Jones Mallard Diary, in *The Children of Pride: A True Story of Georgia and the Civil War*, ed. Robert Manson Myers (New Haven, Conn.: Yale University Press, 1972), 1220–48, December 22, 1864, 1233 (hereafter cited as Jones/Mallard).

6. Catherine Ann Devereux Edmondston, *"Journal of a Secesh Lady": The Diary of Catherine Ann Devereux Edmondston, 1860–1866*, ed. Beth G. Crabtree and James W. Patton (Raleigh, N.C.: Division of Archives and History, 1979), February 26, 1865, 672, and March 15, 1865, 679 (hereafter cited as Edmondston); Ella Gertrude Clanton Thomas, *The Secret Eye: The Journal of Ella Gertrude Clanton Thomas, 1848–1889*, ed. Virginia Ingraham Burr (Chapel Hill: University of North Carolina Press, 1990), late September 1862, 209; Ella Gertrude Clanton Thomas Diaries, 1861–1868 (typescripts), Ella Gertrude Clanton Thomas Papers, David M. Rubenstein Rare Books and Manuscript Library, Duke University, Durham, N.C., September 16, 1864, 192 (hereafter cited as Thomas).

7. Grace Brown Elmore, *A Heritage of Woe: The Civil War Diary of Grace Brown Elmore, 1861–1868*, ed. Marli F. Weiner (Athens: University of Georgia Press, 1997), December 26, 1864, 84–85, and February 11, 1865, 97 (hereafter cited as Elmore).

8. Sarah Morgan, *Sarah Morgan: The Civil War Diary of a Southern Woman*, ed. Charles East (Athens: University of Georgia Press, 1991), June 28, 1862, 139–40 (hereafter cited as Morgan).

9. For Morgan's account of the sacking of her family's house, see Morgan, August 25, 1862, 232–37.

10. Josephine Humphreys, *Like Nowhere Else on Earth* (New York: Viking, 2000), 92.

11. Emma LeConte, *When the World Ended: The Diary of Emma LeConte*, ed. Earl Schenck Miers, foreword by Anne Firor Scott (Lincoln: University of Nebraska Press, 1987), February 5, 1865, 26; DeCaradeuc, February 19, 1865, 71, and August 17, 1864, 55; Anna Maria Green, *The Journal of a Milledgeville Girl, 1861–1867*, ed. James C. Bonner (Athens: University of Georgia Press, 1964), November 17, 1864, 58 (hereafter cited as Green); Stone, April 28, 1865, 333; Morgan, October 5, 1862, 294.

12. Buck, February 25, 1865, 312, and March 3, 1865, 313; Eliza Frances Andrews, *The War-time Journal of a Georgia Girl, 1864–1865*, introduction by Jean V. Berlin (Lincoln: University of Nebraska Press, 1997), May 4, 1865, 211 (hereafter cited as Andrews); Emma Holmes, *The Diary of Miss Emma Holmes, 1861–1866*, ed. John F. Marszalek (Baton Rouge: Louisiana State University Press, 1979), October 4, 1865, 471 (hereafter cited as Holmes); Stone, May 2, 1863, 204, and June 26, 1864, 292–93; Emilie Riley McKinley, *From the Pen of a She-Rebel: The Civil War Diary of Emilie Riley McKinley*, ed. Gordon A. Cotton (Columbia: University of South Carolina Press, 2001), June 21, 1863, 34 (hereafter cited as McKinley). Andrews on frizzing her hair is in Andrews, April 15, 1865, 144.

13. Anne Carson, *Eros the Bittersweet: An Essay* (Princeton, N.J.: Princeton University Press, 1986), 153.

14. DeCaradeuc, April 22, 1865, 73–74.

15. DeCaradeuc, February 14, 1864, 37; March 31, 1864, 39, 47; August 12, 1865, 84; August 20, 1865, 85; September 20, 1865, 88; and October 16, 1865, 89.

16. Green, August 14, 1867, 116; Anna Green (Cook) Diary (typescript), January 30, 1864, MS p. 68, Hargrett Rare Book and Manuscript Library, University of Georgia, Athens, (hereafter cited as Green typescript); Green, August 20, 1864, 54. Tobacco bags, a key item, were also made by Kate Stone, Grace Elmore, and Gertrude Thomas (for her brother).

17. Green, December 31, 1867, 124. On Anna and Houston, see Green, March 29, 1867, 110, and July 24, 1867, 115.

18. Green, March 20, 1866, 109; Green typescript, November 2, 1867, MS p. 223; Green, December 31, 1867, 125. For other examples of Samuel and Anna's lovers' dialogues (also deleted by Green's editor), see Green typescript, September 11 and 17, 1867, MS pp. 216–20; and November 25–December 30, 1867, MS pp. 226–27.

19. Emmala Reed, *A Faithful Heart: The Journals of Emmala Reed, 1865 and 1866*, ed. Robert T. Oliver (Columbia: University of South Carolina Press, 2004), April 6, 1865, 21; May 20, 1865, 91; April 7, 1865, 24; May 20, 1865, 91; and February 7, 1866, 196 (hereafter cited as Reed).

20. Reed, April 8, 1865, 25–26.

21. Reed, April 11, 1865, 32.

22. Holmes, September 20, 1862, 201; August 2, 1864, 365; August 15, 1865, 466; August 2, 1864, 365; August 15, 1864, 371; August 2, 1864, 365; and March 25, 1865, 423.

23. Holmes, March 4, 1865, 402, and August 15, 1865, 466.

24. Lucy Breckinridge, *Lucy Breckinridge of Grove Hill: The Journal of a Virginia Girl, 1862–1864*, ed. Mary D. Robertson (Columbia: University of South Carolina Press, 1994), August 15, 1863, 142 (hereafter cited as Breckinridge).

25. Breckinridge, October 26, 1863, 161; November 2, 1863, 161; July 29, 1864, 201; November 11, 1864, 216; and February 1, 1864, 177.

26. Breckinridge, August 11, 1864, 202, and November 9, 1864, 214–15.

27. Marilynne Robinson, *Gilead* (New York: Farrar, Straus and Giroux, 2004), 203.

28. Morgan, March 18, 1863, 443, and January 22, 1863, 407.

29. Morgan, April 13, 1863, 468.

30. Morgan, October 22, 1862, 314; February 17, 1863, 426; August 24, 1863, 545; and April 16, 1863, 473.

31. Morgan, April 12, 1863, 458.

32. Morgan, April 12, 1863, 459–60. Morgan's son Warrington Dawson *did* cut the passages about kissing Frank from his 1913 edition of her diary.

33. Morgan, January 9, 1863, 386; January 11, 1863, 393; November 15, 1862, 340; December 30, 1862, 380; and February 25 and 26, 1863, 435.

34. Morgan, November 24, 1862, 349; October 7, 1862, 298; October 1, 1862, 286; June 26, 1863, 511; October 1, 1862, 286; and October 17, 1862, 308.

35. Morgan, August 7, 1863, 532, and June 15, 1865, 612.

36. Mary Boykin Chesnut, *The Private Mary Chesnut: The Unpublished Civil War Diaries*, ed. C. Vann Woodward and Elisabeth Muhlenfeld (New York: Oxford University Press, 1984), February 18, 1865, 231; Buck, June 20, 1863, 221, and June 17, 1863, 220.

37. Morgan, September 21, 1862, 270; Holmes, May 24, 1862, 167–68.

38. Andrews, March 22, 1865, 120; Morgan, April 12, 1863, 462, and April 26, 1863, 489.

39. Holmes, March 4, 1865, 405, 407.

40. Morgan, January 22, 1863, 405; April 14, 1863, 469; and January 22, 1863, 405.

41. Holmes, March 4, 1865, 404; Reed, May 1, 1865, 64.

42. McKinley, May 25, 1863, 16.

43. Such depredations were widespread. Eating raw meat and vinegar is in McKinley, June 3, 1863, 22, and the plunging of arms into fruit preserves (and eating raw meat) is in Buck, August 18, 1864, 300.

44. Floride Clemson, *A Rebel Come Home: The Diary and Letters of Floride Clemson, 1863–1866*, ed. Charles M. McGee Jr. and Ernest M. Lander Jr., rev. ed. (Columbia: University of South Carolina Press, 1989), May 7, 1865, 85; Jones/Mallard, December 17, 1864, 1227; DeCaradeuc, February 18, 1865, 68. Grace Elmore thinking about suicide is in Elmore, November 26, 1864, 81–82.

45. Elmore, November 26, 1864, 81; Breckinridge, June 19, 1864, 193; DeCaradeuc, February 18, 1865, 66; Buck, August 18, 1864, 298; Stone, March 22, 1863, 182.

46. Edmondston, August 20, 1864, 604.

47. McKinley, May 22, 1863, 15; Buck, February 20, 1864, 267; Thomas, May 27, 1865, 77.

48. Cornelia Peake McDonald, *A Woman's Civil War: A Diary, with Reminiscences of the War, from March 1862*, ed. Minrose C. Gwin (New York: Gramercy Books, 2003), January 10, 1863, 112 (hereafter cited as McDonald). For a similar confrontation, see McDonald, June 4, 1863, 153.

49. McDonald, February 9, 1863, 120; May 8, 1863, 145; and April 8, 1863, 137.

50. McDonald, February 19, 1863, 122. The valentine is reproduced in the edition of McDonald's diary published by her son; see [Cornelia Peake McDonald], *A Diary with Reminiscences of the War and Refugee Life in the Shenandoah Valley, 1860–1865, [by] Mrs. Cornelia McDonald, Louisville, Kentucky, 1875. Annotated and Supplemented by Hunter McDonald, Nashville, Tenn.* (Nashville: Cullom & Ghertner, 1934), facing p. 137.

51. McDonald, June 14, 1863, 157.

CHAPTER 5

1. George Orwell, *Shooting an Elephant and Other Essays* (New York: Harcourt, Brace, 1945), 8.

2. Cornelia Peake McDonald, *A Woman's Civil War: A Diary, with Reminiscences of the War, from March 1862*, ed. Minrose C. Gwin (New York: Gramercy Books, 2003), February 26, 1863, 125, and February 9, 1863, 121 (hereafter cited as McDonald).

3. Lucy Rebecca Buck, *Shadows on My Heart: The Civil War Diary of Lucy Rebecca Buck of Virginia*, ed. Elizabeth R. Baer (Athens: University of Georgia Press, 1997), June 9, 1863, 208.

4. Emma Holmes, *The Diary of Miss Emma Holmes, 1861–1866*, ed. John F. Marszalek (Baton Rouge: Louisiana State University Press, 1979), April 7, 1865, 435 (hereafter cited as Holmes).

5. McDonald, June 11, 1863, 154; Catherine Ann Devereux Edmondston, *"Journal of a Secesh Lady": The Diary of Catherine Ann Devereux Edmondston, 1860–1866*, ed. Beth G. Crabtree and James W. Patton (Raleigh, N.C.: Division of Archives and History, 1979), February 19, 1865, 668 (hereafter cited as Edmondston).

6. Emma LeConte, *When the World Ended: The Diary of Emma LeConte*, ed. Earl Schenck Miers, foreword by Anne Firor Scott (Lincoln: University of Nebraska Press, 1987), February 19, 1865, 54; Grace Brown Elmore, *A Heritage of Woe: The Civil War Diary of Grace Brown Elmore, 1861–1868*, ed. Marli F. Weiner (Athens: University of Georgia Press, 1997), December 27, 1864, 85, and December 31, 1864, 87 (hereafter cited as Elmore).

7. Ella Gertrude Clanton Thomas Diaries, 1861–1868 (typescripts), Ella Gertrude Clanton Thomas Papers, David M. Rubenstein Rare Books and Manuscript Library, Duke University, Durham, N.C., September 23, 1864, 4–5; September 17, 1864, 199; and December 26, 1864, 30 (hereafter cited as Thomas).

8. Thomas, May 2, 1865, 63–64, and May [?], 1865, 71.

9. Thomas, May 29, 1865, 83.

10. Holmes, May 1865, 444–45.

11. Mary Jones and Mary Sharpe Jones Mallard Diary, in *The Children of Pride: A True Story of Georgia and the Civil War*, ed. Robert Manson Myers (New Haven, Conn.: Yale University Press, 1972), 1220–48, January 21 and 23, 1865, 1247 (hereafter cited as Jones/Mallard).

12. Elizabeth Ingraham, "The Vicksburg Diary of Mrs. Alfred Ingraham (May 2–June 13, 1863)," ed. W. Maury Darst, *Journal of Mississippi History* 44 (May 1982): 148–79, May 21, 1863, 169, 168 (hereafter cited as Ingraham).

13. Ingraham, May 13, 1863, 165.

14. Ingraham, May 13, 1863, 165; May 31, 1863, 173; May 27, 1863, 171; May 31, 1863, 173; and May 13, 1863, 165.

15. Holmes, April 2, 1865, 427–28.

16. Sarah Katherine Stone, *Brokenburn: The Journal of Kate Stone, 1861–1868*, ed. John Q. Anderson, new introduction by Drew Gilpin Faust (Baton Rouge: Louisiana State University Press, 1995), December 29, 1862, 165, and May 22, 1863, 209 (hereafter cited as Stone). Lucy Breckinridge, *Lucy Breckinridge of Grove Hill: The Journal of a Virginia Girl, 1862–1864*, ed. Mary D. Robertson (Columbia: University of South Carolina Press, 1994), June 16, 1864, 193; August 31, 1862, 43; June 16, 1864, 193; and June 19, 1864, 194 (hereafter cited as Breckinridge).

17. Thomas, June [?], 1865, 86; Emmala Reed, *A Faithful Heart: The Journals of Emmala Reed, 1865 and 1866*, ed. Robert T. Oliver (Columbia: University of South Carolina Press, 2004), June 8, 1865, 114.

18. Ellen Douglas, *Can't Quit You, Baby* (New York: Atheneum, 1988), 127.

19. Holmes, January 21, 1863, 224.

20. Elmore, February 21, 1865, 102, 104; Stone, April 10, 1863, 187.

21. Jones/Mallard, December 13, 1864, 1222.

22. Jones/Mallard, January 6, 1865, 1241; Ingraham, May 2, 1863, 152.

23. Eliza Frances Andrews, *The War-time Journal of a Georgia Girl, 1864–1865*, introduction by Jean V. Berlin (Lincoln: University of Nebraska Press, 1997), May 31, 1865, 277; Stone, June 3, 1863, 216; Jones/Mallard, January 7, 1865, 1242, and January 11, 1865, 1244; Elmore, December 26, 1864, 84.

24. Edmondston, December 12, 1860, 23. Edmondston's breakfast story is from the same date, pp. 20–21.

25. Edmondston, March 26, 1862, 141.

26. For examples of references to Harriet Stowe and *Uncle Tom's Cabin*, see Edmondston, December 12, 1860, 23; Thomas, September 23, 1864, 5; and Mary Boykin Chesnut, *The Private Mary Chesnut: The Unpublished Civil War Diaries*, ed. C. Vann Woodward and Elisabeth Muhlenfeld (New York: Oxford University Press, 1984), June 1, 1865, 254 (hereafter cited as Chesnut).

27. Sarah Morgan, *Sarah Morgan: The Civil War Diary of a Southern Woman*, ed. Charles East (Athens: University of Georgia Press, 1991), April 19, 1863, 481 (hereafter cited as Morgan).

28. Edmondston, February 27, 1865, 673.

29. Ingraham, June 2, 1863, 175 (her Robinson Crusoe reference is from May 13, 1863, 165); Stone, April 25, 1863, 198.

30. Stone, April 25, 1863, 195–96.

31. Chesnut, May 13, 1865, 243; Elmore, December 24, 1864, 83; Stone, September 5, 1864, 298. For Gertrude Thomas on insurrection, see Thomas, July 22, 1865, 88.

32. Ingraham, May 28, 1863, 172; May 27, 1863, 170; and May 11, 1863, 163.

33. Ingraham, May 8, 1863, 159; May 31, 1863, 173; and May 27, 1863, 171.

34. For Ellen and other workers, see Chesnut, February 16, 1865, 230.

35. Edmondston, October 1, 1865, 717–18.

36. Thomas, September 17, 1866, 123–24.

37. Saidiya V. Hartman, *Scenes of Subjection: Terror, Slavery, and Self-Making in Nineteenth-Century America* (New York: Oxford University Press, 1997), 26, 34, 50.

38. Edmondston, October 1, 1865, 719.

39. Holmes, March 11, 1865, 413; March 4, 1865, 400; and April 2, 1865, 430.

40. Breckinridge, December 16, 1864, 219.

41. Alice Munro, *The View from Castle Rock* (New York: Alfred A. Knopf, 2006), 300.

42. Morgan, January 30, 1863, 414.

43. Morgan, January 30, 1863, 417.

44. Morgan, January 30, 1863, 417. I borrow the term "social intelligence" from Nancy Sherman, "Empathy, Respect, and Humanitarian Intervention," *Ethics and International Affairs* 12 (1998): 103–19.

45. Thomas, September 17, 1864, 195, and September 23, 1864, 5.

46. Thomas, September 23, 1864, 5, and September 30, 1864, 6. She was reading a new novel: E. W. Warren, *Nellie Norton, or, Southern Slavery and the Bible. A Scriptural refutation of the principal arguments upon which the abolitionists rely* [. . .] (Macon, Ga.: Burke, Boykin, 1864).

47. Thomas, October 9, 1865, 88, 89, and October 14, 1865, 90.

48. Thomas, November 3, 1868, 16–17.

49. Thomas, November 3, 1868, 17.

CHAPTER 6

1. Michael Ondaatje, *Divisadero* (New York: Alfred A. Knopf, 2007), 136.

2. Marilynne Robinson, *The Death of Adam: Essays on Modern Thought* (Boston: Houghton Mifflin, 1998), 237.

3. Emmala Reed, *A Faithful Heart: The Journals of Emmala Reed, 1865 and 1866*, ed. Robert T. Oliver (Columbia: University of South Carolina Press, 2004), January 14, 1866, 151 (hereafter cited as Reed); Floride Clemson, *A Rebel Come Home: The Diary and Letters of Floride Clemson, 1863–1866*, ed. Charles M. McGee Jr. and Ernest M. Lander Jr., rev. ed. (Columbia: University of South Carolina Press, 1989), February 19, 1865, 76.

4. Grace Brown Elmore, *A Heritage of Woe: The Civil War Diary of Grace Brown Elmore, 1861–1868*, ed. Marli F. Weiner (Athens: University of Georgia Press, 1997), December 31, 1864, 87, and March 6, 1865, 110 (hereafter cited as Elmore).

5. Elmore, March 4, 1865, 108; Emma Holmes, *The Diary of Miss Emma Holmes, 1861–1866*, ed. John F. Marszalek (Baton Rouge: Louisiana State University Press, 1979), November 12, 1864, 384 (hereafter cited as Holmes); Catherine Ann Devereux Edmondston, *"Journal of a Secesh Lady": The Diary of Catherine Ann Devereux Edmondston, 1860–1866*, ed. Beth G. Crabtree and James W. Patton (Raleigh, N.C.: Division of Archives and History, 1979), July 28, 1865, 717 (hereafter cited as Edmondston).

6. Reed, January 14, 1866, 151; Ella Gertrude Clanton Thomas Diaries, 1861–1868 (typescripts), Ella Gertrude Clanton Thomas Papers, David M. Rubenstein Rare Books and Manuscript Library, Duke University, Durham, N.C., September 17, 1864, 201 (hereafter cited as Thomas); Elizabeth Ingraham, "The Vicksburg Diary of Mrs. Alfred Ingraham (May 2–June 13, 1863)," ed. W. Maury Darst, *Journal of Mississippi History* 44 (May 1982): 148–79, May 31, 1863, 173 (hereafter cited as Ingraham); Edmondston, October 31, 1863, 486; Thomas, November 21, 1864, 19; Mary Jones and Mary Sharpe Jones Mallard Diary, in *The Children of Pride: A True Story of Georgia and the Civil War*, ed. Robert Manson Myers (New Haven, Conn.: Yale University Press, 1972): 1220–48, January 17, 1865, 1246–47 (hereafter cited as Jones/Mallard); Thomas, September 17, 1864, 200.

7. Lucy Rebecca Buck, *Shadows on My Heart: The Civil War Diary of Lucy Rebecca Buck of Virginia*, ed. Elizabeth R. Baer (Athens: University of Georgia Press, 1997), July 12, 1863, 231 (hereafter cited as Buck); Edmondston, January 2, 1863, 331; Elmore, December 23, 1861, 29; Cornelia Peake McDonald, *A Woman's Civil War: A Diary, with Reminiscences of the War, from March 1862*, ed. Minrose C. Gwin (New York: Gramercy Books, 2003), April 4, 1863, 135; David Golightly Harris [and Emily Liles Harris], *Piedmont Farmer: The Journals of David Golightly Harris, 1855–1870*, ed. Philip N. Racine (Knoxville: University of Tennessee Press, 1990), January 1, 1865, 357 (hereafter cited as Harris).

8. Ingraham, May 2, 1863, 152; Jones/Mallard, December 21, 1864, 1232.

9. Jones/Mallard, December 21, 1864, 1232; Ingraham, May 8, 1863, 162.

10. Jones/Mallard, December 22, 1864, 1234.

11. Jones/Mallard, January 7, 1865, 1242, and January 17, 1865, 1247.

12. Pauline DeCaradeuc Heyward, *A Confederate Lady Comes of Age: The Journal of Pauline DeCaradeuc Heyward, 1863–1888*, ed. Mary D. Robertson (Columbia: University of South Carolina Press, 1992), December 26, 1864, 61, and May 12, 1864, 45 (hereafter cited as DeCaradeuc); Thomas, October 9, 1865, 89.

13. Edmondston, September 6, 1864, 613.

14. Harris, August 27, 1864, 340; Elmore, October 1, 1865, 130; Emma LeConte, *When the World Ended: The Diary of Emma LeConte*, ed. Earl Schenck Miers, foreword by Anne Firor Scott (Lincoln: University of Nebraska Press, 1987), January 28, 1865, 21–22; Lucy

Breckinridge, *Lucy Breckinridge of Grove Hill: The Journal of a Virginia Girl, 1862–1864*, ed. Mary D. Robertson (Columbia: University of South Carolina Press, 1994), July 3, 1864, 197.

15. Elmore, October 1, 1865, 130.

16. Elmore, March 22, 1867, 138–39, and February 27, 1868, 169.

17. DeCaradeuc, December 26, 1864, 61; January 4, 1864, 33; and March 18, 1865, 71.

18. Buck, July 11, 1863, 231; June 17, 1864, 284; August 20, 1864, 301; March 6, 1865, 313; April 30, 1864, 271; and September 25, 1863.

19. Anna Maria Green, *The Journal of a Milledgeville Girl, 1861–1867*, ed. James C. Bonner (Athens: University of Georgia Press, 1964), July 24, 1867, 115; April 12, 1865, 72; and May 12, 1867, 114.

20. Sarah Morgan, *Sarah Morgan: The Civil War Diary of a Southern Woman*, ed. Charles East (Athens: University of Georgia Press, 1991), January 23, 1863, 410–11 (hereafter cited as Morgan).

21. Morgan, February 25, 1863, 434.

22. Morgan, June 14, 1863, 504; September 29, 1863; and July 25, 1896, 565.

23. Morgan, November 9, 1863, 576.

24. Morgan, January 17, 1864, 591.

25. William Maxwell, *So Long, See You Tomorrow* (New York: Alfred A. Knopf, 1980), 27; Thomas, July 22, 1866, 112; Sarah Katherine Stone, *Brokenburn: The Journal of Kate Stone, 1861–1868*, ed. John Q. Anderson, new introduction by Drew Gilpin Faust (Baton Rouge: Louisiana State University Press, 1995), July 1, 1861, 34; Edmondston, January 21, 1863, 344; Holmes, March 9, 1861, 13.

26. Elmore, April 2, 1865, 113.

27. Thomas, July 22, 1866, 103; July 9, 1866, 101–2; and July 22, 1866, 114. For her champagne cork vulgarity and details of her Macon trip, see Thomas, January 1, 1866, 100, and July 22, 1866, 103–14.

28. Thomas, October 14, 1865, 91.

INDEX

58–59, 64, 96–97, 107, 129; and religious faith, 139–40; and the sublime, 48–49, 64; and writing, 29, 31, 44–45, 48–49, 52. *See also* Army, Confederate States; Army, United States; Confederate States of America; Slavery; Soldiers

Class. *See* Social class

Clemson, Floride, xx, 51, 106; and diary keeping, 2–3, 29, 35, 42–43, 146; and end of war, 64–65, 140; and fear of rape, 96; and wartime change, 59

Conecuh County, Ala., 17

Confederate States of America, 20, 39, 40, 61, 63, 65, 79, 140; defeat of, 24, 26, 32, 49, 64–65, 115, 127, 136, 145; and fortunes of war, x, 21, 29, 143; support of, 32–33, 49, 62, 73, 74, 93, 97. *See also* Army, Confederate States

Cook, Samuel, 10, 81, 86

Crouch, 93

Cynthia, 108–9, 118–19, 156

Dabney ("Old Dabney"), 124–25

Daniel, 109–10, 128–29

Davis, Jefferson, 93

Dawson, Warrington, 14–19

DeCaradeuc, James Achille, 73–74

DeCaradeuc, Pauline, xxi, 4, 22, 73; and diary keeping, 27, 33, 41; and end of war, 64–65, 66; and fear of rape, 96; and men, 77–78, 79–80, 86; and religious faith, 145; and slaves, 105; and Union soldiers, 62, 96; and wartime change, 58, 61, 150

Diaries: editorial transformations of, 1, 7–9, 11–14, 18, 21, 106, 153; and emotion, 32–33, 150–54; and femininity, 4, 146–49; as first drafts, xvi, 42–43, 115, 152, 155; as historical text and source, xii–xiii, xv, 1, 9, 12, 14–15, 18, 29, 48, 103, 138, 152, 155, 157; and "just reading," 4, 6, 11–12, 14, 34, 65, 74, 103, 108, 115, 130–31; as literary creations, ix, xi, 10–11, 13, 27, 28–29, 41–46, 48, 52–53, 59, 68, 76, 109, 128–30, 132, 137; "original" texts of, 7, 9–11, 16, 21, 23, 38; and "readability," 11–13, 16, 19,

23, 65, 71, 103, 139, 157; and reading, ix, xii, 2, 6, 8, 13–14, 26, 41, 48, 155–57; and religious faith, 139–46, 153; and scale, 5–8, 32, 52–53, 125, 154–55; and stories, 5, 8, 16, 28–29, 45, 65–66, 72, 103–4, 115, 126–30, 139; and subjectivity, 2, 6–7, 11, 26, 29, 30, 33, 35–36, 44–45, 117–18; and trivia, 12–13, 15–16, 19, 20–21, 23, 26, 34, 41, 71–72; and voice, 2–5, 11, 15, 16, 33, 52, 68; and writing, ix, xiii, xv, 4, 27–29, 30–31, 34–40, 42, 44, 137, 154. *See also individual diarists*

Dillard, Annie, 10, 45

Dolly, 121

Douglas, Ellen, 117

Downs, Mrs., 95

Dupres, Lieutenant, 94

Edmondston, Catherine Devereux, xxi; and cause of war, 97; and diary keeping, 2, 9–10, 30–31, 35, 37, 38–39, 41, 44, 127; and end of war, 65–66, 127, 142, 143; and femininity, 146; and husband's army service, 74; and religious faith, 143, 155; and slaves, 108, 121, 123, 127–29, 130; and wartime change, 48, 61, 68

Edmondston, Patrick Muir, 37, 74

Ellen, 126

Elmore, Grace Brown, xxi, 3; and diary keeping, 2–3, 9, 33, 36, 42–43; and end of war, 66, 69; and fear of rape, 96; and femininity, 147, 149; and men, 74–75, 96, 148; and religious faith, 2, 141, 143; and slaves, 108–9, 118, 120, 124; and wartime change, 50, 61, 148–49, 156–57

Elsy, 113–14, 125–26

Emancipation. *See* Slavery: disintegration of

Emma, 114

Empathy: diarists', with men, 73, 76, 79, 86, 94, 97; diarists', with slaves, 111, 118, 121–22, 126, 130, 132–33, 134; and the diary, xi–xii, 14, 21, 26, 46, 66, 86, 111, 125; limits of, xii, 39, 54, 76, 86, 106, 130, 134–35; and living in the present, xi, 10,

9 781469 640969